The **music**socket.com
# Music Industry Directory
# 2021

The **music**socket.com

# Music Industry Directory 2021

EDITOR
J. PAUL DYSON

JP&A
Dyson

Published in 2020 by JP&A Dyson
27 Old Gloucester Street, London WC1N 3AX, United Kingdom
Copyright JP&A Dyson

https://www.jpandadyson.com
https://www.musicsocket.com

ISBN 978-1-909935-34-1

**Registered with the IP Rights Office**
**Copyright Registration Service**
**Ref: 3231987728**

# Foreword

This directory includes hundreds of listings of **record labels** and **managers**, updated in **MusicSocket**'s online databases between 2018 and 2020.

It also provides free access to the entire current databases, including over 1,800 record labels, and over 700 managers, with dozens of new and updated listings every month.

For details on how to claim your free access please see the back of this book.

## Included in the subscription

A subscription to the full website is not only free with this book, but comes packed with all the following features:

### Advanced search features

- Save searches and save time – set up to 15 search parameters specific to your work, save them, and then access the search results with a single click whenever you log in. You can even save multiple different searches if you have different types of work you are looking to place.
- Add personal notes to listings, visible only to you and fully searchable – helping you to organise your actions.
- Set reminders on listings to notify you when to submit your work, when to follow up, when to expect a reply, or any other custom action.
- Track which listings you've viewed and when, to help you organise your search – any listings which have changed since you last viewed them will be highlighted for your attention!

### Daily email updates

As a subscriber you will be able to take advantage of our email alert service, meaning you can specify your particular interests and we'll send you automatic email updates when we change or add a listing that matches them. So if you're interested in labels dealing in hard rock in the United States you can have us send you emails with the latest updates about them – keeping you up to date without even having to log in.

### User feedback

Our databases include a user feedback feature that allows our subscribers to leave feedback on each listing – giving you not only the chance to have your say about the markets you contact, but giving a unique artist's perspective on the listings.

## *Save on copyright protection fees*

If you're sending your work away to record labels and managers you should first consider protecting your copyright. As a subscriber to **MusicSocket** you can do this through our site and save 10% on the copyright registration fees normally payable for protecting your work internationally through the Intellectual Property Rights Office (https://www.Copyright RegistrationService.com).

For details on how to claim your free access please see the back of this book.

# Contents

# Protecting Your Copyright

Protecting your copyright is by no means a requirement before submitting your work, but you may feel that it is a prudent step that you would like to take before allowing strangers to hear your material.

These days, you can register your work for copyright protection quickly and easily online. The Intellectual Property Rights Office operates a website called the "Copyright Registration Service" which allows you to do this:

- *https://www.CopyrightRegistrationService.com*

This website can be used for material created in any nation signed up to the Berne Convention. This includes the United States, United Kingdom, Canada, Australia, Ireland, New Zealand, and most other countries. There are around 180 countries in the world, and over 160 of them are part of the Berne Convention.

Provided you created your work in one of the Berne Convention nations, your work should be protected by copyright in all other Berne Convention nations. You can therefore protect your copyright around most of the world with a single registration, and because the process is entirely online you can have your work protected in a matter of minutes.

# US Record Labels

*For the most up-to-date listings of these and hundreds of other record labels, visit https://www.musicsocket.com/recordlabels*

*To claim your **free** access to the site, please see the back of this book.*

## Acony Records

PO Box 60007
Nashville, TN 37206
*Email:* information@aconyrecords.com
*Website:* http://www.aconyrecords.com

*Genres:* Folk; Roots

Folk and roots label based in Nashville, Tennessee.

## American Gramaphone

9130 Mormon Bridge Road
Omaha, NE 68152
*Email:* mailbox@mannheimsteamroller.com
*Website:* http://www.
mannheimsteamroller.com

*Genres:* Classical

*Contact:* Chip Davis

Label based in Omaha, Nebraska.

## Amulet Records, Inc.

*Email:* billy@amuletrecords.com
*Website:* http://www.amuletrecords.com
*Website:* https://www.facebook.com/Amulet-
Records-2071064413172768/

*Genres:* Experimental; Avant-Garde

*Contact:* Billy Martin

Experimental record label specialising in percussion and avant-garde.

## Arista Nashville

*Website:* https://www.
sonymusicnashville.com/label/arista-
nashville/

*Genres:* Country

Record label specialising in Country music.

## Better Looking Records

*Website:* https://betterlookingrecords.com
*Website:* https://www.facebook.com/
betterlookingrecords

*Genres:* Indie; Rock

Indie and rock label based in Los Angeles, California.

## Big Machine Records

1219 16th Avenue South
Nashville, TN 37212
*Email:* chris.stacey@bmlg.net
*Website:* http://www.bigmachinerecords.com
*Website:* http://www.facebook.com/
bigmachinerecords

*Genres:* Country

*Contact:* Chris Stacey

Country music label based in Nashville Tennessee.

## Blue Note Label Group
1750 North Vine Street
Hollywood, CA 90028-5274
*Website:* http://www.bluenote.com
*Website:* https://www.facebook.com/
bluenote

*Genres:* Jazz; Pop; R&B

Record label based in New York,
specialising in Jazz.

## BMG
1745 Broadway, 19th Floor
New York, NY 10019

LOS ANGELES:
6100 Wilshire Boulevard, Suite #1600
Los Angeles, CA 90048

NASHVILLE:
29 Music Square East
Nashville, TN 37203
*Email:* info.us@bmg.com
*Website:* https://www.bmg.com

*Genres:* All types of music

International record label with US offices in
New York, LA, and Nashville.

## Bolero Records
18653 Ventura Boulevard, Suite 314
Tarzana, CA 91356
*Email:* info@bolero-records.com
*Website:* https://www.bolero-records.com

*Genres:* World; Jazz; Latin; New Age

Independent record label based in Tarzana,
California, specialising in Nuevo Flamenco,
Traditional Flamenco, World, Jazz, Latin
and New Age.

## Brash Music
c/o New Music
888 3rd Street NW, Suite A
Atlanta, GA 30318
*Email:* info@brashmusic.com
*Website:* http://www.brashmusic.com
*Website:* https://www.facebook.com/Brash-
Music-168206919862613/

*Genres:* All types of music

Record label based in Atlanta, Georgia. Not
accepting new music as at January 2018.

## Bridge Nine Records
119R Foster Street, Building 4 Suite 3
Peabody, MA 01960
*Fax:* +1 (978) 532-3806
*Email:* chris@bridge9.com
*Email:* rushton@bridge9.com
*Website:* http://www.bridge9.com
*Website:* https://www.facebook.com/bridge9

*Genres:* Hardcore

*Contact:* Chris Wrenn; Bryan Rushton

Record label based in Peabody,
Massachusetts.

## Bright Antenna Records
146 East Blithedale Avenue
Mill Valley, CA 94941
*Email:* info@brightantenna.com
*Website:* http://www.brightantenna.com
*Website:* https://soundcloud.com/
brightantenna

*Genres:* Rock

Accepts submissions via Soundcloud only.
No physical submissions.

## Brunswick Record Corporation
157 E. Franklin St., Suite 5
Chapel Hill, NC 27514
*Fax:* +1 (984) 999-4339
*Website:* https://brunswickrecords.com

*Genres:* R&B

Record label based in Chapel Hill, North
Carolina.

## Brushfire Records
424 North Larchmont Avenue
Los Angeles, CA 90004-3014
*Fax:* +1 (323) 957-9931
*Website:* http://brushfirerecords.com
*Website:* https://www.facebook.com/
brushfirerecords

*Genres:* All types of music

Record label founded in Hawaii in 2002, and now based in Los Angeles. Strives to make music and films that are positive and works to connect like-minded musicians and artists in the surf community and beyond.

## Bullet Tooth
ATTENTION A&R
23 Farm Edge Lane
Tinton Falls, NJ 07724
*Fax:* +1 (732) 542-7957
*Email:* demo@bullettooth.com
*Email:* info@bullettooth.com
*Website:* http://bullettooth.com

*Genres:* Rock; Hardcore; Metal; Emo; Punk

*Contact:* Josh Grabelle

Handles rock and all sub-genres. Send demo on CD by post, or send email with info, Myspace links, Bio, etc. Do not email MP3s! Include band name, contact name, phone number, email address, Myspace, and street address either on the CD itself, or on the packaging. Considers bands from overseas. Only interested in hard working bands. See website for full submission guidelines.

## Burnt Toast Vinyl
PO Box 42188
Philadelphia, PA 19101
*Email:* btv@burnttoastvinyl.com
*Website:* http://www.burnttoastvinyl.com
*Website:* https://www.facebook.com/burnttoastvinyl

*Genres:* Alternative; Singer-Songwriter

Record label based in Philadelphia.

## Cantaloupe Music
80 Hanson Place, Suite 702
Brooklyn, NY 11217
*Fax:* +1 (718) 852-7732
*Email:* info@cantaloupemusic.com
*Website:* http://www.cantaloupemusic.com

*Genres:* Classical; Electronic; Jazz; New Age; Punk; Rock; World

*Contact:* Cantaloupe A&R

Send demos by email or by US mail. All submissions listened to, but response not guaranteed. Include details of past and upcoming performances.

## Cantora
New York
*Email:* hello@cantora.com
*Website:* http://cantora.com
*Website:* https://www.facebook.com/WeAreCantora

*Genres:* Progressive Pop

Record label based in New York, releasing artists who make forward-thinking pop music.

## Canvasback Music
1633 Broadway 10th Floor
New York, NY 10019-6708
*Fax:* +1 (212) 405-5427
*Email:* steve@canvasbackmusic.com
*Website:* http://www.canvasbackmusic.com
*Website:* https://www.facebook.com/canvasbackmusic/

*Genres:* All types of music

*Contact:* Steve Ralbovsky

Record label based in New York.

## Canyon
1761 West University Drive, Suite 145
Tempe, Arizona 85281
*Email:* canyon@canyonrecords.com
*Website:* https://www.canyonrecords.com
*Website:* https://www.facebook.com/canyonrecords

*Genres:* Regional; World

Native American record label.

## Capitol Christian Music Group
PO Box 74008453
Chicago, IL 60674-8453
*Website:* http://www.capitolchristianmusicgroup.com
*Website:* https://www.facebook.com/capitolchristiandistribution

*Genres:* Christian; Gospel

Christian record label based in Chicago, Illinois. Unsolicited demos will not be responded to.

## Capitol Music Group

1750 Vine Street
Los Angeles, CA 90028
*Website:* http://www.capitolrecords.com
*Website:* https://www.facebook.com/capitolrecords

*Genres:* Dance; Indie; Pop; Rock; Urban

Accepts submissions through established sources (managers, etc.) only. All other material returned without being listened to.

## Carnival Music

24 Music Square West #200
Nashville, TN 37203-3204
*Email:* info@carnivalmusic.net
*Email:* fliddell@carnivalmusic.net
*Website:* http://www.carnivalmusic.net
*Website:* https://soundcloud.com/carnivalmusic

*Genres:* Americana; Country; Indie; Pop; Rock

*Contact:* Frank Liddell; Travis Hill

Describes itself as neither a record label or publishing company, but doing the work of both.

## Carpark Records

PO Box 42374
Washington, DC 20015
*Email:* carparkrecords@gmail.com
*Website:* http://carparkrecords.com
*Website:* https://soundcloud.com/carparkrecords

*Genres:* Alternative; Rock

Independent record label based in Washington DC.

## Carved Records

*Email:* info@carvedrecords.com
*Website:* http://www.carvedrecords.com
*Website:* https://www.facebook.com/carvedrecords

*Genres:* All types of music

Record label describing itself as being "powered by a family of music industry professionals, musicians and entrepreneurs who offer unparalleled expertise in A&R, Digital and Physical Sales, Promotion, Press, and Brand Marketing, as well as New Media and Social Network Marketing."

## Cascine

New York, NY
*Email:* demos@cascine.us
*Email:* info@cascine.us
*Website:* http://www.cascine.us
*Website:* https://soundcloud.com/cascine

*Genres:* Alternative Pop; Electronic

Independent record label based in New York. Known for its consistently stylish brand of alternative pop and electronic music. Send demos by email.

## Cash Money Records

Miami, FL
*Website:* http://www.cashmoney-records.com
*Website:* https://www.facebook.com/cashmoneyrecords

*Genres:* Hip-Hop; Urban; Pop

Record label based in Miami, Florida.

## Cheap Lullaby Records

5115 Excelsior Boulevard #242
Minneapolis, MN 55416-2906
*Fax:* +1 (310) 622-4189
*Email:* joe@cheaplullaby.com
*Website:* http://www.cheaplullaby.com

*Genres:* All types of music

Record label based in Minneapolis, Minnesota.

## Chesky Records

1650 Broadway, Suite 900
New York, NY 10019
*Email:* info@chesky.com
*Website:* http://www.chesky.com

*Genres:* Classical; Jazz; World

Record label based in New York, specialising in classical, jazz, and world music.

## Chiaroscuro Records
100 WVIA Way
Pittston, PA 18640
*Email:* info@chiaroscurojazz.org
*Website:* http://www.chiaroscurojazz.com

*Genres:* Jazz

Jazz label based in Pittston, Pennsylvania.

## Chicago Kid Records
2420 N. Catalina Street
Los Angeles, CA 90027
*Email:* Chicagokid1@earthlink.net
*Website:* http://www.chicagokidrecords.com

*Genres:* All types of music

Record label based in Los Angeles. Send query by post with CD, Tape, or DAT of your best material, bio, photo, and contact info.

## Cleopatra Records
11041 Santa Monica Blvd PMB #703
Los Angeles, CA 90025
*Fax:* +1 (310) 312-5653
*Email:* cleoinfo@cleorecs.com
*Website:* http://www.cleorecs.com
*Website:* https://www.facebook.com/CleopatraRecords
*Website:* https://myspace.com/cleorecs

*Genres:* Metal; Punk; Pop; Electronic; Rap; Hip-Hop; Jazz; Gothic; Reggaeton; Industrial

Record label based in Los Angeles.

## Collect Records
67 West Street, Suite 401-04
Brooklyn, NY 11222
*Website:* http://collectrecords.org
*Website:* https://soundcloud.com/collectrecords

*Genres:* All types of music

An independent record company based in Brooklyn, New York.

## Columbia Records
550 Madison Avenue
New York, NY 10022-3211

WEST COAST OFFICE:
9830 Wilshire Boulevard
Beverly Hills, CA 90212
*Website:* http://www.columbiarecords.com
*Website:* https://www.facebook.com/columbiarecords/

*Genres:* All types of music

Record label with offices in New York and LA, dealing in all genres.

## Communion Records US
Brooklyn, NY
*Email:* info@communionmusic.com
*Website:* https://www.facebook.com/CommunionMusic

*Genres:* All types of music

Artist-led organisation combining elements of live promotion, publishing and recording to create a hub for artists to develop and flourish. Founded in London in 2006.

## Compass Records
916 19th Avenue South
Nashville, TN 37212
*Fax:* +1 (615) 320-7378
*Email:* submissions@compassrecords.com
*Email:* info@compassrecords.com
*Website:* http://compassrecords.com
*Website:* https://www.facebook.com/CompassRecordsGroup

*Genres:* Blues; Folk; Americana; Jazz; Pop; Alternative; Roots; World; Celtic

Record label based in Nashville, Tennessee. No hip hop, rap, hard rock, or commercial country. Send query by email with link to music online. Explain why you think this label is right for you and vice versa, and provide details of last two years of touring history.

## Compound Entertainment
1755 Broadway
New York, NY 10019

*Email:* info@compoundent.com
*Website:* http://compoundent.com

*Genres:* Pop; Urban

Record label based in New York.

## Concord Music Group

100 North Crescent Drive
Garden Level
Beverly Hills, CA 90210
*Fax:* +1 (310) 385-4134
*Email:* submissions@
concordmusicgroup.com
*Website:* http://www.
concordmusicgroup.com
*Website:* https://twitter.com/ConcordRecords

*Genres:* Jazz; Pop; Rock; R&B; Blues; Soul;
Classical; World; Latin

Record label based in Beverly Hills,
California. Describes itself as "one of the
largest independent record and music
publishing companies in the world".

## Crosscheck Records

Silver Lake
Los Angeles, CA
*Website:* http://www.cmhlabelgroup.com/

*Genres:* Punk; Rap

Rap and punk label based in Silver Lake, Los
Angeles.

## Crush Music

New York
*Email:* info@crushmusic.com
*Website:* https://www.crushmusic.com

*Genres:* Pop; Rock; Punk; Singer-Songwriter

Record label based in New York.

## Curb Records

48 Music Square East
Nashville, TN 37203
*Email:* curb@curb.com
*Website:* http://www.curb.com

*Genres:* Christian; Country; Pop Rock;
Classical; Dance; Instrumental; Jazz;
Soundtracks; Urban; R&B

*Contact:* Mike Curb

Christian and Country label based in
Nashville, Tennessee.

## Dangerbird Records

3801 Sunset Boulevard
Los Angeles, CA 90026
*Email:* info@dangerbird.com
*Website:* http://www.dangerbirdrecords.com
*Website:* https://www.facebook.com/
dangerbirdrecords

*Genres:* Alternative; Indie; Rock

Record label based in Los Angeles,
California. Not accepting unsolicited demos
as at June 2018.

## Daptone Records

115 Troutman
Brooklyn, NY 11206
*Fax:* +1 (718) 366-3783
*Email:* info@daptonerecords.com
*Website:* http://daptonerecords.com
*Website:* https://www.facebook.com/
daptonehouseofsoul

*Genres:* All types of music

Record label based in Brooklyn, New York.

## Dauman Music

137 North Larchmont
Los Angeles, CA 90004-3704
*Email:* jason@daumanmusic.com
*Website:* http://www.daumanmusic.com

*Genres:* Dance

*Contact:* Jason Dauman

Record label based in Los Angeles. Founder
has procured songs for artists including U2,
Bruce Springsteen, Garth Brooks, Billy
Steinberg and Tom Kelly, Burt Bacharach
and Carole Bayer Sager.

## Decca Records US

*Website:* http://www.deccarecordsus.com

*Genres:* Mainstream

Releases music that appeals to a mainstream,
broad audience.

## Deep South Records

PO Box 17737
Raleigh, NC 27619

NASHVILLE
PO Box 121975
Nashville, TN 37212
*Email:* Info@DeepSouthEntertainment.com
*Website:* http://deepsouthentertainment.com
*Website:* https://www.facebook.com/
deepsouthent

*Genres:* Rock

A record label, artist management firm,
talent agency, and concert production
company with offices in Raleigh, NC and
Nashville, TN.

## Delmark Records

4121 N. Rockwell
Chicago, IL 60618
*Fax:* +1 (773) 887-0329
*Email:* online@delmark.com
*Website:* http://www.delmark.com

*Genres:* Blues; Jazz

Blues and jazz record label based in
Chicago, Illinois.

## Delos

PO Box 343
Sonoma, CA 95476
*Fax:* +1 (415) 358-5959
*Email:* delosmusicproductions@gmail.com
*Website:* https://delosmusic.com
*Website:* https://soundcloud.com/delos-radio

*Genres:* Classical

Classical music label based in Sonoma,
California.

## Delta Groove Music

16555 Sherman Way, Suite B2
Van Nuys, CA 91406
*Fax:* +1 (818) 907-1620
*Email:* info@deltagroovemusic.com
*Website:* http://deltagroovemusic.com

*Genres:* Blues; Roots

Describes itself as the West Coast leader in
roots and blues music.

## Delved in Dreams, inc.

PO Box 11653
South Bend,IN 46634
*Email:* delvedindreamsplus@gmail.com
*Website:* https://www.
delvedindreamsmusic.com

*Genres:* Christian Classic Electronic
Industrial Mainstream Progressive Soulful
Regional Traditional Tribal Ambient
Classical Country Cuban Dance Ethnic Folk
Fusion Gospel Indie Instrumental Jazz Pop
Nostalgia New Age Techno Swing Soul
Roots Rhythm and Blues Singer-Songwriter
Reggae

*Contact:* Pamela Carl

An independent label who handles digital
distribution. We get our artists on all major
sites such as itunes, Amazon, CDbaby,
Spotify and others. We market all of our
artists' music, this includes radio, reviews,
and social media.

## Derrty Entertainment

9648 Olive Blvd # 230
St Louis, MO 63132-3002
*Email:* BluBolden@DerrtyEnt.com
*Email:* Taj@DerrtyEnt.com
*Website:* http://www.derrtyent.com
*Website:* http://www.facebook.com/pages/
DERRTY-ENT/89589703772

*Genres:* Urban; Hip-Hop

*Contact:* Blu Bolden; Taj McDade

Record labal based in St Louis, Missouri.

## Dewey Dog Records

263 West 21st Street, 1st Floor, Front
Erie, PA 16502
*Email:* joe@deweydogrecords.com
*Website:* http://www.deweydogrecords.com

*Genres:* Alternative Avant-Garde Electronic
Funky Progressive Soulful Tribal Urban
Blues Dance Deep Funk Ethnic Folk Funk
Hip-Hop Indie Jazz Latin R&B Punk Rap
Remix Singer-Songwriter Soul Techno

*Contact:* Joe Kotyuk

An independent, developmental record label
that specializes in artist / band development

for new and some ignored older talent.

Excited to be the first record label headquartered in the Erie, Pa., with a major branch office in Terra Haute, In., to initiate an all digital strategic marketing, publicity, and distribution plan for all Single, EP and LP releases.

We have been producing top quality commercial releases for some of the most talented artists, producers, and independent record labels around.

Takes a hybrid approach to making records, working with a huge collection of the best software and plugins, as well as splitting out key tracks, groups, or even the whole mix to analog mixers, compressors, delays and other processors to find that perfect sound for each track of an album.

Our "Old School" techniques, combined with today's technology is what sets us apart from other Independent Labels.

Encourages artists to be as creative as they can be and that's the key to the Label's fast growth in such a competitive market.

### DFA Records
225 West 13th Street
New York, NY 10011
*Email:* hold.on@dfarecords.com
*Website:* http://www.dfarecords.com
*Website:* https://www.facebook.com/dfarecords
*Website:* http://www.myspace.com/dfarecords

*Genres:* Indie; Disco House; Electronic

*Contact:* Jonathan Galkin; James Murphy; Tim Goldsworthy

Record label based in New York. Not accepting demos as at July 2018.

### DigSin
Nashville, TN
*Email:* jay@digsin.com
*Website:* http://digsin.com
*Website:* http://www.musicxray.com/

profiles/2512?afid=ef81d670cce8012eea2b1231381bf5de

*Genres:* All types of music

*Contact:* Jay Frank

A new model record label based in Nashville, Tennessee. Distributes music for free to those who subscribe to the label. Submit online (see website).

### Direct Management Group
8332 Melrose Ave, Top Floor
Los Angeles, CA 90069
*Website:* http://directmanagement.com

*Genres:* All types of music

International entertainment company with broad-based success in the representation of music artists.

### Dirty Canvas Music
New York
*Email:* shep.goodman@gmail.com
*Website:* https://www.facebook.com/DirtyCanvasProductions/

*Genres:* Alternative Rock; Pop

*Contact:* Shep Goodman

Full scale music production company based in NY.

### Disney Music Group
500 South Buena Vista Street
Burbank, CA 91521
*Fax:* +1 (818) 560-3230
*Website:* https://www.waltdisneystudios.com/disney-music-group/

*Genres:* All types of music

Record label arm of children's entertainment multimedia giant based in Burbank, California.

### Disruptor Records
25 Madison Avenue
New York, NY 10016
*Email:* info@disruptorrecords.com
*Website:* http://disruptorrecords.com

*Website:* https://soundcloud.com/
disruptorrecs

*Genres:* Dance; Pop

Record label based in New York. Joint
venture with Sony Music Entertainment.

## Disturbing Tha Peace Records (DTP)

1451 Woodmont Lane NW Suite A 29th
floor
Atlanta, GA 30318
*Email:* alamodtp@gmail.com
*Website:* http://dtprecords.com
*Website:* http://facebook.com/dtprecords

*Genres:* Urban

*Contact:* Ken Bailey; Sean Taylor; Erica
Novich

Record label based in Atlanta, Georgia.

## DM Music Group

265 South Federal Highway, #352
Deerfield Beach, FL 33441
*Email:* mark@dmrecords.com
*Email:* david@dmrecords.com
*Website:* http://www.dmrecords.com

*Genres:* Dance; Pop; R&B; Country Rap

*Contact:* Mark Watson; David Watson

Independent music content company based
in South Florida. Aims to exploit the full
spectrum of revenue opportunities within the
industry. Seeks talented, unique, new, and
authentic country rap artists and songwriters
for upcoming compilations and album
projects.

## DO IT Records

80 Cabrillo Highway, Suite Q429
Half Moon Bay, CA
*Email:* doitmanagement@xtra.co.nz
*Website:* http://www.doitmanagement.com
*Website:* http://www.myspace.com/
doitmanagement

*Genres:* All types of music

*Contact:* Paul Marshall

I offer services such as; International artist
management, concert promoter and record
label. I am originally from London, England.

We strive to enhance the lives and careers of
the music artists we represent, to be
approachable and amicable in all business
dealings and to provide the best possible
value for money. Our goal is to build a
lasting trust and partnership with our artists.
We will connect our artists with publishers,
tour promoters, sponsors and marketing
opportunities to further their careers. In
addition, we will seek to develop new
products for the mutual benefit of the
company and its artists. Last but not least,
we are committed to assisting our artists to
effortlessly export their music
internationally.

## Doghouse Records

118 16th Avenue S, Suite 4-144
Nashville, TN 37203-3100
*Email:* info@doghouserecords.com
*Website:* http://doghouserecords.com
*Website:* http://www.facebook.com/
doghouserecords
*Website:* http://www.myspace.com/
doghouserecords

*Genres:* Alternative; Rock; Punk; Hardcore

Record label based in New York.

## Domino Record Co. Ltd

*Website:* http://www.dominorecordco.us

*Genres:* Electronic; Indie; Punk; Rock

Record label with offices in the US and UK.

## DOMO Records, Inc.

11022 Santa Monica Blvd. #300
Los Angeles, CA 90025
*Fax:* +1 (310) 966-4420
*Email:* newtalent@domomusicgroup.com
*Website:* http://www.domomusicgroup.com
*Website:* https://soundcloud.com/domo-
records

*Genres:* Contemporary; Classical;
Electronic; Folk; Indie; New Age; Pop;
Rock; Singer-Songwriter; World; Ambient;
Soundtracks

*Contact:* A&R

Record company based in Los Angeles, California. Prefers to receive links to music online (FaceBook / MySpace, etc.) by email or via online submission form, but will not download music files or accept files attached to emails. Also accepts CDs – ensure your contact details are written on the CD itself. Response only if interested.

## Don Giovanni Records
PO Box 628
Kingston, NJ 08528
*Email:* info@dongiovannirecords.com
*Email:* dongiovannirecords@gmail.com
*Website:* http://www.dongiovannirecords.com
*Website:* https://www.facebook.com/dongiovannirecords/

*Genres:* Punk

Punk label based in Kingston, New Jersey. Happy to listen to tracks by post or by email (no MP3s), though has never previously signed a band from a demo submission alone.

## Don Rubin Productions
250 West 57th
New York, NY 10001
*Email:* drubin6573@aol.com

*Genres:* Pop; Rock

Record label based in New York.

## Dorado Music (US)
4770 Biscayne Blvd. Suite 900
Miami, FL 33137
*Email:* contact@dorado.net
*Website:* https://dorado.net
*Website:* https://www.facebook.com/doradorecords/

*Genres:* Acid Jazz; Drum and Bass; Jazz

Label with offices in London and Miami.

## Dovecote Records
231 Norman Ave # 102
Brooklyn, NY 11222
*Email:* info@dovecoterecords.com

*Website:* http://www.dovecoterecords.com
*Website:* https://soundcloud.com/dovecoterecords/

*Genres:* Indie; Rock

Independent record label and artist management company based in New York City.

## Downtown Records
New York, NY
*Email:* hello@downtownrecords.com
*Website:* http://downtownrecords.com
*Website:* https://www.facebook.com/DowntownRecords

*Genres:* All types of music

Independent record label based in New York.

## Drag City
P.O. Box 476867
Chicago, IL 60647

UK OFFICE:
Drag City Inc.
Unit 409
Bon Marche Centre
241-251 Ferndale Rd
London, SW9 8BJ
*Fax:* +1 (312) 455-1057
*Email:* press@dragcity.com
*Email:* webmaster@dragcity.com
*Website:* http://www.dragcity.com

*Genres:* Pop; Rock; Alternative; Hard Rock; Experimental

Record label with offices in Chicago and London. No longer accepts demos "unless they're amazing".

## DRG Records Incorporated
22 Harbor Park Drive
Port Washington, NY 11050
*Fax:* +1 (516) 484-2365
*Email:* info@drgrecords.com
*Website:* https://www.drgrecords.com

*Genres:* Soundtracks

Focuses on Broadway, vocal artists, cabaret and soundtracks.

## Dualtone Records
3 Mcferrin Ave
Nashville, TN 37206
*Fax:* +1 (615) 320-0692
*Email:* info@dualtone.com
*Website:* http://www.dualtone.com
*Website:* http://www.facebook.com/
dualtonemusic

*Genres:* Americana; Folk; Indie Rock;
Singer-Songwriter

American-based independent record label
specializing in folk, singer/songwriter,
Americana and indie rock.

## Duck Down Music
*Email:* demos@duckdown.com
*Email:* info@duckdown.com
*Website:* http://www.duckdown.com
*Website:* https://soundcloud.com/duckdown

*Genres:* Urban; Hip-Hop

Urban record label based in New York. For
beats and demos, send query by email with:

1) Artist Name
2) Hometown
3) Age
4) SoundCloud page
5) YouTube channel
6) Twitter, Facebook, Instagram pages
7) Phone number

## Earache Records Inc.
4402 11th Street, #400A
Long Island City, NY 11101
*Email:* al@earache.com
*Website:* http://www.earache.com
*Website:* https://www.facebook.com/
earacherecords/
*Website:* http://www.myspace.com/
earacherecords

*Genres:* Metal; Rock; Blues Rock; Extreme
Metal

*Contact:* Al Dawson

American office of a UK label. Submit
demos via form on website.

## Earwig Music Company, Inc.
2054 W. Farwell Avenue, Suite G
Chicago, IL 60645
*Email:* info@earwigmusic.com
*Website:* https://www.earwigmusic.com
*Website:* https://www.facebook.com/
earwigmusicpage/

*Genres:* Blues; Jazz

Founded in 1978 as a record label and artist
management company. Also offeres music
career consulting and music marketing
services.

## East of Sideways Music
*Email:* ContactEOS@eastofsideways.com
*Website:* https://www.eastofsideways.com
*Website:* https://www.youtube.com/user/
barrykeenan

*Genres:* Blues; Country; Electronic; Jazz;
Latin; Pop; Rap; Hip-Hop; Rock; Urban

"All of the songs in our catalog are lyrically
well-written, with exceptional melodies, and
top notch instrumental and production
values.

Our music is distinctive, affecting, and
thought provoking."

## Eclipse Records, inc.
c/o A&R Submissions
P.O. Box 51
Pompton Plains, NJ 07444-0051
*Website:* https://www.eclipserecords.com/
*Website:* https://www.facebook.com/
eclipserecords

*Genres:* Alternative; Rock

Record label based in Pompton Plains, New
Jersey. Submit through form on website, or
by post. See website for full submission
guidelines.

## ECR Music Group
511 Avenue of the Americas, Suite #K144
New York, NY 10011
*Email:* contact@ecrmusicgroup.com
*Website:* http://www.ecrmusicgroup.com
*Website:* https://www.facebook.com/
ecrmusicgroup

*Genres:* Pop; Rock

Record label based in New York. Describes itself as one of the world's leading independent music companies.

## Elektra Music Group
3400 West Olive Avenue, 2nd Floor
Burbank, CA 91505
*Website:* http://www.elektramusicgroup.com

*Genres:* All types of music

Music group with offices in Burbank, California, New York, and Nashville, Tennessee.

## Elm City Music
New Haven, CT
*Website:* http://elmcitymusic.net
*Website:* https://www.facebook.com/ElmCityMusicRecords/

*Genres:* All types of music

*Contact:* Michael Caplan

Full service music and entertainment company based in New Haven, Connecticut.

## Emblem Music Group
23679 Calabasas Rd #739
Calabasas CA 91302
*Email:* info@emblem-music.com
*Website:* http://www.emblem-music.com

*Genres:* All types of music

Record label based in Calabasas, California.

## The End Records
PO Box 20529
New York, NY 10023
*Email:* all@theendrecords.com
*Website:* http://www.theendrecords.com
*Website:* https://www.facebook.com/theendrecords/
*Website:* http://www.myspace.com/theendrecords

*Genres:* Rock; Metal; Indie; Alternative

Indepdent record label based in New York, specialising in rock and alternative music.

## Entertainment One (eOne)
10 Harbor Park Drive
Port Washington, New York 11050
*Website:* https://www.entertainmentone.com
*Website:* https://www.facebook.com/EntertainmentOneGroup/

*Genres:* All types of music

Entertainment company with interests in film, television, and music, and offices in multiple locations in North America and around the world.

## Epic Records Group
25 Madison Avenue, 10th Floor
New York, NY 10022-3211

CALIFORNIA OFFICE:
9830 Wilshire Boulevard,
Beverly Hills, CA 90212
*Website:* http://www.epicrecords.com

*Genres:* All types of music

*Contact:* Farra Matthews, VP A&R; Michael Klein, A&R Operations

Label with offices in New York and Beverly Hills, California. Handles all genres, but in particular pop, hip-hop, rock, alternative, and electronica. Accepts approaches via known managers/agents only.

## Epitaph
2798 Sunset Boulevard
Los Angeles, CA 90026
*Website:* http://www.epitaph.com
*Website:* https://www.facebook.com/epitaphrecords

*Genres:* Punk; Indie; Hardcore; Emo; Garage; Alternative Rock; Post Hardcore; Punk Rock; Hip-Hop

*Contact:* Brett Gurewitz

Record label based in Los Angeles, California. Submit links to music online via demo submission form on website.

## Equal Vision Records
P.O. Box 38202
Albany, NY 12203-8202
*Fax:* +1 (518) 458-1312

*Email:* music@equalvision.com
*Email:* info@equalvision.com
*Website:* http://www.equalvision.com
*Website:* https://soundcloud.com/equalvision

*Genres:* Alternative; Indie; Metal; Punk; Rock

Label based in Albany, New York. No physical demos. Send email with links to your music online (no downloads), plus bio.

## Ernest Jenning Record Co.
Brooklyn, NY
*Email:* info@ernestjenning.com
*Website:* http://www.ernestjenning.com
*Website:* https://www.facebook.com/ErnestJenning

*Genres:* Modern Pop; Rock

Independent record label based in Brooklyn, New York. Send demos by email.

## Everloving
2658 Griffith Park Boulevard #115
Los Angeles, CA 90039
*Email:* andy@everloving.com
*Email:* jp@everloving.com
*Website:* http://www.everloving.com
*Website:* http://soundcloud.com/everloving

*Genres:* All types of music

*Contact:* Andy Factor (Partner); JP Plunier (Partner)

Record label based in Los Angeles, California. No longer accepts demos by post. All submissions must be made via Soundcloud dropbox.

## Fade To Silence
*Email:* info@fadetosilencerecords.com
*Website:* http://www.fadetosilencerecords.com
*Website:* https://www.facebook.com/fadetosilencerecords

*Genres:* All types of music

Independent label / digital services/ music publishing.

## Fair Trade
*Website:* http://www.fairtradeservices.com

*Genres:* Christian

Christian record label that aims to foster relationships with artists in a spirit of partnership and fairness.

## Famous Records
4577 N. Nob Hill Road, Suite 201
Sunrise, FL 33351
*Fax:* +1 (954) 368-2740
*Email:* famousfontana1@gmail.com
*Email:* jeffrey@famousmusicgroup.com
*Website:* http://www.famousmusicgroup.com
*Website:* https://soundcloud.com/famousfontana

*Genres:* All types of music

Record label based in Sunrise, Florida. Considers all genres of music. Send query by email with MP3s or links to music online.

## Fat Possum Records
PO Box 1923
Oxford, MS 38655
*Fax:* +1 (662) 234-2899
*Email:* matthew@fatpossum.com
*Email:* bruce_w@fatpossum.com
*Website:* http://www.fatpossum.com
*Website:* https://soundcloud.com/fatpossum

*Genres:* Blues; Indie

*Contact:* Matthew Johnson; Bruce Watson

Record label based in Oxford, Mississippi.

## Fearless Records
5870 W Jefferson Blvd, Suite E
Los Angeles, CA 90016
*Email:* demos@fearlessrecords.com
*Email:* info@fearlessrecords.com
*Website:* http://www.fearlessrecords.com
*Website:* https://www.facebook.com/fearlessrecords

*Genres:* Indie; Punk; Rock; Hardcore; Pop; Alternative

*Contact:* Bob B (President/A&R)

Record label based in Los Angeles, California. Send demos by email with links to music online, or by post. Include contact information, 3-4 of your best songs, band bio and band photo.

## Ferret Music
1290 Ave of the Americas, 24th Floor
New York, NY 10104
*Email:* ferretstyle@ferretstyle.com
*Website:* http://ferretstyle.com
*Website:* https://www.youtube.com/profile?user=FERRETMUSICNJ
*Website:* http://www.myspace.com/ferretmusic

*Genres:* Alternative Rock; Hard Rock; Metal

Record label based in New York. Send query by email with links to online community pages only. No links to MP3s, EPKs, etc. Do not chase for response.

## Fervor Records
*Email:* info@fervor-records.com
*Website:* http://www.fervor-records.com

*Genres:* Indie; Contemporary; Traditional; Rock

A boutique indie label representing emerging artists and an extensive catalogue of vintage recordings from 1921 to 1995.

## Fool's Gold
147 Grand St
11249 Brooklyn, New York
*Email:* demos@foolsgoldrecs.com
*Website:* https://foolsgoldrecs.com
*Website:* https://www.facebook.com/foolsgoldrecords

*Genres:* All types of music

Record label based in Brooklyn. Send query by email with links to music online. MP3 attachments will be deleted.

## Frenchkiss Records
New York
*Email:* info@frenchkissrecords.com
*Website:* http://www.frenchkissrecords.com
*Website:* https://www.facebook.com/frenchkissrecords

*Genres:* All types of music

Record label based in New York.

## Friendly Fire Recordings
3727 25th Street
San Francisco, CA 94110
*Email:* info@friendlyfirerecordings.com
*Website:* http://www.friendlyfirerecordings.com
*Website:* https://soundcloud.com/friendlyfirerecordings

*Genres:* All types of music

Record label based in San Francisco. Prefers queries by email with links to music online (no MP3 attachments), but will also consider CDs by post.

## Frontier Records
PO Box 22
Sun Valley, CA 91353
*Email:* info@frontierrecords.com
*Website:* http://www.frontierrecords.com
*Website:* https://www.facebook.com/thefrontierrecords?ref=ts

*Genres:* Punk Rock; Classic Punk; Alternative Rock

Punk label based in Sun Valley, California. Not accepting demos as at May 2018, but is interested in re-releasing vintage punk or alternative rock. Contact by email.

## Fueled By Ramen
1633 Broadway 10th floor
New York, NY 10019
*Email:* erick@fueledbyramen.com
*Website:* http://www.fueledbyramen.com
*Website:* http://www.facebook.com/fueledbyramen

*Genres:* All types of music

Record label based in New York. Send demo by post with bio, contact information, touring information, and more. Do not send emails about demo submissions.

## Funzalo Records
PO Box 571567
Tarzana, CA 91357
*Email:* dan@mikesmanagement.com
*Website:* http://funzalorecords.com

*Website:* https://www.facebook.com/
funzalorecords/

*Genres:* Americana; Folk; Indie; Rock

*Contact:* Mike Lembo; Dan Agnew

Send submissions via online submission form. Submissions without music links will be deleted. No rap music.

## Get Hip Recordings

R.J. Casey Industrial Park
1800 Columbus Avenue
Pittsburgh, PA 15233
*Email:* gregg@gethip.com
*Email:* barbara@gethip.com
*Website:* http://www.gethip.com
*Website:* https://www.facebook.com/
GetHipRecordings

*Genres:* Folk; Punk; Rock; Indie

*Contact:* Gregg Kostelich; Barbara Garcia-Bernado

Record label based in Pittsburgh. Also acts as a distributor.

## Ghostly International

PO Box 220395
Brooklyn, NY 11222
*Email:* booking@ghostly.com
*Website:* https://ghostly.com

*Genres:* Electronic; Indie; Hip-Hop; Pop; Rap; Rock

Label based in Brooklyn, New York.

## Glassnote

NEW YORK
770 Lexington Avenue, 16th Floor
New York, NY 10065

LOS ANGELES
2220 Colorado Avenue, Suite 200
Santa Monica, CA 90404
*Fax:* +1 (646) 237-2711
*Email:* demos@glassnotemusic.com
*Website:* http://glassnotemusic.com
*Website:* https://soundcloud.com/
glassnotemusic

*Genres:* All types of music

*Contact:* Attn: Demo Submissions

Record label with offices in New York, Los Angeles, London, and Toronto. Send demos by post to the New York address or send queries by email with MP3 attachments or links to music online.

## GNP Crescendo Records

*Email:* gnp@pacificnet.net
*Website:* http://store.gnpcrescendo.com
*Website:* https://www.facebook.com/
gnpcrescendo/

*Genres:* Blues; Country; Dance; Electronic; Folk; Jazz; Latin; Pop; Rock; Soundtracks; World

Label based in Los Angeles, California.

## Gotee Records

*Email:* music@gotee.com
*Website:* https://www.gotee.com

*Genres:* R&B; Reggae; Rap; Rock

Submit music by email.

## Green Linnet

Compass Records
916 19th Avenue South
Nashville, TN 37212
*Fax:* +1 (615) 320-7378
*Email:* submissions@compassrecords.com
*Email:* info@compassrecords.com
*Website:* http://www.greenlinnet.com
*Website:* http://www.myspace.com/
greenlinnetrecords

*Genres:* Folk; World; Celtic

Record label based in Nashville, Tennessee. Describes itself as "the best-known brand in Celtic music". Send query by email with links to website with your music, bio, photos, and upcoming tour dates. Include details of why your think your music is right for this label, and the last 2 years of touring history. If you send in a CD and printed material, this will significantly slow down the review process.

## Hacienda Records
1236 South Staples Street
Corpus Christi, TX 78404
*Fax:* +1 (361) 882-3943
*Email:* sales@haciendarecords.com
*Email:* hacienda@haciendarecords.com
*Website:* http://hacienda-records.
myshopify.com
*Website:* https://www.facebook.com/
haciendarecords

*Genres:* Latin; Gospel

Record label based in Corpus Christi, Texas, producing Latin, Tejano, Traditional Tex-Mex, Conjunto and Norteño music, as well as Banda, Merengue, Duranguense, Rock En Español, Gospel and Christmas music.

## Harbour Records
*Email:* info@harbourrecordings.com
*Website:* http://harbourrecordings.com

*Genres:* Electronic; Pop; Rock

Independent boutique record label founded in 2012.

## Headliner Records / George Tobin Music
102 NE 2nd Street
Boca Raton, FL 33432
*Email:* georgetobinmusic@aol.com
*Website:* http://www.headlinerrecords.com

*Genres:* Alternative; Pop; R&B

*Contact:* George Tobin

Record label based in Boca Raton, Florida. Claims to be responsible for the sale of over 25 million records worldwide. Accepts demos and promotion packages.

As at June 2018 this label is conducting a professional talent search for young unsigned male pop singers and vocal groups between the ages of 14-22. No rap. See website for details.

## Hidden Beach Recordings
*Email:* admin@hiddenbeach.com
*Website:* http://www.hiddenbeach.com

*Genres:* Gospel; Jazz; R&B; Hip-Hop; Rap

California-based record label. See website for more details.

## HighNote Records
106 West 71st Street
New York, NY 10023
*Fax:* +1 (212) 877-0407
*Email:* jazzdepo@ix.netcom.com
*Website:* http://www.jazzdepot.com
*Website:* https://www.facebook.com/
HighNoteRecords

*Genres:* Jazz

Jazz record label based in New York.

## Highwheel Records
*Email:* info@highwheelrecords.com
*Website:* http://highwheelrecords.com

*Genres:* Alternative; Rock

Boutique label offering high quality, independently spirited records.

## Hit City USA
Los Angeles, CA
*Website:* http://www.hitcityusa.com
*Website:* http://www.facebook.com/
hitcityusa

*Genres:* Alternative; Pop; R&B

Describes itself as a record label and cultural hub, based in LA.

## Hit World Records
Los Angeles, CA / Houston, TX
*Email:* hitworldrecords@gmail.com
*Website:* http://www.hitworldrecords.com

*Genres:* Pop; Urban

Record label with offices in Los Angelse, California, and Houston, Texas.

## Hollywood Records
*Website:* http://www.hollywoodrecords.com
*Website:* https://www.facebook.com/
HollywoodRecords

*Genres:* All types of music

Record label with a roster that spans genres.

## Hopeless Records

*Email:* ar@hopelessrecords.com
*Email:* info@hopelessrecords.com
*Website:* http://hopelessrecords.com
*Website:* https://www.facebook.com/
hopelessrecords

*Genres:* Hardcore; Indie; Metal; Punk; Rock;
Ska

Record label based in Van Nuys, California.
Contact by email only, including bio, links to
MySpace and Youtube videos, etc. electric
press kit if you have one, and/or 2-4 MP3
tracks (maximum). No physical submissions.

## Hydra Head Records

Los Angelese, CA
*Website:* http://hydrahead.com
*Website:* https://www.facebook.com/
hydrahead

*Genres:* Heavy Metal; Experimental;
Hardcore

Independent record label based in LA,
specialising in heavy and experimental
music.

## Iamsound

Los Angeles, CA
*Email:* hello@iamsound.com
*Website:* https://iamsound.com
*Website:* https://www.facebook.com/
iamsoundrecords

*Genres:* All types of music

Record label, agency and visual art studio
based in Los Angeles.

## Idol Records

Attn: A & R
PO Box 140344
Dallas, TX 75214
*Email:* info@idolrecords.com
*Website:* http://www.idolrecords.com
*Website:* http://www.facebook.com/
idolrecordsgroup
*Website:* http://www.myspace.com/
idolrecords

*Genres:* Indie; Pop; Punk; Rap; Hip-Hop;
Rock;; Americana; Instrumental

*Contact:* Erv Karwelis

Send demo with contact information along
with a bio, recent photo, web address, press
kit and upcoming show dates. No material
returned. Response not guaranteed unless
interested.

## In the Red Records

PO Box 50777
Los Angeles, CA 90050
*Email:* info@intheredrecords.com
*Website:* https://intheredrecords.com

*Genres:* Garage; Punk; Rock and Roll

Record label based in Los Angeles,
California.

## Infidel Records

931 Madison Street
Hoboken, NJ 07030
*Website:* http://infidelrecords.com

*Genres:* All types of music

Record label based in New Jersey.

## Innovative Leisure

2658 Griffith Park Boulevard #324
Los Angeles, CA 90039
*Email:* info@innovativeleisure.net
*Website:* https://www.innovativeleisure.net

*Genres:* All types of music

Independent record label based in Los
Angeles, California.

## Inspired Studios Inc.

8854 Via Brilliante
Wellington, FL 33411
*Fax:* +1 (561) 333-9143
*Email:* dkasen@inspired-studios.com
*Website:* http://www.inspired-studios.com

*Genres:* All types of music

Music company based in Wellington,
Florida.

## Intelligent Noise

Los Angeles, CA
*Email:* shannon@intelligentnoise.com

*Website:* http://intelligentnoise.com
*Website:* https://www.facebook.com/
intelligentnoise

*Genres:* All types of music

Indie label based in LA.

## Interscope Geffen A&M
2220 Colorado Avenue
Santa Monica, CA 90404
*Website:* https://www.interscope.com
*Website:* https://www.facebook.com/
interscope

*Genres:* Hip-Hop; Indie; Pop; Rap; Rock

Record label based in Santa Monica,
California.

## Ipecac Recordings
*Email:* info@ipecac.com
*Website:* http://www.ipecac.com
*Website:* https://www.facebook.com/ipecac

*Genres:* Rock

Aims to be an honest, artist friendly label run
on a shoe string with no outrageous
promotional or production costs.

## Jaggo Records, LLC
*Email:* jaggo@jaggo.com
*Website:* http://www.jaggo.com

*Genres:* Jazz; Hip-Hop; Pop; R&B; Rock;
Soul; World

Record label based in California, boasting
120 years of collective experience in the
industry. Aims to build lasting careers for
artists.

## Jagjaguwar
213 S. Rogers Street
Bloomington, IN 47404
*Email:* info@jagjaguwar.com
*Website:* http://jagjaguwar.com
*Website:* https://www.facebook.com/
Jagjaguwar/

*Genres:* Alternative; Folk; Indie

Record label based in Bloomington, Indiana.

## Javotti Media
*Email:* info@javottimedia.com
*Website:* http://www.javottimedia.com
*Website:* https://www.facebook.com/
javottimedia/

*Genres:* Urban

No audio files by email.

## K Records
PO Box 7154
Olympia, WA 98507
*Email:* info@krecs.com
*Email:* promo@krecs.com
*Website:* https://www.krecs.com
*Website:* https://www.facebook.com/
box7154/

*Genres:* All types of music

*Contact:* Calvin Johnson

Record label based in Olympia, Washington.
Not accepting demos as at March 2019.
Check website for current status.

## Kanine Records
*Email:* info@KanineRecords.com
*Website:* http://kaninerecords.com
*Website:* https://www.facebook.com/
kaninerecords

*Genres:* Indie; Pop; Punk; Rock

Record label based in Brooklyn, New York.
Not accepting demos as at March 2019.

## Keyframe Music
*Email:* keyframe@yahoo.com
*Website:* http://keyframe-entertainment.com
*Website:* https://www.facebook.com/
keyframe.entertainment/

*Genres:* Electronic; Trance

Produces, finances, and distributes cutting-
edge projects in a variety of media.

## Kill Rock Stars
107 SE Washington Street, Suite 155
Portland, OR 97214
*Fax:* +1 (360) 357-6408
*Email:* krs@killrockstars.com
*Email:* portia@killrockstars.com

*Website:* https://www.killrockstars.com
*Website:* http://www.myspace.com/
killrockstars5rc

*Genres:* Indie; Punk

*Contact:* Portia Sabin, President

Only willing to consider bands who are touring and who will be playing in Portland. Send email with links to music online and details of tour dates, and date playing in Portland. No demos by post.

## Killroom Records
Seattle, WA
*Email:* killroomrecords@gmail.com
*Website:* http://www.killroomrecords.com
*Website:* https://www.facebook.com/
killroomrecords/

*Genres:* All types of music

*Contact:* Troy Nelson; Ben Jenkins

Record label based in Seattle, Washington.

## King Street Sounds
New York, NY
*Email:* rich@kingstreetsounds.com
*Website:* https://www.kingstreetsounds.com
*Website:* https://soundcloud.com/
kingstreetsounds

*Genres:* Electronic; Dance

Record label based in New York. Send demos by email.

## Kirtland Records
Dallas, TX 75226
*Fax:* +1 (214) 849-9807
*Email:* music@kirtlandrecords.com
*Website:* http://kirtlandrecords.com
*Website:* https://www.facebook.com/
KirtlandRecords/

*Genres:* Alternative; Pop; Rock

*Contact:* John Kirtland

Record label based in Dallas, Texas.

## Knife Fight Media
*Email:* alexander@knifefightmedia.com
*Website:* http://www.knifefightmedia.com
*Website:* https://www.facebook.com/
knifefightmedia

*Genres:* Electronic; Metal; Punk; Rock

Record label based in Red Bank, New Jersey.

## Lakeshore Entertainment
9268 West Third Street
Beverly Hills, CA 90210
*Email:* MusicDept@
lakeshoreentertainment.com
*Website:* http://www.lakeshorerecords.com

*Genres:* Soundtracks

Independent music division of film production company.

## Lamon Records
PO Box 1907
Mt Juliet, TN 37121
*Email:* dave@lamonrecords.com
*Website:* http://www.lamonrecords.com

*Genres:* Blues; Christian; Country; Folk; Gospel; Latin; Roots

Label with offices in Nashville, Hollywood, and Charlotte. Submit via online submission form.

## Landslide Records
PO Box 15117
Fernandina Beach, FL 32035
*Email:* mrland@mindspring.com
*Website:* http://www.landsliderecords.com
*Website:* https://myspace.com/
landsliderecordsoriginal

*Genres:* Americana; Blues; Folk; Jazz; Rock

*Contact:* Landslide Records

Record label based in Fernandina Beach, Florida.

## Lava Records
1755 Broadway
New York, NY 10019
*Website:* http://www.lavarecords.com

*Website:* https://www.facebook.com/
LavaRecordsUS

*Genres:* All types of music

Record label based in New York. Discovered and championed artists who went on to sell in excess of 100 million records around the world in the label's first nine years of existence.

## Le Grand Magistery, LLC
PO Box 611
Bloomfield Hills, MI 48303
*Email:* magistery@aol.com
*Website:* http://www.magistery.com

*Genres:* Alternative; Rock

Record label based in Bloomfield Hills, Michigan.

## Lightning Rod Records
718 Thompson Lane
Suite 108 – PMB 181
Nashville, TN 37204
*Email:* info@lightningrodrecords.com
*Website:* https://www.
lightningrodrecords.com
*Website:* https://www.facebook.com/
lightningrodrecords

*Genres:* Americana; Rock; Roots

Record label based in Nashville, Tennessee.

## Lightyear Entertainment
*Website:* http://www.lightyear.com
*Website:* https://www.facebook.com/
lightyearent

*Genres:* All types of music

Los Angeles and New York based entertainment company. Describes itself as "a multi-layered entertainment company that creates and acquires a mix of music and video product with two key common elements: high quality and strong niche appeal."

## Little Fish Records
PO Box 19164
Cleveland, OH 44119

*Email:* littlefishrecords@gmail.com
*Website:* http://www.littlefishrecords.com
*Website:* https://www.facebook.com/
LittleFishRecords

*Genres:* Regional; Reggae; World; Americana; Blues; Folk; Jazz; Rock

Cleveland-based record label, "committed to presenting the finest local and regional sounds within a wide variety of musical genres".

## LML Music
Post Office Box 48081
Los Angeles, CA 90048
*Fax:* +1 (323) 856-9204
*Email:* lee@lmlmusic.com
*Website:* http://www.lmlmusic.com

*Genres:* Contemporary; Pop; Traditional

Record label based in Los Angeles. Send demo with press kit by post. Include SASE if return of material required.

## Loma Vista
*Website:* https://www.
lomavistarecordings.com
*Website:* https://twitter.com/LomaVistaRC

*Genres:* All types of music

Record label based in California.

## Lookout! Records
*Website:* https://www.lookoutrecords.com

*Genres:* Punk; Rock

Punk/rock label based in Berkely, California.

## Lost Highway Records
*Website:* https://www.umgnashville.com
*Website:* https://www.facebook.com/
UMGNashville

*Genres:* Country; Roots; Rock; Americana; Folk

Label based in Nashville, Tennessee.

## LoveCat Music

*Email:* lovecatmusic@gmail.com
*Website:* http://www.lovecatmusic.com
*Website:* https://www.facebook.com/
LoveCatMusic

*Genres:* Pop; Rock; Dance; Latin; World;
R&B; Jazz; Reggaeton; Latin Hip-Hop; Rap;
Hip-Hop

Independent record label and music
publisher, founded in 1999. License original
songs for use in films, TV, advertisement,
trailers and games. Particularly interested in
songs with the themes of freedom, moving /
action. happiness / joy, and friends / family.
Cannot use cover versions or songs that
include samples from other songs.

## Lovelane Music Group

Sherman Oaks, CA 91423
*Email:* lovelanemusic@gmail.com

*Genres:* Blues; Funk; R&B

Record label based in Sherman Oaks,
California.

## Lovitt Records

Post Office Box 100248
Arlington, VA 22210-9998
*Fax:* +1 (703) 824-0511
*Website:* http://www.lovitt.com
*Website:* https://www.facebook.com/
lovittrecords

*Genres:* Indie; Punk

Record label based in Arlington, Virginia.
Accepts demos by post but has never yet
signed a band from a demo – usually this
happens by bands being seen at shows, doing
shows with bands already on the roster, etc.

## Loyalty Over Royalty Records

*Email:* loyaltyoverroyaltyrecs@gmail.com
*Website:* https://www.facebook.com/
LoyaltyOverRoyaltyRecords

*Genres:* All types of music

*Contact:* Warren Wells

An independent record label and concert
promotion company founded in 2019 in
Toronto, Canada. As an indie label and
booking company, we are dedicated to
promoting shows and artists we love in
North America and beyond.

## Machin Entertainment

11135 Weddington St. #424
N Hollywood, CA 91601
*Fax:* +1 (270) 717-8862
*Email:* info@machinentertainment.com
*Website:* http://machinentertainment.com

*Genres:* All types of music

Provides fast and easy digital distribution to
independent labels and artists.

## Mad Decent

*Website:* https://maddecent.com
*Website:* https://www.facebook.com/
maddecent

*Genres:* Black Metal; Glam; House;
Underground

Record label based in Los Angeles,
California. On a mission is to highlight
underground, genre-blurring sounds.

## Mad Dragon Music Group

3501 Market St
19104 Philadelphia, PA
*Email:* mdmg@drexel.edu
*Website:* http://www.maddragonmusic.com
*Website:* https://www.facebook.com/
MADDragonMusicGroup/

*Genres:* Alternative; Rock

Record label based in Philadelphia,
Pennsylvania. Send query through online
web form with links to music online.

## Maggie's Music

PO Box 490
Shady Side, MD 20764
*Email:* mail@maggiesmusic.com
*Website:* https://www.maggiesmusic.com

*Genres:* Celtic; Acoustic

Celtic record label based in Shady Side,
Maryland.

## Magna Carta Records

East Rochester, NY
*Email:* info@magnacarta.net
*Website:* https://magnacartarecords.
bandcamp.com

*Genres:* Progressive Metal; Rock

Independent record label based in East
Rochester, New York. Best known for
progressive rock / metal.

## Mandala Records

*Website:* http://mandalarecords.com

*Genres:* All types of music

See website for details.

## Maranatha Music

*Email:* info@maranathamusic.com
*Email:* jakob@maranathamusic.com
*Website:* https://www.maranathamusic.com
*Website:* https://www.facebook.com/
maranathamusicofficial/

*Genres:* Christian; Gospel

Christian music label founded in 1971.

## Marsalis Music

323 Broadway
Cambridge, MA 02139
*Fax:* +1 (617) 354-2396
*Email:* info@marsalismusic.com
*Website:* https://www.marsalismusic.com

*Genres:* Jazz

*Contact:* Branford Marsalis

Jazz label based in Cambridge,
Massachusetts. Currently closed to new
artists as at September 2019.

## Mascot Label Group

118 East 28th Street, Suite 701
New York, NY 10016
*Email:* questions@mlgmerch.com
*Website:* https://usa.mascotlabelgroup.com
*Website:* http://www.facebook.com/
mascotlabelgroup

*Genres:* All types of music

Record label with offices in New York and
the Netherlands.

## Mass Appeal Records

*Website:* http://www.massappealrecords.com
*Website:* https://www.facebook.com/
MassAppealRecs/

*Genres:* Urban; Hip-Hop

Independent record label.

## Matador Records

304 Hudson Street, 7th Floor
New York, NY 10013
*Fax:* +1 (212) 995-5883
*Email:* info@matadorrecords.com
*Website:* https://www.matadorrecords.com

*Genres:* Indie

Indie label based in New York. Not
accepting unsolicited demo submissions as at
June 2019.

## Maybach Music Group

*Website:* https://www.facebook.com/
MaybachMusicGroup
*Website:* https://www.instagram.com/
untouchablemmg/

*Genres:* Hip-Hop; Rap

Rap and hip-hop record label.

## Megaforce Records

*Website:* http://www.megaforcerecords.com
*Website:* https://www.facebook.com/
OfficialMegaforceRecords/

*Genres:* Rock

Rock record label based in New York.

## Merge Records

*Email:* merge@mergerecords.com
*Website:* https://www.mergerecords.com
*Website:* https://soundcloud.com/
mergerecords

*Genres:* Indie; Rock; Singer-Songwriter

Record label founded in Chapel Hill, North
Carolina, in 1989. No unsolicited demos.

## Metal Blade Records, Inc.

5160 Van Nuys, Blvd #301
Sherman Oaks, CA 91403
*Email:* metalblade@metalblade.com
*Website:* https://www.metalblade.com

*Genres:* Hardcore; Metal; Rock

Closed to unsolicited demos as at July 2019.
Check website for current status.

## Metropolis Records

PO Box 974
Media, PA 19063
*Email:* demo@metropolis-records.com
*Email:* info@metropolis-records.com
*Website:* http://www.metropolis-records.com
*Website:* https://www.facebook.com/
MetropolisRecords

*Genres:* Alternative; Indie

*Contact:* Attn: Demos

Send submissions on CD or CD-R by post,
with brief bio and contact information
(marked for the attention of "Demos"), or
send email with soundcloud links. Do not
send email attachments (these will be deleted
without being opened). Response only if
interested.

## Metropolitan Groove Merchants (MGM)

604 Gallatin Ave, Suite 206
Nashville TN 37206
*Email:* usa@thegroovemerchants.com
*Website:* https://www.
thegroovemerchants.com
*Website:* https://www.facebook.com/
mgmdistribution

*Genres:* All types of music

US office of Australian record label. Send
demos through submission form on website.

## Middle West

*Email:* info@middlewestmgmt.com
*Website:* http://www.middlewestmgmt.com
*Website:* https://www.facebook.com/
middlewestmgmt

*Genres:* All types of music

Artist management company founded in
2010 in the Midwest.

## Milan Records

Burbank, CA 91505
*Email:* jc.chamboredon@milanrecords.com
*Website:* https://www.milanrecords.com

*Genres:* Electronic; Soundtracks; World

Label based in Burbank, California.

## The Militia Group

*Fax:* +1 (562) 491-0470
*Email:* contact@themilitiagroup.com
*Website:* http://www.themilitiagroup.com

*Genres:* Folk; Indie; Pop; Rock; Singer-
Songwriter

Record label based in California.

## Mind of a Genius Records

Los Angeles, CA
*Website:* https://www.mindofagenius.com

*Genres:* All types of music

Record label based in Los Angeles,
California.

## Minty Fresh Records

Chicago, IL
*Email:* info@mintyfresh.com
*Website:* http://www.mintyfresh.com
*Website:* https://www.facebook.com/
mintyfreshrecords
*Website:* http://www.myspace.com/
mintyfreshrecords

*Genres:* Alternative; Electronic; Indie; Pop;
Punk; Rock

Accepts submissions as links to music online
only. No attachments.

## Mixpak

Brooklyn, NY
*Email:* info@mixpakrecords.com
*Website:* http://mixpakrecords.com
*Website:* https://soundcloud.com/mixpak

*Genres:* All types of music

Brooklyn-based globally-minded endeavour without genre boundaries or confines – delivering music from rappers, underground club producers and experimental electronic artists alike.

## Mom + Pop
New York, NY
*Website:* http://www.momandpopmusic.com
*Website:* https://www.facebook.com/momandpopmusic

*Genres:* All types of music

Independent record label based in New York.

## Moodswing Records
*Website:* http://www.moodswingrecords.com
*Website:* https://www.facebook.com/Moodswing-Records-178415592209351/
*Website:* https://myspace.com/moodswingrecords

*Genres:* Punk; Avant-Garde; World

Record label founded in 1994 in Atlanta.

## Morphius Records
Morphius-A&R/Demo Submissions
100 East 23rd Street,
Baltimore, MD 21218
*Fax:* +1 (410) 662-0116
*Email:* info@morphius.com
*Website:* http://morphius.com

*Genres:* Experimental; Hip-Hop; Punk; Rock

Record label based in Baltimore, Maryland. Send demo package by post. Wait two weeks before following up. See website for more details.

## Mosaic Records
425 Fairfield Avenue, Suite 421
Stamford, CT 06902
*Fax:* +1 (203) 323-3526
*Email:* info@mosaicrecords.com
*Website:* http://www.mosaicrecords.com
*Website:* http://www.facebook.com/pages/Mosaic/268268936547980

*Genres:* Jazz

Jazz record label based in Stamford, Connecticut.

## Moth Man Records
*Email:* joe@mothmanrecords.com
*Website:* https://mothmanrecords.com

*Genres:* Alternative Thrash Psychedelic Acoustic Hard Heavy Funky Melodic Modern Post Progressive Americana Emo Funk Garage Guitar based Hardcore Indie Lo-fi Melodicore Pop Punk Rock Rock and Roll Rockabilly Shoegaze

*Contact:* Joe

A recording studio located in a Milwaukee basement specializing in indie rock and related genres. When I have time, I record music projects that I enjoy for free. Feel free to message me or send your demos.

## Motown Gospel
101 Winners Circle
Brentwood, TN 37027
*Email:* info@motowngospel.com
*Website:* https://www.motowngospel.com
*Website:* https://www.facebook.com/MotownGospel

*Genres:* Gospel

Gospel label based in Brentwood, Tennessee.

## Motown
*Website:* https://www.motownrecords.com
*Website:* https://www.facebook.com/MotownRecords

*Genres:* All types of music

Record label based in New York.

## MPress Records
118 E 28th St. #1010
New York, NY 10016
*Email:* info@mpressrecords.com
*Website:* http://mpressrecords.com
*Website:* http://www.facebook.com/mpressrecords

*Genres:* All types of music

*Contact:* Jojo Gentry

Record label based in New York.

## Music Plant Group
*Website:* http://www.musicplantrecords.com
*Website:* https://www.facebook.com/musicplantrecords/

*Genres:* Dance; Hip-Hop; Latin; R&B

Record label of over 25 years standing.

## Mute Records
*Email:* demos@mute.com
*Email:* mute@mute.com
*Website:* http://mute.com
*Website:* https://soundcloud.com/muterecords

*Genres:* Alternative

Send query by email with links to up to four tracks online. No file attachments or submissions by post.

## Nacional Records
*Email:* hearme@nacionalrecords.com
*Email:* info@nacionalrecords.com
*Website:* http://www.nacionalrecords.com
*Website:* https://www.facebook.com/nacionalrecords

*Genres:* Latin

Send query by email with links to music online. Response not guaranteed.

## Naxos Records
1810 Columbia Ave, Suite 28
Franklin, TN 37064
*Fax:* +1 (615) 771-6747
*Email:* naxos@naxosusa.com
*Website:* https://www.naxos.com
*Website:* https://www.facebook.com/Naxos/

*Genres:* Classical

The world's leading classical music label as measured by the number of new recordings it releases and the depth and breadth of its catalogue.

## Neon Gold
New York, NY
*Website:* http://neon.gold

*Website:* https://soundcloud.com/neongoldrecords

*Genres:* All types of music

Record label based in New York.

## Nervous Records NYC
150 Broadway, Suite 1007
New York, New York
*Fax:* +1 (212) 888-3182
*Email:* info@nervousnyc.com
*Email:* andrew@nervousnyc.com
*Website:* http://nervousnyc.com
*Website:* https://soundcloud.com/nervous-records
*Website:* http://www.myspace.com/nervousrecords

*Genres:* Underground Dance; Hip-Hop; Electronic; House; Uptempo; Chill; Downtempo

Record label based in New York, describing itself as one of the longest standing independent record labels in the US.

## Nettwerk Records
3900 West Alameda Ave, Suite 850
Burbank, CA 91505

NEW YORK:
33 Irving Place
New York, NY 10003

BOSTON:
15 Richdale Ave., Unit 203
Cambridge, MA 02140
*Fax:* +1 (747) 477-1093
*Email:* info@nettwerk.com
*Website:* http://www.nettwerk.com

*Genres:* Contemporary; Alternative; Americana; Blues; Christian; Electronic; Folk; Indie; Latin; Pop; Singer-Songwriter

Record label with offices in Burbank, New York, Boston, Vancouver, London, and Hamburg.

## New Earth Records
3980 N. Broadway Suite 103-223
Boulder, CO 80304

Administrative Offices:
PO Box 3388
Ashland, OR 97520
*Website:* https://www.newearthrecords.com

*Genres:* Chill; New Age; Trance; World; Electronic

Independent record label with offices in Boulder, Colorado, and Ashland, Oregon. Specialises in visionary music.

## New Heights Entertainment
*Email:* info@newheightsent.com
*Website:* http://newheightsent.com

*Genres:* All types of music

Privately held personal management and consulting firm with its core business focusing on Music Production, Artist Management, Live Entertainment, Music Producers, Songwriters, Record Label Management, Music Publishing, Brand Development and Strategic Guidance for Entertainment Content and IP Creators.

## New West Records LLC
*Email:* info@newwestrecords.com
*Website:* http://www.newwestrecords.com
*Website:* https://www.facebook.com/newwestrecords

*Genres:* Americana; Blues; Country; Folk; Indie; Rock; Roots

Label boasting a number of Grammy-award winning artists.

## Newvelle Records
*Email:* info@newvelle-records.com
*Website:* https://www.newvelle-records.com
*Website:* https://www.facebook.com/NewvelleRecords

*Genres:* Jazz

A premium, subscription-based record label that releases new music exclusively on vinyl.

## Nine Mile Records (NMR)
Austin, TX
*Email:* info@ninemilerecords.com
*Website:* http://www.ninemilerecords.com

*Genres:* Indie; Pop; Rock

Record label based in Austin, Texas.

## No Quarter
1717 Green Street #5
Philadelphia, PA 19130
*Email:* noquarter@noquarter.net
*Website:* https://www.noquarter.net

*Genres:* All types of music

Record label based in Philadelphia.

## No Sleep
Costa Mesa, CA
*Email:* hello@nosleeprecords.com
*Email:* info@nosleeprecords.com
*Website:* https://nosleeprecords.com
*Website:* https://www.facebook.com/nosleeprecords

*Genres:* Indie; Hardcore; Experimental; Hip-Hop

Record label based in Costa Mesa, California.

## Nonesuch Records
New York
*Email:* info@nonesuch.com
*Website:* http://www.nonesuch.com
*Website:* https://www.facebook.com/NonesuchRecords

*Genres:* Classical; Contemporary; Jazz; Traditional Americana; World; Mainstream; Alternative; Singer-Songwriter; Pop

Founded as a classical label in 1964, now including jazz, contemporary, world, and mainstream.

## NorthSide
*Website:* https://noside.com

*Genres:* Regional; Roots

A label to bring Nordic roots music to North American audiences.

## Not Not Fun
*Email:* notnotfunrecords@gmail.com
*Website:* http://www.notnotfun.com

*Website:* https://soundcloud.com/not-not-fun-1

*Genres:* All types of music

Send query by email with links to music online.

## Oglio Entertainment
3540 West Sahara Avenue #308
Las Vegas, NV 89102
*Email:* getinfo14@oglio.com
*Website:* https://www.oglio.com

*Genres:* Alternative; Electronic; Hip-Hop; Rap; Rock

*Contact:* Carl Caprioglio; Mark Copeland

Management company based in Las Vegas, Nevada.

## Omnium Records
Minneapolis, MN
*Website:* http://omniumrecords.com
*Website:* https://www.facebook.com/OmniumRecords

*Genres:* World Rock

*Contact:* Drew Miller

Releases world music that rocks.

## Omnivore Recordings
4470 W. Sunset Boulevard, Suite 209
Los Angeles, CA 90027
*Website:* http://omnivorerecordings.com
*Website:* https://www.facebook.com/omnivorerecordings

*Genres:* All types of music

Record label based in Los Angeles. Closed to submissions as at February 2020.

## One Little Independent Records US
*Email:* paulj@olirecords.com
*Email:* samb@olirecords.com
*Website:* https://www.olirecords.com/
*Website:* https://www.facebook.com/olirecords

*Genres:* Electronic; Folk; Indie; Pop; Punk; Rap; Hip-Hop; Rock; Singer-Songwriter; World

Inspired by the DIY principles and anarchistic ideals of independent labels. Since its inception the label has prided itself on giving complete control to artists it feels deserve a shot at a wider audience.

## Orange Recordings
Seattle
*Email:* rons@orangerecordings.com
*Website:* http://www.orangerecordings.com

*Genres:* Blues; Folk; Indie; Punk; Rock

Record label based in Seattle. Send query by email in first instance, selling your band, providing details, where you've played and who with, etc. and explaining why you and this particular label would be a good match. Do not send MP3s or MPEGs.

## Paper Garden Records
170 Tillary Street, Apt 608
Brooklyn, NY 11201
*Email:* demos@papergardenrecords.com
*Email:* info@papergardenrecords.com
*Website:* http://papergardenrecords.com
*Website:* https://soundcloud.com/papergardenrecords

*Genres:* All types of music

Record label based in Brooklyn, New York. Send demos by email.

## Parasol
303 West Griggs Street
Urbana, IL 61801
*Email:* parasol@parasol.com
*Email:* promo@parasol.com
*Website:* https://www.parasol.com
*Website:* https://www.facebook.com/ParasolLG/

*Genres:* Alternative; Folk; Indie; Pop; Rock; Roots; Singer-Songwriter

Independent record label based in Urbana, Illinois.

## Park the Van Records

*Email:* jeff@parkthevan.com
*Website:* https://www.parkthevan.com
*Website:* https://www.facebook.com/
parkthevan

*Genres:* Alternative; Pop; Rock

Record label originally started in New
Orleans in 2004.

## Parliament Record Group

357 S. Fairfax Ave. #430+1
Los Angeles, CA 90036
*Fax:* +1 (323) 653-7670
*Email:* parlirec@aol.com
*Website:* http://www.parliamentrecords.com

*Genres:* Blues; Gospel; Hip-Hop; R&B;
Soul

Send 3-10 tracks on CD by post, including
lyric sheet and SASE.
If you are a producer of tracks we would
love to hear your music. We are always
looking for new producers to work with our
artists.

## Partisan Records

281 N 7th Street, #2
Brooklyn, NY 11211
*Website:* https://partisanrecords.com

*Genres:* All types of music

Record label with offices in Brooklyn and
London. Not accepting demos as at March
2020.

## Pavement Music

6348 N Milwaukee Ave., Suite 301
Chicago, IL 60646
*Email:* info@pavementmusic.com
*Website:* https://www.pavementmusic.com/
*Website:* https://www.facebook.com/
Pavementent

*Genres:* Underground Heavy Metal; Rock

*Contact:* Rob Bolfer (A&R Manager)

Specialises in the development and
distribution of underground heavy metal.

## Peek-A-Boo Records

5808 Vicstone Ct.
Culver City, CA 90232
*Website:* http://www.peekaboorecords.com

*Genres:* Pop; Rock

Record label based in Culver City,
California.

## Penalty Entertainment

*Website:* http://penaltyent.com

*Genres:* Hip-Hop; Urban

*Contact:* Neil Levine

A full service entertainment company
consisting of a record label, music publisher,
label services, merchandise and
management.

## Phase One Network

*Website:* https://www.phaseonenetwork.net

*Genres:* All types of music

Music asset management company, owning
and controlling the assets of over 20 labels.

## Photo Finish Records

New York
*Email:* hello@photofinishrecords.com
*Website:* https://www.
photofinishrecords.com
*Website:* https://www.facebook.com/
photofinishrecords

*Genres:* All types of music

Record label based in New York.

## Pinch Hit Records

2400 West Carson Street Suite 223 Torrance,
CA 90501
*Website:* http://pinchhit.com

*Genres:* Alternative; Indie; Pop

*Contact:* David Lebental

Record label based in Torrance, California,
specialising in alternative and pop music.

## Playing In Traffic Records
*Website:* https://playingintrafficrecords.com
*Website:* https://www.facebook.com/
playingintrafficrecords

*Genres:* All types of music

Record label founded in 2009.

## Plug Research
*Email:* submissions@plugresearch.com
*Email:* contact@plugresearch.com
*Website:* http://www.plugresearch.com
*Website:* https://soundcloud.com/
plugresearch-music
*Website:* https://myspace.com/
plugresearchmusic

*Genres:* Electronic; Indie; Rock

Send a private soundcloud link. A four
sentence paragraph about yourself. Include a
link to your personal facebook and twitter
pages. No mp3 as attachments.

## +1 Records
New York
*Email:* info@plusonemusic.net
*Website:* http://plusonemusic.net
*Website:* https://soundcloud.com/
plusonemusic

*Genres:* All types of music

Record label based in New York.

## Polo Grounds Music
*Email:* info@pologroundsmusic.com
*Website:* https://pologroundsmusic.com
*Website:* https://www.facebook.com/Polo-
Grounds-Music-360463501306366/

*Genres:* Gospel; Pop; R&B; Rap; Hip-Hop;
Reggae; Reggaeton; Urban

New York based record-breaking imprint
boasts streaming numbers of nearly 40
billion (and counting) and sales well over 92
million singles and 16 million albums
worldwide.

## Pop Cautious Records
*Email:* tyler@popcautiousrecords.com
*Website:* https://www.

popcautiousrecords.com
*Website:* https://soundcloud.com/
popcautiousrecords

*Genres:* Alternative; Folk; Indie; Rock

*Contact:* Tyler Porterfield

We accept links to music via our website and
email. You can also use submission
websites.

Please, email us before attempting to mail a
CD or Vinyl.

## Poptown Records
Po Box 51
Lincolndale, NY 10540
*Email:* info@PoptownRecords.com
*Website:* http://www.poptownrecords.com

*Genres:* Pop; Rock

Record label based in Lincolndale, New
York.

## PPL Entertainment Group
*Email:* pplzmi@aol.com
*Website:* http://www.pplzmi.com

*Genres:* All types of music

Record label based in Beverly Hills,
California.

## PRA Records
*Email:* pra@prarecords.com
*Website:* http://www.prarecords.com
*Website:* https://twitter.com/prarecords

*Genres:* Jazz

*Contact:* Patrick Rains; Stephanie Pappas

Record label based in New York with sister
management arm.

## Prosthetic Records
11664 National Blvd., #413
Los Angeles, CA 90064
*Email:* info@prostheticrecords.com
*Website:* https://www.prostheticrecords.com/
*Website:* https://www.facebook.com/
prostheticrecords

*Genres:* Hard Rock; Heavy Metal

Heavy music label based in LA.

## Provident Label Group
*Website:* https://www.
providentlabelgroup.com/
*Website:* https://www.facebook.com/
ProvidentLabelGroupSonyMusic/

*Genres:* Christian; Gospel

Includes a number of labels and is itself a
division of a multinational music company.

## PS Classics
*Website:* http://www.psclassics.com
*Website:* https://www.facebook.com/
psclassics/

*Genres:* Soundtracks; Pop; Americana

Label celebrating the heritage of Broadway
and American popular song.

## Pure Noise
*Website:* http://www.purenoise.net
*Website:* https://www.facebook.com/
PureNoiseRecords

*Genres:* All types of music

Submit demos using form on website.

## Putumayo World Music
413 Carpenter Road
Charlotte, VT 05445
*Fax:* +1 (212) 460-0095
*Email:* submissions@putumayo.com
*Email:* info@putumayo.com
*Website:* https://www.putumayo.com

*Genres:* Blues; Folk; Latin; World

Send demo by email or on CD by post.

## Pyramid Records
11077 Biscayne Boulevard, Suite 200
Miami, Florida 33161
*Website:* http://pyramidrecords.net
*Website:* https://www.facebook.com/
pyramidrecords

*Genres:* Rock; R&B; Urban; Hip-Hop; Rap;
Gospel; Country; Contemporary; Reggae

Combines recording, touring, merchandising
and television into a single co-ordinated
entity.

## Q Division Records
363 Highland Avenue
Somerville, MA 02144
*Fax:* +1 (617) 625-2224
*Email:* info@qdivision.com
*Website:* http://www.qdivisionrecords.com

*Genres:* Rock; Indie; Pop

*Contact:* A&R

Send demo by post, via sonicbids, or send a
link to your music online by email. Do not
email MP3s or other music files. Prefers
bands that play regularly in front of people.
Unlikely to sign a band without seeing them,
and due to travel budget constraints this
generally means most bands are based in the
North East. See website for detailed FAQs.

## Quality Control
*Email:* QUALITYCONTROL@
UMGSTORES.com
*Website:* https://qualitycontrolmusic.com
*Website:* https://www.facebook.com/
RealQualityControl/

*Genres:* Hip-Hop; Urban

Independent record label.

## Quango Music Group
Los Angeles, CA
*Email:* info@quango.com
*Website:* http://www.quango.com
*Website:* https://www.facebook.com/
quangomusic

*Genres:* Chill; Electronic

Label based in Los Angeles, California,
dealing in chilled-out electronica.

## Quark Records
Post Office Box 452
Newtown, CT 06470-0452
*Email:* ar@quarkmusicgroup.com

*Email:* webmaster@quarkmusicgroup.com
*Website:* http://www.quarkmusicgroup.com/
*Website:* https://www.facebook.com/groups/
80122004353/

*Genres:* Electronic

Record label based in Newtown,
Connecticut. Send query by email with links
to music online. Response not guaranteed.

## Quarterback Records
P.O. Box 40465
Nashville, TN 37204
*Email:* allums@quarterbackrecords.com
*Website:* http://www.
quarterbackrecords.com/

*Genres:* Country

Country label based in Nashville, Tennessee.

## R.O.A.D. (Riding on a Dream) Records
PO Box 68096
Nashville, TN 37206
*Email:* bluesland@comcast.net
*Email:* fred@blueslandproductions.com
*Website:* http://www.
blueslandproductions.com

*Genres:* Blues; Soul; Americana Roots

*Contact:* Fred James

Blues label based in Nashville, Tennessee.
Describes itself as "one of the world's
foremost independent music companies
devoted to Blues, Soul and American Roots
music". Send query by email in first
instance.

## Radical Records
222 Dean Street #1
Brooklyn, NY 11217
*Email:* bryoonie222@gmail.com
*Website:* https://www.facebook.com/
radicalrecordsnyc/

*Genres:* Punk Rock

Record label based in New York. Deals
almost exclusively in punk rock.

## Radikal Records
*Website:* http://www.radikal.com
*Website:* https://soundcloud.com/
radikalrecords

*Genres:* Dance; Electronic; Pop

Interested in dance, pop, and electronic
music. Must have vocals. Send streaming
links through form on website. No CDs or
MP3 downloads.

## Rainman Records
*Website:* https://rainmanrecords.com

*Genres:* Blues; Metal; Pop; Rock;
Americana Blues Rockabilly Rock and Roll
Classic

Record label based in Beverly Hills,
California, we handle classic rock bands and
put out DVDs by classic rock bands.

## Rampage Records
48 Kelley Ave
Battle Creek, MI 49017
*Email:* officialrampagerecords@gmail.com
*Website:* https://www.facebook.com/
RealRampageRecords/
*Website:* https://www.reverbnation.com/
label/officialrampagerecords

*Genres:* All types of music

*Contact:* Chandler Culler

An independent record. For all business
inquiries please email or phone.

## Razor & Tie
*Website:* http://www.razorandtie.com
*Website:* https://www.facebook.com/
RazorandTie

*Genres:* Alternative; Folk; Gospel; Indie;
Metal; Pop; Rock; Singer-Songwriter;
Urban; World

Label which has enjoyed success in a variety
of genres, achieving Platinum sales and
Grammy awards. Includes a children's
division.

## RCA Records
550 Madison Avenue
New York, NY 10022
*Website:* https://www.rcarecords.com
*Website:* https://www.facebook.com/
rcarecords

*Genres:* Hip-Hop; Pop; R&B; Rock; Roots;
Urban

Record label based in New York.

## Red Bull Records
3535 Hayden Avenue #350
Culver City, CA 90232-2412
*Email:* customercare@redbullrecords.com
*Website:* http://redbullrecords.com
*Website:* https://www.facebook.com/
RedBullRecords/

*Genres:* All types of music

Record label based in Culver City,
California. Submit demo using form on
website (see "Demo Submissions" link at
bottom of page).

## Red House Records
916 19th Avenue South
Nashville, TN 37212
*Fax:* +1 (615) 320 7378
*Email:* info@compassrecords.com
*Email:* comments@compassrecords.com
*Website:* http://www.redhouserecords.com
*Website:* https://www.redhouserecords.com/
about/

*Genres:* Blues; Folk; Roots; Acoustic;
Singer-Songwriter; Traditional; Instrumental

Aims to provide a home and environment in
which creative artists can make albums in
total freedom, without interference from
"mogul types" just looking for the next hit
single. A&R submissions may be sent by
post on CD or by email as an MP3 streaming
link.

## Red Parlor Records
PO Box 362
Green Farms, CT 06838
*Email:* office@redparlor.com
*Website:* http://www.redparlor.com

*Genres:* Acoustic Soulful Singer-Songwriter
Rock Americana Blues

*Contact:* Steven Goff

Record label with international distribution,
based in New York. No unsolicited material,
but accepts queries.

## Region Liberty Records
101 NW 47th Terrace
Miami, FL 33127
*Email:* Regionlibertyllc@gmail.com
*Email:* bookingmarcusj@gmail.com
*Website:* https://region-liberty-records.
business.site/
*Website:* https://www.hiclipart.com/free-
transparent-background-png-clipart-dpcfb

*Genres:* Urban R&B

*Contact:* A&R

Named the best record label of Miami in
2019. Has since also expanded into artist
management and PR. Artists and producers
signed as partner label distributed artist. This
all but ensures that whatever the fate of the
declining music industry, Miami will most
likely remain a hip-hop power center for
years to come.

## Reservoir Music
276 Pearl St.
Kingston, NY 12401
*Fax:* +1 (845) 338-4266
*Email:* mfeldmanmd@hvc.rr.com
*Website:* http://www.reservoirmusic.com

*Genres:* Jazz

*Contact:* Mark Feldman

Jazz label based in Kingston, New York.

## Righteous Babe Records
*Email:* steve@righteousbabe.com
*Website:* https://www.righteousbabe.com/

*Genres:* Alternative; Folk; Jazz; Latin; Punk;
Rock

International record label with offices in
Buffalo, NY, and London.

## Rise Records, Inc.
*Website:* https://riserecords.com
*Website:* https://www.facebook.com/
RiseRecords

*Genres:* All types of music

Indie record label. Send query through form on website with link to music online.

## Sequoia Records
*Website:* http://www.sequoiarecords.com

*Genres:* Electronic; Folk; New Age; World; Ambient; Trance; Dance; Chill; Lounge; Celtic

Dedicated to creating music to enlighten the mind, nourish the soul and celebrate life. For 26 years, Sequoia has consistently created groundbreaking recordings that have defined and transcended Ambient, Worldbeat, Native/Drumming , Trance/Dance, Chill-Out/Lounge, Celtic and Healing/Meditative music.

## SGNB Records
9971 E Ida Pl
Englewood, CO 80111
*Email:* info@sgnbrecords.com
*Email:* tracey@tacmusicmanagement.com
*Website:* http://sgnbrecords.com/
*Website:* https://tacmusicmanagement.com/

*Genres:* Country; Blues; Guitar based; Metal; Rock; Rock and Roll; Rockabilly; Roots; Singer-Songwriter; Americana

*Contact:* Tracey Chirhart

Indie record label service based in Denver CO. Label releases singles only and focuses on southern rock, hard rock, country and blues rock and metal. The label's focus is "new" sound of southern rock. Parent company offers artist management, consulting, marketing, promo, branding and tour planning/booking. No long-term contracts, artist keeps rights to their music and services available on a monthly basis or as needed depending on artists needs and goals.

## Six Lowa Records
*Email:* info@sixlowarecords.com
*Email:* beats@sixlowarecords.com
*Website:* http://sixlowarecords.com
*Website:* https://www.facebook.com/
SixLowaRecords/

*Genres:* R&B; Rap; Reggae; Hip-Hop

An independent record label based in Lower Manhattan, New York that focuses heavy on the internet as a way to market, promote, and distribute digital music.

## Sony Masterworks
*Website:* https://www.
sonymusicmasterworks.com/

*Genres:* Classical; Jazz

Record label based in New York.

## Sony Music Latin
*Website:* https://www.sonymusiclatin.com
*Website:* https://www.facebook.com/
sonymusiclatin

*Genres:* Latin

Latin music label.

## Spitslam
*Website:* https://slamjamz.com

*Genres:* Urban

Urban record label established in 1996.

## Sunset Music Supervision
1928 The Woods II
Cherry Hill, NJ 08003
*Email:* submissions@
sunsetmusicsupervision.com
*Email:* sunsetcorporate@
sunsetcorporationamerica.com
*Website:* http://sunsetmusicsupervision.com
*Website:* http://sunset-usa.com

*Genres:* All types of music

*Contact:* Don Lichterman

World-Renowned Music Licensing Placements and Global Distribution for Creative and Commercial Uses. Available

Tracks by Award-Winning Artists, Composers, Bands, and Orchestras. High-Quality Music for Major Films, TV Shows, Commercials, and Branding -- Fun, Creative, User-Friendly.

## Sunset Recordings

1928 The Woods II
Cherry Hill, NJ 08003
*Email:* artistdevelopment@
sunsetrecordings.com
*Email:* sunsetcorporate@
sunsetcorporationamerica.com
*Website:* http://sunsetrecordings.com
*Website:* http://sunset-usa.com

*Genres:* All types of music

*Contact:* Don Lichterman

An American based record label that operates its business worldwide. It was founded in 2009 as his rock, alternative and pop label.

## Sunset Special Markets (SSM)

1928 The Woods II
Cherry Hill, NJ 08003
*Email:* artistdevelopment@
sunsetspecialmarkets.com
*Email:* sunsetcorporate@
sunsetcorporationamerica.com
*Website:* http://sunsetspecialmarkets.com
*Website:* http://sunset-usa.com

*Genres:* All types of music

*Contact:* Don Lichterman

Opened its door's 2008/2009 when the founder started to put together a new label with licensed product.

Produces, develops and releases special market products, boxed sets, greatest hits titles, stand up comedy LP's, live recordings, collectible releases and exclusive special markets products in the world entertainment.

## Swade Records

106 Virginia Road
Pittsburgh, PA 15237
*Website:* https://www.swaderecords.com

*Genres:* Alternative Modern Mainstream Americana Blues Garage Guitar based Rock Rock and Roll Ska

*Contact:* Tony Vinski

An independent record label founded in 2004 that is based in Pittsburgh, PA. We focus on, but are not limited to, rock & roll, alternative, indie, punk, and ska music. Most of our releases feature Pittsburgh musicians but our intention is not to be a Pittsburgh-only label by any means.

## Tama Industries Record Label

*Email:* info@tamaindustriesrecordlabel.com
*Website:* https://www.
tamaindustrieslabel.com

*Genres:* Acoustic Christian Classic Commercial Hard Modern New Wave Non-Commercial Underground Urban Soulful Club Country Blues Dance Dubstep Gospel Gothic Hardcore Hip-Hop Indie Instrumental Jazz Latin Metal New Age Pop R&B Punk Ragga Rap Reggae Reggaeton Relaxation Rock Rock and Roll Rhythm and Blues Singer-Songwriter Spoken Word Techno Trip Hop World

Delivers innovative, customization, complete record deals, and music distribution packages to musicians around the world. For 5 years, we've worked closely with our artists and producers to provide an easy and effective all-in-one Record Deal portfolio. Our music goes to one million sites in 250 countries and territories, and the largest global music distribution network of retailers, broadcasters, licencors and channels.

More than just a label. Winning the hearts of many musicians we hold no fear in our explanation of what makes our company the best. Our contract is simple, sweet and to the point. Holding the highest payouts to signed talents. Prides itself in supporting its hometown of San Antonio Texas and its local police department "SAPD". Connecting San Antonio's start-up companies and musicians in promotion are the greatest achievement for us.

What we do!

We put together many programs for uprising talents such as a housing program and TV networks for actors, actress, and musicians. Since the high calling for our services, we have connected a future for many. Getting a record deal should be simple for any artist trying to thrive. You should be able to sign a contract with any label without being asked for money or to prove yourself. Partnering with our label is simple; sign our e-agreement and receive an email on next steps and how to get started.

Each Artist will receive a login to their accounting software to revive monthly and quarterly payments. Payroll link to fill out there 1099's and more. Don't wait we work around the clock so you can do what you love. We provide instant results and proof of placement and income.

## Tonally Records
*Email:* contact@tonallyrecords.com
*Website:* https://www.facebook.com/tonallyrecords

*Genres:* All types of music

*Contact:* Christian Tobon

Independent record label and owns a publishing subsidiary.

## Turkey Vulture Records
129 Phelps Avenue, Suite 240
Rockford, IL 61108
*Email:* info@turkeyvulturerecords.com
*Website:* http://www.turkeyvulturerecords.com
*Website:* https://www.facebook.com/turkeyvulturerecords

*Genres:* All types of music

A worldwide independent label specializing in rock, metal, hardcore, punk, emo, and alternative bands.

## Undertow Records
*Email:* hello@undertowmusic.com
*Website:* http://undertowmusic.com
*Website:* http://facebook.com/undertowmusic

*Genres:* Blues; Indie; Rock; Roots

*Contact:* Bob Andrews; Jayne Ballantyne; Ward Gollings; Chris Grabau; Mark Ray

Unlikely to take on any new acts, so don't send CDs by post or MP3s by email. Send email query with links to your music online, but response not guaranteed.

## United Riot Records
*Email:* UNITEDRIOT1@gmail.com
*Email:* unitedriotrec@aol.com
*Website:* https://unitedriotrecords.com
*Website:* https://www.facebook.com/unitedriotrecords
*Website:* https://myspace.com/unitedriotrecords

*Genres:* Hardcore; Punk; Rock and Roll; Ska; Metal

A label dedicated to the underground music scene. Mainly interested in Hardcore, Punk and Oi! but always interested in all types of music such as Rock n' Roll, Ska, Metal or just plain good music.

## Universal Music Group
2220 Colorado Avenue
Santa Monica, CA 90404
*Email:* communications@umusic.com
*Website:* https://www.universalmusic.com
*Website:* https://www.facebook.com/UniversalMusicGroup

*Genres:* All types of music

International music group. Accepts demos only through a manager, agent, producer, radio DJ or other industry professional.

## Universal Music Latin Entertainment
*Website:* http://www.universalmusica.com
*Website:* https://www.facebook.com/universalmusica

*Genres:* Latin

A record company specialised in producing and distributing Latin Music in the US and Puerto Rico.

## Varese Sarabande Records
*Email:* cary.mansfield@
varesesarabande.com
*Website:* https://www.varesesarabande.com/

*Genres:* Soundtracks

*Contact:* Cary Mansfield

Record label of new and classic soundtracks.

## Water Music Records
Los Angeles
*Email:* info@watermusicrecords.com
*Website:* http://watermusicrecords.com
*Website:* https://www.facebook.com/
WaterMusicDance

*Genres:* Dance; Electronic; Pop; Rock

Record label based in Los Angeles, California.

## Yellow Dog Records
1910 Madison Avenue #671
Memphis, TN 38104
*Website:* http://yellowdogrecords.com
*Website:* http://facebook.com/ydrecords

*Genres:* Blues; Folk; Jazz; Roots; Soul; Americana

Record label based in Memphis, Tennessee.

# UK Record Labels

*For the most up-to-date listings of these and hundreds of other record labels, visit https://www.musicsocket.com/recordlabels*

*To claim your **free** access to the site, please see the back of this book.*

## !K7 Records
217 Chester House
Kennington Park
1-3 Brixton Road
London
SW9 6DE
*Website:* http://www.k7.com
*Website:* https://soundcloud.com/k7-records

*Genres:* Electronic

Record label with offices in Berlin, New York, and London. Send query via online form, with details about yourself, how you can be contacted, and why you think your music is special. Response not guaranteed.

## 0114 Records
*Email:* 0114records.submissions@
gmail.com
*Website:* https://0114records.com

*Genres:* Alternative; Rock; Folk; Garage; Hard Rock; Indie; Punk; Reggae; Singer-Songwriter; Ska

Independent record label based in Sheffield. Accepts soundcloud and youtube links by email from UK residents over 18 with original music.

## 2020 Vision Recordings Ltd
*Website:* https://www.2020recordings.com
*Website:* https://www.facebook.com/
2020VisionRecordings/

*Genres:* Dance; Electronic

Send demos through online form on website.

## 37 Degrees
*Email:* hi@37d.co
*Website:* https://www.37d.co
*Website:* https://www.facebook.com/37dgrs/

*Genres:* All types of music

Record label and management service. Send query by email with links to music online.

## 3tone Records
Saint Nicholas Street
Bristol
BS1 1TG
*Email:* demo@3tonerecords.co.uk
*Email:* info@3tonerecords.co.uk
*Website:* http://www.3tonerecords.co.uk
*Website:* https://www.facebook.com/
3toneRecords/

*Genres:* All types of music

Independent record label based in Bristol. Send demos by email.

## Abattoir Blues
*Email:* abattoirbluesrecords@hotmail.com
*Website:* http://www.
abattoirbluesrecords.com
*Website:* https://soundcloud.com/abattoir-blues-records

*Genres:* Blues; Rock; Alternative; Garage; Guitar based; Psychedelic; Punk; Punk Rock

Record Label based in Manchester – promoters of scuzz, blues, psych, rock. Send query by email with links to music online.

## Accidental Records Ltd
*Email:* info@accidentalrecords.com
*Website:* http://www.accidentalrecords.com
*Website:* https://www.facebook.com/accidentalrecords

*Genres:* All types of music

Send demos by email with the words "Demo submission" in the subject line and links to streaming music online. No audio files.

## Acorn Records
*Email:* acornrecords@hotmail.com
*Website:* https://twitter.com/acornrecordsuk

*Genres:* All types of music

Send query by email with MP3 attachments.

## Adapted Vinyl
*Email:* sb@adaptedvinyl.com
*Website:* http://www.adaptedvinyl.com

*Genres:* Electronic

Record label dedicated to releasing high quality electronic music.

## The Adult Teeth Recording Company
*Email:* hello@adultteeth.co.uk
*Website:* http://www.adultteeth.co.uk
*Website:* https://www.facebook.com/adultteeth/

*Genres:* Alternative Rock; Experimental Pop; Indie; Electronic; Ambient

Record label founded in 2012, dealing in alternate rock, experimental pop, indie, electronic, ambient and spoken word. Formats: vinyl, CD, cassette and digital.

## Akira
*Email:* stevie@akirarecords.com
*Email:* info@akirarecords.com

*Website:* http://akirarecords.com
*Website:* https://soundcloud.com/akira-records

*Genres:* Folk; Rock; Indie; Electronic

Label and Production House intent on exposing the best new talents and the most exciting music. Send query by email with links to music online. No MP3 attachments.

## Alex King Records
*Website:* https://sites.google.com/view/akingrecords/contact-us

*Genres:* Electronic Experimental Psychedelic Uptempo Urban; Club Dance Disco Drum and Bass Dub Dubstep Garage Glitch Grime Hardcore IDM House Melodicore Pop R&B Remix Trance Techno

Artists receive at least 75% of royalties, although most of the time it will be higher. We do not charge for distribution.

We are semi-open. Send demos via form on website.

## ALM Records
*Email:* alm-records@outlook.com
*Website:* https://alm-records.co.uk
*Website:* https://www.facebook.com/ALMRecords

*Genres:* Metal; Rock

Record label based in North East England, looking to sign local rock and metal bands.

## Alya Records
Room 16
The John Banner Centre
620 Attercliffe Road
Sheffield
S9 3QS
*Email:* autumn@dmfdigital.com
*Email:* hello@alyarecords.com
*Website:* http://www.alyarecords.co.uk
*Website:* https://www.facebook.com/AlyaRecords/

*Genres:* All types of music

Record label based in Sheffield. Send demos via upload page on website.

## AnalogueTrash Ltd
83 Ducie Street
Manchester
M1 2JQ
*Email:* hello@analoguetrash.com
*Website:* http://www.analoguetrash.com
*Website:* https://soundcloud.com/
analoguetrash

*Genres:* Alternative

Record label based in Manchester. Send demos by email.

## Anchorage Records
Glasgow
*Email:* anchoragerecords@gmail.com
*Website:* https://anchoragerecords.
wordpress.com

*Genres:* All types of music

Record label based in Glasgow. Prefers rock music, but will consider all genres. Send query by email with MP3s or links to music online.

## Associated Music International (AMI) Media
Red Bus House
34 Salisbury Street
London
NW8 8QE
*Fax:* +44 (0) 20 7723 3064
*Email:* eliot@amimedia.co.uk
*Website:* http://www.amimedia.co.uk

*Genres:* All types of music

Send query by email with bio and links to streamable music online.

## At the Helm Records
Brighton
East Sussex
BN1
*Email:* jeremy@atthehelmrecords.com
*Website:* http://www.atthehelmrecords.com
*Website:* https://soundcloud.com/at-the-helm-records

*Genres:* Americana

Independent record label based in Brighton, specialising in "un-scrubbed" Americana.

## Atlantic Records
27 Wright's Lane
London
W8 5SW
*Website:* http://atlanticrecords.co.uk

*Genres:* All types of music

UK branch of international record label. Send demos by post on CD.

## Audio Vendor
*Email:* contact@audiovendor.com
*Website:* http://www.audiovendor.com
*Website:* https://soundcloud.com/
audiovendor

*Genres:* Experimental; Folk; Indie; Rock

Independent record label made up of independent artists, songwriters and producers. Send query by email with MP3 attachments or links to music online.

## Audiorec Limited
Lynton House
304 Bensham Lane
Thornton Heath
Surrey
CR7 7EQ
*Email:* info@audiorec.co.uk
*Email:* info@audiorec.co.in
*Website:* http://www.audiorec.co.uk

*Genres:* Regional

Record label handling Indian music, with offices in the UK and India.

## Aveline Records
London
*Email:* info@avelinerecords.com
*Website:* http://www.avelinerecords.com
*Website:* https://twitter.com/avelinerecords

*Genres:* Americana; Country; Folk; Singer-Songwriter

London-based independent record label.

## Avenoir Records
40 Hawkes Way
Kent
ME15 9ZL

*Email:* enquiries@avenoirrecords.com
*Website:* https://avenoirrecords.com
*Website:* https://twitter.com/AvenoirOfficial

*Genres:* All types of music

Music company based in London, offering artist management, music production, and record label. Send demos by post.

## Axtone
*Email:* contact@axtone.com
*Website:* https://www.axtone.com

*Genres:* Dance; House; Disco; Dubstep; Electronic; Techno; Trance

Send demos via online submission system. See website for details.

## Bad Bat Records
Chester
*Email:* badbatrecords@gmail.com
*Website:* https://badbatrecords.
bandcamp.com
*Website:* https://soundcloud.com/
badbatrecords

*Genres:* Alternative; Electronic; Ambient; Experimental; Dance

Independent record label specialising in alternative, electronic, ambient, dance and experimental music. Looking for artists to support and release.

## Bamboleo Records
London
*Email:* demos@bamboleorecords.com
*Email:* info@bamboleorecords.com
*Website:* http://www.bamboleorecords.com

*Genres:* House; Techno; Funk

Record label based in London. Send demos by email.

## Battle Worldwide
Brighton
*Email:* hello@
battleworldwiderecordings.com
*Website:* http://
battleworldwiderecordings.com
*Website:* https://soundcloud.com/battle

*Genres:* All types of music

Independent record label and publishing (music and literature) company based in Brighton. Send query by email with links to streaming music online. Response only if interested.

## Bear Love Records
*Email:* bearloverecords@hotmail.co.uk
*Website:* http://bearloverecords.
bigcartel.com

*Genres:* Alternative; Americana; Folk

Accepts approaches from bands and artists who play regular gigs. Send query by email with links to music online.

## Beatphreak
Manchester
*Email:* hello@beatphreak.co.uk
*Website:* http://beatphreak.co.uk
*Website:* https://soundcloud.com/beatphreak

*Genres:* Dance

Dance label based in Manchester. Send query by email with MP3 demos.

## Bella Union
120-124 Curtain Road
London
EC2A 3SQ
*Email:* simon@bellaunion.com
*Email:* mark@bellaunion.com
*Website:* https://bellaunion.com
*Website:* https://www.facebook.com/
bellaunionrecs

*Genres:* All types of music

*Contact:* Simon

Not accepting unsolicited demos as at September 2020, due to overwhelming level of submissions.

## Bespoke Records
20B Preston Park Avenue
Brighton
BN1 6HL
*Email:* info@bespokerecords.com
*Website:* http://www.bespokerecords.com

*Website:* https://www.facebook.com/
bespokerecords

*Genres:* All types of music

Indie label on a crusade to change the music industry. Aims to value creatives above their creative products. No unsolicited submissions.

## Beta Recordings
*Email:* demos@john-b.com
*Website:* https://www.beta-recordings.com/
*Website:* https://www.facebook.com/
betarecordings/

*Genres:* Dance; Drum and Bass; Techno; House; Atmospheric Drum and Bass; Melodic Drum and Bass; Electronic; Dance Rock

*Contact:* John B

Send soundcloud links by email.

## BFS Records
Blackfrog Studios Ltd
Unit 9 Jefferson Way
Thame, Oxfordshire
OX9 3SZ
*Email:* zoe@bfsrecords.co.uk
*Email:* info@bfsrecords.co.uk
*Website:* https://www.bfsrecords.co.uk
*Website:* https://www.facebook.com/
BFSrecordsuk

*Genres:* All types of music

*Contact:* Zoe Bourke

Record label based in Thame, Oxfordshire. Send query by email with links to your social media and music online.

## Big Bear Records
PO Box 944
Edgbaston
Birmingham
West Midlands
B16 8UT
*Email:* admin@bigbearmusic.com
*Website:* http://www.bigbearmusic.com
*Website:* http://www.
birminghamjazzfestival.com

*Genres:* Jazz; Swing; Blues

Possibly the UK's longest-established independent record label, has recorded jazz, swing and blues [and a little bit of rock] for more than 40 years. It is now available on iTunes world-wide as well as being conventionally distributed.

## Bingo Records
Sheffield
*Email:* bingorecs@gmail.com
*Website:* https://www.bingorecords.
bandcamp.com
*Website:* https://facebook.com/bingorecs

*Genres:* Indie Pop; Folk; Shoegaze; Electronic

Independent record label based in Sheffield. Send queries and demos by email.

## Birdland Records
*Email:* hq@birdlandrecords.com
*Website:* https://birdlandrecords.com
*Website:* https://soundcloud.com/
birdlandrecords

*Genres:* Singer-Songwriter

Independent record label. Send query by email with links to music online.

## Black Bleach Records
Manchester
*Email:* blackbleachrecords@gmail.com
*Website:* http://blackbleachrecords.com
*Website:* https://www.facebook.com/
blackbleachrecords

*Genres:* Alternative; Electronic; Garage; Indie; Post Punk; Punk; Punk Rock; Shoegaze

Indie label based in Manchester.

## Black Tragick Records
Belfast
*Email:* blacktragickrecords@gmail.com
*Website:* https://www.facebook.com/
blacktragickrecords
*Website:* https://twitter.com/blacktragician

*Genres:* Doom; Folk; Metal

Record label based in Belfast.

## Blak Hand Records
*Email:* blakhandrecords@gmail.com
*Website:* https://blakhandrecords.
bandcamp.com
*Website:* https://www.facebook.com/
blakhandrecords

*Genres:* Garage; Rock; Alternative; Guitar
based; Psychedelic Rock; Punk

Independent cassette label based in the UK,
specialising in psych, garage, rock and fuzz.

## Blue Shell Music
Derry
*Email:* jonny@blueshellmusic.com
*Website:* https://www.facebook.com/
BlueShellMusicManagement

*Genres:* Pop

Record label and management based in
Derry, Northern Ireland. Send query by
email in first instance and submit demo upon
request.

## Blues Matters Records
PO Box 18
Bridgend
CF33 6YW
*Email:* alan@bluesmatters.com
*Website:* http://www.bluesmatters.com
*Website:* https://www.facebook.com/
bluesmattersmagazine/

*Genres:* Blues; Rhythm and Blues

*Contact:* Alan Pearce

Describes itself as one of the most
recognizable Blues magazines in the world.

## Bluesky Pie Records
Folkestone
Kent
*Email:* spies@blueskypierecords.com
*Email:* press@blueskypierecords.com
*Website:* https://www.facebook.com/
blueskypierecords/

*Genres:* All types of music

Not-for-profit, ethical record label. Send
query by email with MP3s or links to music
online.

## Box Records
Newcastle Upon Tyne
*Email:* matt@box-records.com
*Website:* http://box-records.com

*Genres:* Experimental; Folk; Psychedelic
Rock; Underground; Punk; Doom;
Alternative Folk

Record label based in Newcastle. Send query
by email with links to music online.

## Breakfast Records LLP
Bristol
*Email:* dan@breakfastrecords.co.uk
*Email:* josh@breakfastrecords.co.uk
*Website:* http://breakfastrecords.co.uk
*Website:* https://www.facebook.com/
breakfastlabel

*Genres:* Folk; Garage; Guitar based; Indie;
Punk; Punk Rock

*Contact:* Dan Anthony; Josh Jarman

Record label based in Bristol. Send demos
by email.

## Brightonsfinest
Brighton
*Email:* theteam@brightonsfinest.com
*Website:* https://www.brightonsfinest.com
*Website:* https://soundcloud.com/
BrightonsFinest

*Genres:* Alternative; Dance; Electronic;
Folk; Indie; Pop; Rock

An online music magazine and record label.
Send query by email with MP3s or links to
music online.

## Brock Wild
London
*Email:* brockwildrec@gmail.com
*Website:* http://www.brockwildrec.com
*Website:* https://soundcloud.com/
brockwildrec

*Genres:* House; Acid

Management company based in London.
Send query by email with links to music
online.

## BS1 Records
*Email:* info@bs1records.com
*Website:* https://bs1records.com
*Website:* https://soundcloud.com/bs1records

*Genres:* Drum and Bass

Drum & Bass label. Send email with links to music online for consideration.

## Bubblewrap Collective
The Laundry
Rear of 35 Romilly Cres
Canton
Cardiff
CF11 9NP
*Email:* rich@bubblewrapcollective.co.uk
*Website:* http://www.
bubblewrapcollective.co.uk
*Website:* https://soundcloud.com/
bubblewrapcollective

*Genres:* Folk; Indie; Electronic; Alternative

A collective of Cardiff creatives, aiming to create the perfect balance between a design studio and record label. Send demos on CD by post.

## Bucks Music Group
Roundhouse
212 Regents Park Road Entrance
London
NW1 8AW
*Fax:* +44 (0) 20 7229 6893
*Email:* recordings@bucksmusicgroup.co.uk
*Email:* info@bucksmusicgroup.co.uk
*Website:* http://www.bucksmusicgroup.com
*Website:* https://www.facebook.com/
bucksmusicgroup/

*Genres:* All types of music

Independent music publisher based in London, operating a number of labels.

## Bush Bash Recordings
London
*Email:* recordings@bushbash.biz
*Website:* https://www.
bushbashrecordings.com
*Website:* https://facebook.com/BushBashrecs

*Genres:* Garage; Grime; Hip-Hop; House; R&B; Rap; Urban

Record label based in London.

## Button Up Records
51 King Street
Coatbridge
ML5 1JF
*Email:* buttonupinfo@hotmail.com
*Website:* https://www.buttonuprecords.co.uk/
*Website:* https://www.facebook.com/
buttonuprecords

*Genres:* All types of music

*Contact:* Garry John Kane

Record label based in Coatbridge. Send query by email with links to music online or MP3s. We are very open minded.

## Canigou Records
*Email:* canigourecords@gmail.com
*Website:* http://canigourecords.co.uk
*Website:* https://soundcloud.com/
canigourecords

*Genres:* Ambient; Electronic; Folk; Lo-fi; Shoegaze

Record label and community of musicians and visual artists. Send query by email with MP3s or links to music online.

## Catskills Records
3 Brooker Street
Hove
BN3 3YX
*Email:* info@catskillsrecords.com
*Website:* https://www.catskillsmusic.com
*Website:* https://www.facebook.com/
catskillsrecords

*Genres:* All types of music

Record label based in London and Brighton.

## CCT Records
45 Staple Lodge Road
Northfield
Birmingham
B31 3BZ
*Website:* http://milwaukie2003.wixsite.com/
cctrecords

*Genres:* Alternative; Electronic; Ambient; Dubstep; Hip-Hop; Techno

Record label based in Birmingham. Send query via online form with links to music online, or submit files via website dropbox.

## Chalkpit Records Ltd
*Email:* chalkpitrecords@gmail.com
*Website:* https://www.chalkpitrecords.com

*Genres:* Alternative; Funk; Indie; Pop; Soul

*Contact:* Silas Gregory

Record label based on the Isle of Wight. Send query by email with MP3 attachments or links to music online.

## ChillnBass
*Email:* Patrick@chillnbass.com
*Email:* Clement@chillnbass.com
*Website:* http://www.chillnbass.com/
*Website:* https://twitter.com/Patitude1

*Genres:* Commercial; Dance

*Contact:* Patrick Ruane; Clement Ignace

Label with studios in Paris and London.

## Circus Recordings
*Website:* http://www.circusrecordings.com
*Website:* https://www.facebook.com/CircusRecordings

*Genres:* House; Techno

Send query via Facebook or contact page of website, with links to music online.

## Cold Spring
62 Victoria Street
Glossop
Derbyshire
SK13 8HY
*Email:* demos@coldspring.co.uk
*Email:* info@coldspring.co.uk
*Website:* http://coldspring.co.uk

*Genres:* Ambient; Industrial; Noise Core; Power Electronic; Doom; Experimental; Soundtracks

Record label / mailorder store / distributor based in Derbyshire. Send demos by post or send links to music online by email, but do not send attachments by email. Replies to all demos, but do not expect an immediate reply.

## Coloursounds
Leeds
*Website:* https://soundcloud.com/coloursoundsuk
*Website:* https://www.facebook.com/coloursoundsuk

*Genres:* Electronic; House; Disco; Indie; Pop

Works closely with emerging artists that represent the best of Electronic music; House, Nu Disco, Indie, Pop.

## Columbia Records
9 Derry Street
London
W8 5HY
*Website:* http://www.columbia.co.uk
*Website:* https://www.facebook.com/ColumbiaRecordsUK/

*Genres:* All types of music

UK office of the oldest surviving brand name in pre-recorded sound.

## Come Play With Me
Leeds
*Email:* tony@cpwm.co
*Email:* sam@cpwm.co
*Website:* http://cpwm.co
*Website:* https://www.facebook.com/ComePlayWith

*Genres:* All types of music

Record label based in Leeds. Accepts submissions from artists in the Leeds area (including Bradford, Calderdale, Kirklees, Barnsley, Wakefield, Selby, York, Harrogate, and Craven). Submit via online submission form on website.

## Copro Productions
P.O. Box 4429
Henley-on-Thames
Oxfordshire

RG9 1GH
*Fax:* +44 (0) 1491 412571
*Website:* http://www.coprorecords.co.uk
*Website:* http://www.myspace.com/
coprorecords

*Genres:* Heavy Metal; Punk; Rock; Indie;
Guitar based

*Contact:* A&R Department

Send demos by post on audio CD with
contact name, band name, email address and
phone number written clearly on the CD
itself, not just the packaging. Include band
bio and photo. No submissions by email, and
will not listen to music online / check out
your website. Do not query or follow-up by
phone. Will contact if interested.

## Crucial Records
*Email:* crlabelinfo@crucial-records.com
*Website:* http://www.crucial-records.com

*Genres:* All types of music

Mainly interested in rock, metal etc. music
with social or political ideas being a big part
of the song.

## Dance To The Radio
Munro House
Duke St
Leeds
LS9 8AG
*Email:* sally@futuresoundgroup.com
*Email:* sam@futuresoundgroup.com
*Website:* http://www.dancetotheradio.com
*Website:* https://www.facebook.com/
dancetotheradio

*Genres:* Experimental; Indie

Music group including label, publishing, and
artist management. Send demos by email.

## Decca Records
364–366 Kensington High Street
London
W14 8NS
*Website:* http://decca.com
*Website:* https://www.facebook.com/
deccarecords

*Genres:* All types of music

Describes itself as a legendary British record
label, which has been home to "some of the
greatest recording artists ever".

## Deek Recordings
*Website:* http://www.deekrecordings.co.uk
*Website:* https://soundcloud.com/
deekrecordings

*Genres:* All types of music

*Contact:* Nathan Jenkins

Send query by email with links to music
online.

## Defenders Ent
Industrial Estate
3A Juno Way
London
SE14 5RW
*Email:* music@defendersent.com
*Email:* info@defendersent.com
*Website:* https://defendersent.com
*Website:* https://www.facebook.com/
DefendersEnt

*Genres:* Dance; Reggae; R&B; Rap

Record label based in London. Send query
by email with links to music online. No MP3
attachments.

## Delphian Records
34 Wallace Avenue
The Meadows
Wallyford
East Lothian
EH21 8BZ
*Email:* info@delphianrecords.co.uk
*Website:* https://www.delphianrecords.com
*Website:* https://www.facebook.com/
delphianrecords/

*Genres:* Classical

*Contact:* Paul Baxter

Describes itself as one of the UK's foremost
independent classical record labels.

## Deltasonic Records
*Email:* annheston@live.com
*Website:* http://deltasonicrecords.co.uk

*Website:* https://www.facebook.com/
deltasonicrecords/

*Genres:* All types of music

Record label based in Liverpool, founded by a former Polygram music scout. Send Soundcloud link via contact form on website.

## Demon Music Group
BBC Worldwide Ltd
Television Centre
101 Wood Lane
London
W12 7FA
*Email:* info@demonmusicgroup.co.uk
*Website:* http://www.
demonmusicgroup.co.uk
*Website:* https://www.facebook.com/
DemonMusicGroup

*Genres:* Alternative; Indie

Describes itself as the UK's largest independent record company. Specialises in the reissues of catalogue titles so does not sign new acts.

## Denizen Recordings
Nottingham
*Email:* denizendemos@denizen.uk.com
*Email:* kristi@denizen.uk.com
*Website:* http://denizenrecordings.uk.com
*Website:* https://soundcloud.com/
denizenrecordings

*Genres:* All types of music

*Contact:* Kristi Genovese

Send demos by email as MP3 attachments up to 10MB maximum, or upload to the dropbox.

## Detour Records
PO Box 18
Midhurst
West Sussex
GU29 9YU
*Fax:* +44 (0) 1730 815422
*Email:* Detour@btinternet.com
*Website:* http://www.detour-records.co.uk
*Website:* https://www.facebook.com/pages/
Detour-Records-Official/672613086164448

*Genres:* Punk

Label dealing in Mod and Punk. Send demo by post.

## Different Records
*Email:* differentdemos@pias.com
*Email:* hi@differentrecords.com
*Website:* http://www.differentrecordings.com
*Website:* https://www.facebook.com/
differentrecordings/

*Genres:* Alternative Hip-Hop; Electronic; Experimental; Urban

Send queries by email with links to music online.

## Dipped in Gold Recordings
*Email:* paulriddlesworth@hotmail.com
*Website:* https://www.
dippedingoldrecordings.com
*Website:* https://www.facebook.com/
DippedInGoldRec

*Genres:* Indie

"Sole purpose is putting out bloody good records by bloody good people..."

## Dirty Bingo Records
Flat 254 Hardy House
Poynders Garden
Clapham
London
SW4 8PQ
*Email:* dirtybingorecords@greedbag.com
*Website:* https://dirtybingorecords.
greedbag.com

*Genres:* Alternative; Electronic; Indie; Indie Pop

Record label based in London. Send query by email with MP3 or links to music online.

## Disconnect Disconnect Records
*Email:* disconnectdisconnect@hotmail.co.uk
*Website:* https://
disconnectdisconnectrecords.bigcartel.com
*Website:* https://www.facebook.com/
disconnectdisconnectrecords

*Genres:* Emo; Pop Punk; Post Punk; Punk; Punk Rock; Hardcore

Will accept soundcloud links by email, but prefers physical submissions by post. Send email or facebook message requesting postal address.

## Discovering Arts Music Group (DAMG)

*Email:* discovering@damg.co.uk
*Website:* http:// discoveringartsmusicgroup.com
*Website:* https://soundcloud.com/damg-records

*Genres:* All types of music

Media company offering management, publishing, record company, and more. Always on the lookout for new talent: use demo submission form on website.

## Distinctive Records

*Website:* http://www.distinctiverecords.com
*Website:* https://www.facebook.com/ distinctiverecs

*Genres:* Acid; Dance; House; Break Beat

proud upholder of Acid house and rave, and likes submissions form this genre.

## DJD Music Ltd

2A Fairfield Road
Heysham
*Email:* djd@gmx.com
*Website:* https://www.djdmusicltd.com
*Website:* https://www.facebook.com/ ukglobal.uk/

*Genres:* Acoustic Alternative Avant-Garde Electronic Hard Heavy Ambient Dance Hip-Hop Indie Instrumental Metal Pop Punk R&B Rap Reggae New Wave Industrial Experimental Progressive Folk Guitar based Lounge Roots Singer-Songwriter Soul Spoken Word Synthpop

*Contact:* David John Duckworth

An artist product promotion and online digital distribution company integrated into an Independent UK and International record label. The company caters specifically for unsigned artists, focusing on the traditional ideals of a standard record label but working more closely with the increasingly popular and fast-growing online marketplace. Alongside their distribution aspects, the company offers other services. For further information and details. Visit our website and other locations on the internet by searching through Google.

## Doing Life Records

Liverpool
*Email:* doinglifeltd@gmail.com
*Website:* https://doingliferecords. bandcamp.com
*Website:* https://www.facebook.com/ doingliferecords/

*Genres:* Alternative; Emo; Indie; Rock; Singer-Songwriter

Not-for-profit label focused on community and developing the next generation of alternative Liverpool musicians. Send query by email with links to music / EPK online. No attachments.

## Don't Try

Suffolk
*Email:* ben@donttryrecords.com
*Website:* https://www.donttryrecords.com
*Website:* https://www.facebook.com/ donttryuk

*Genres:* Alternative; Indie; Pop

An independent record label, music PR agency and management service based in Suffolk. Send query by email with links to music online.

## Donut Records

Bristol
*Email:* donutrecords@hotmail.com
*Website:* https://donutrecords.bandcamp.com
*Website:* https://soundcloud.com/donut-records

*Genres:* Indie; Psychedelic Rock; Rock and Roll

Independent record label based in Bristol, releasing quarterly compilations of unsigned artists. Send query by email with links to music online. No MP3 attachments.

## Dose Entertainment
Keys Court
82-84 Moseley St
Birmingham
B12 0RT
*Email:* info@doseentertainments.com
*Website:* https://www.
doseentertainments.com/doseent-the-label

*Genres:* Hip-Hop; R&B; Rap

Independent record label founded in 2017 in Birmingham. Send query by email. Prefers links to music online, but will accept MP3s.

## Double Denim Records
*Email:* new@doubledenimrecords.com
*Website:* http://doubledenimrecords.com
*Website:* https://www.facebook.com/doubledenimrecords

*Genres:* Electronic; Pop

Record label founded in 2010. Send query by email with links to music online.

## Dove Records
*Email:* vjartistmanagement@yahoo.com
*Website:* https://www.facebook.com/vjmediadoverecords

*Genres:* Contemporary Christian; Gospel; Rap; Reggae

Send query by email with links to music and videos online.

## Dr Johns Surgery Records
*Email:* drjohnssurgeryrecords@gmail.com
*Website:* https://www.facebook.com/drjohnssurgery1
*Website:* https://www.facebook.com/drjohnssurgery1

*Genres:* All types of music

Independent record label run for the artists, not personal gain. Submit demos via form on website.

## Dreamscope Media Group (DMG)
71-75 Shelton Street
Covent Garden
London
WC2H 9JQ
*Email:* info@dreamscopemediagroup.co.uk
*Website:* https://www.dreamscopemediagroup.co.uk
*Website:* https://www.facebook.com/DreamscopeMG

*Genres:* Country; Folk; Pop; R&B; Rock; Soul

Record label based in London. No unsolicited post. Accepts queries by email only.

## Droma Records
*Email:* dromarecords@gmail.com
*Website:* https://dromarecords.bandcamp.com

*Genres:* All types of music

Record label based in the West Midlands. Always interested in a chat about a potential new project. Send query by email or via website.

## Eastzone Records
53 Corbet Avenue
Sprowston
Norwich
NR7 8HS
*Website:* http://www.eastzonerecords.co.uk

*Genres:* All types of music

*Contact:* Kingsley Harris

Record label based in Norwich.

## Easy Life Records
*Email:* info@easyliferecords.com
*Website:* http://easyliferecords.com
*Website:* https://www.facebook.com/easyliferecords/

*Genres:* Alternative

Independent label formed in 2014. Send query via online submission form with links to social media and your music online.

## Electric Honey Music

*Email:* electrichoney1992@gmail.com
*Website:* https://www.facebook.com/
electrichoneymusic
*Website:* https://www.twitter.com/
ElectricHoney25

*Genres:* All types of music

College record label based in Glasgow,
Scotland. Run by Music Business students.
Send query by email with band name, short
bio, your location, and links to your music
online.

## Elevate Records

*Website:* https://www.elevaterecords.co.uk
*Website:* https://soundcloud.com/
elevaterecordsuk

*Genres:* Drum and Bass

Submit demos via online submission system.
See website for details.

## Elliptic Records

*Email:* adrian@ellipticrecords.com
*Email:* demos@ellipticrecords.com
*Website:* http://www.ellipticrecords.com
*Website:* https://soundcloud.com/
ellipticrecords

*Genres:* All types of music, except:
Americana Black Metal Black Origin Blue
Beat Blues Break Beat C-DUB Classical
Country Cuban Dancehall Doom Drum and
Bass Dub Dubstep Emo Ethnic Folk Fusion
Garage Gospel Gothic Grime Grind Guitar
based Hardcore Hi-NRG Hip-Hop IDM
Indie Instrumental Jazz Jungle Latin
Melodicore Metal MOR Mystical New Age
Noise Core Nostalgia Pop Psychebilly Punk
R&B Ragga Rap Reggae Reggaeton
Relaxation Remix Rock Rock and Roll
Rockabilly Roots Rhythm and Blues Singer-
Songwriter Shoegaze Ska Skool Soul
Soundtracks Spoken Word Surf Swing
Synthpop Trip Hop World

*Contact:* Adrian Fern

Label dealing in House (Minimal / Deep /
Glitch). Send query by email with links to
music online.

## Emerald Music (Ireland) Ltd

120a Coach Road
Templepatrick
Ballyclare
Co Antrim
BT39 0HB
Northern Ireland
*Fax:* +44 (0) 28 9443 2162
*Email:* info@emeraldmusic.co.uk
*Email:* sales@emeraldmusic.co.uk
*Website:* http://www.
emeraldmusiconline.com

*Genres:* Celtic; Country; Folk; Gospel;
Regional; Pop; Rock; Traditional; World

Label based in Co Antrim, Northern Ireland.
Roots in Irish music, later expanding to
cover a range of Scottish music.

## End Of The Trail Records

Hastings
*Email:* kelly@endofthetrailcreative.co.uk
*Website:* https://www.
endofthetrailcreative.co.uk
*Website:* https://www.facebook.com/
endofthetrailcreative

*Genres:* All types of music

Management company and record label
based in Hastings. Send demos by email.

## Endearment Records

*Email:* endearmentrecords@gmail.com
*Website:* https://www.facebook.com/
endearmentrecords

*Genres:* Indie

Record label releasing mainly indie music,
but willing to consider all genres. Send query
by email with links to music online.

## Eromeda Records

*Email:* eromedarecords@gmail.com
*Website:* https://eromedaentertainment.com
*Website:* https://www.facebook.com/
EromedaEntertainment

*Genres:* All types of music, except: R&B;
Pop

Diverse media company which operates as a music label and as a film and music video production company.

## Eton Messy Records
Bristol / London
*Email:* etonmessysubmissions@gmail.com
*Email:* info@etonmessy.com
*Website:* https://www.etonmessy.com
*Website:* https://www.facebook.com/Etonmessy

*Genres:* Dance; Electronic

Record label based in Bristol and London. All submissions must be streaming links and photos on flickr or similar. Submit details by email.

## Everyday Records
*Email:* info@everydayrecords.com
*Email:* media@everydayrecords.com
*Website:* https://www.everydayrecords.com
*Website:* https://www.facebook.com/EverydayRecords

*Genres:* Acoustic Alternative Classic Contemporary Mainstream Melodic Progressive Soulful Blues Classical World Swing Soundtracks Soul Singer-Songwriter Rhythm and Blues Roots Rockabilly Rock and Roll Pop R&B New Age MOR Jazz Instrumental Indie Guitar based Folk

An independent record company, run by in-house composers and songwriters and based in the North of England.

## Evil Genius Records
68a Kingston Road
Leatherhead
KT22 7BW
*Email:* info@egrltd.com
*Website:* https://www.egrltd.com

*Genres:* All types of music

Send demos by post or by email as links to music online.

## Evil Twin Records
*Email:* info@eviltwinrecords.com
*Website:* http://www.eviltwinrecords.com

*Website:* https://eviltwinrecords.bandcamp.com

*Genres:* Electronic; Hip-Hop; Reggae; Soul

Record label concentrating mainly on hip-hop.

## Expansion Records
London
*Email:* ralph@passionmusic.co.uk
*Website:* https://expansionrecords.com
*Website:* https://facebook.com/expansionrecs

*Genres:* Modern Soul; Classic Soul; Jazz; Funk

*Contact:* Ralph Tee

Record label describing itself as the UK's number one label for modern soul, classic soul, and smooth jazz.

## Explosive Beatz Records
Birmingham
*Email:* djpariswwalker@gmail.com
*Website:* https://explosivebeatz.com
*Website:* https://www.facebook.com/ExplosiveBeatzMusic/

*Genres:* Dance; Hip-Hop; R&B

Record label based in Birmingham. Send query by email with bio and MP3 attachment.

## F&G Dj Trade
*Email:* gavino@fgmusica.com
*Website:* http://www.fgmusica.com
*Website:* https://www.facebook.com/fgdjtrade

*Genres:* House; Electronic

*Contact:* Francesca Nesi; Gavino Prunas

Record label based in London.

## Fabyl
London
*Email:* info@fabyl.co.uk
*Website:* https://www.facebook.com/FabylRecordings
*Website:* https://soundcloud.com/fabyl-1

*Genres:* Dance; Hip-Hop; Grime; Indie; Pop; Rock; Singer-Songwriter; Soul; Urban

Record label based in London, describing itself as a "bastard child of Rock and Hip Hop". Send query by email with links to music online.

## Fame Throwa Records
*Fax:* +44 (0)
*Email:* famethrowauk@gmail.com
*Website:* https://www.famethrowa.com
*Website:* https://www.facebook.com/famethrowarecords

*Genres:* All types of music

A collective that seeks to support and promote South-East London's wealth of independent music. Send query by email.

## FatCat Records
PO Box 3400
Brighton
BN1 4WG
*Email:* info@fat-cat.co.uk
*Website:* https://www.fat-cat.co.uk
*Website:* https://soundcloud.com/fatcatrecords

*Genres:* All types of music

Send submissions by email with brief description and private listening link, or by post.

## Filter Records
19A Douglas Street, Unit B
London
SW1P 4PA
*Email:* contact@dorado.net
*Website:* http://www.dorado.net
*Website:* https://www.facebook.com/doradorecords/

*Genres:* Electronic

Concentrates on DJs and electronic music.

## Fine Chooned
*Email:* info@finechooned.com
*Website:* http://www.finechooned.com
*Website:* http://soundcloud.com/fine-chooned

*Genres:* Electronic; Funky; Progressive; Tribal; Soulful; Urban; Club; House

Fresh progressive and funky tech house label from the UK. Featuring new but experienced house music producers.

## Fire Records
*Email:* james@firerecords.com
*Website:* http://www.firerecords.com
*Website:* https://soundcloud.com/firerecords

*Genres:* Experimental; New Wave; Post Punk; Psychedelic Rock

*Contact:* James Nicholls

Send query by email with links to music online. No physical submissions.

## First Word Records
*Email:* info@firstwordrecords.com
*Email:* aly@firstwordrecords.com
*Website:* http://www.firstwordrecords.com
*Website:* https://www.facebook.com/firstwordrecords

*Genres:* Hip-Hop; Funk; Jazz; Soul; Reggae; Break Beat

Send demos on CD with bio by post, including SAE if return of CD required.

## Flowers in the Dustbin
Glasgow
*Email:* info@flowersinthedustbin.org
*Website:* http://flowersinthedustbin.org
*Website:* https://soundcloud.com/flowersinthedustbin

*Genres:* All types of music

*Contact:* Stephen McKee

Record label based in Glasgow. Send query by email with links to music online.

## Focused Silence
*Email:* hello@focusedsilence.com
*Website:* https://www.focusedsilence.com
*Website:* https://soundcloud.com/focused-silence

*Genres:* Experimental; Electronic; Jazz; Avant-Garde

*Contact:* Andy Backhouse

Independent record label, publisher and music supervisor, releasing and licensing various electronic, folio and jazz music. Submit demo via we transfer. See website for details.

## Forward Motion Records (UK)
*Email:* fwdmotionrecs@yahoo.com
*Website:* https://fwdmotionrecs.wixsite.com/forwardmotionuk
*Website:* https://www.facebook.com/Forward-Motion-Records-UK-409609599823223/

*Genres:* House; Break Beat; Funky House; Electronic; Hard House; Tribal House

House Music record label based in the North of England. Submit demo via link on website.

## 4AD
*Email:* demos@4ad.com
*Email:* 4ad@4ad.com
*Website:* https://www.4ad.com
*Website:* https://www.facebook.com/fourad

*Genres:* Alternative

Send demos by email.

## Fox Records
*Email:* jd@foxrecords.net
*Website:* http://www.foxrecords.limitedrun.com
*Website:* https://www.facebook.com/foxrecordings/

*Genres:* Alternative

Alternative label accepting queries with SoundCloud links by email.

## Freaks R Us
*Email:* tim@freaksrus.net
*Website:* http://www.freaksrus.net
*Website:* https://www.facebook.com/freakartists

*Genres:* Alternative; Electronic; Experimental; Post Punk

Record label and artist management. Send query by email with MP3 attachments or links to music online.

## From Concentrate
*Email:* hello@fromconc.com
*Website:* https://www.facebook.com/fromconcentratemusic
*Website:* https://soundcloud.com/fromconcentrate

*Genres:* Garage; Pop; Soul

Record label and events collective.

## Full Time Hobby
18 Ashwin Street
London
E8 3DL
*Email:* info@fulltimehobby.co.uk
*Website:* http://www.fulltimehobby.co.uk
*Website:* https://soundcloud.com/fulltimehobby

*Genres:* Alternative Rock; Folk; Singer-Songwriter

Record label based in London, with the aim of releasing interesting, inspiring and exciting music. Prefers queries by email with links to music online, but will also accept CDs with 3-4 of your best tracks on them.

## Futurist Recordings
*Email:* shawndavis22@hotmail.com
*Website:* https://milwaukie2003.wixsite.com/futuristrecordings
*Website:* https://www.facebook.com/Futuristrecordings/

*Genres:* Experimental; Acid House; Techno; Underground

Deep cutting edge experimental techno and acid house label. Submit demo via online submission form on website.

## Gameplan Records
*Email:* hello@gameplanrecords.com
*Website:* https://www.gameplanrecords.com
*Website:* https://soundcloud.com/user-575401443

*Genres:* All types of music

Record label, also offering artist development services.

## Ganbei Records
Shelton Street
London
*Email:* info@ganbeirecords.com
*Email:* paul@ganbeirecords.com
*Website:* http://www.ganbeirecords.com
*Website:* https://ganbeirecords.
bandcamp.com

*Genres:* Alternative; Folk; Post Punk; Psychedelic Rock; Rock

Record label that aims to help musicians release and promote their music. Send query by email with links to music online.

## Geilston Records
*Email:* geilstonrecords@gmail.com
*Website:* https://www.facebook.com/
GeilstonRecords/
*Website:* https://twitter.com/GeilstonRecords

*Genres:* Emo; Indie; Punk

Independent record label from the West of Scotland.

## God Unknown Records
*Email:* godunknownrecs@gmail.com
*Website:* http://www.godunknownrecs.com
*Website:* https://www.facebook.com/
godunknownrecords

*Genres:* Experimental; Psychedelic Rock; Garage

Describes itself as "a label bringing you the best heavy and far out sounds around".Send query by email with links to music online.

## Gotham Records
*Email:* barry@barrytomes.com
*Website:* http://www.gotham-records.com
*Website:* https://www.facebook.com/barry.
tomes

*Genres:* Pop; Rock; Dance; Reggae

*Contact:* Barry Tomes

Record label based in Birmingham.

## Graphite Records
c/o Northern Music Co.
1st & 2nd Floor
5 Victoria Road
Saltaire
Shipley
West Yorkshire
BD18 3LA
*Fax:* +44 (0) 1274 730097
*Email:* andy@northernmusic.co.uk
*Email:* george@northernmusic.co.uk
*Website:* http://www.graphiterecords.net
*Website:* https://soundcloud.com/
graphiterecordsltd

*Genres:* Alternative; Rock; Metal

Independent record label based in Shipley. Send demos by email.

## Harbourtown Records
36 The Gill
Ulverston
Cumbria
LA12 7BP
*Email:* info@harbourtownrecords.com
*Website:* http://www.
harbourtownrecords.com

*Genres:* Acoustic; Folk; Roots; Traditional

Record label based in Cumbria. Send demo with bio by post.

## Harmor Records
London
*Email:* contact@harmorrecords.com
*Website:* https://harmorrecords.com

*Genres:* Alternative; Dance; Electronic; House; IDM

Submit demos through form on website.

## Haystack Records
Manchester
*Email:* enquiries@haystackrecords.co.uk
*Website:* https://www.haystackrecords.co.uk
*Website:* https://soundcloud.com/haystack-records

*Genres:* Folk; Acoustic

Independent record label specialising in British Folk and Acoustic music. Send query by email with links to music online.

## Heavy Metal Records Ltd
152 Goldthorn Hill
Penn
Wolverhampton
WV2 3JA
*Email:* submissions@revolverrecords.com
*Website:* http://heavymetalrecords.co.uk
*Website:* http://revolverrecords.com
*Website:* http://myspace.com/ heavymetalrecords

*Genres:* Heavy Metal; Punk; Rock; Thrash; Classic; Metal; Ska

The original and the best... Heavy Metal Records! We've signed almost every style of rock and metal in the past four decades. Maybe you're what we're after next?

## Heist or Hit Records
12 Hilton Street
Manchester
M1 1JF
*Email:* team@heistorhitrecords.com
*Website:* http://www.heistorhitrecords.com
*Website:* https://www.facebook.com/ heistorhitrecords

*Genres:* Acoustic; Alternative; Indie

Independent record label based in Manchester. Send postcard with email address and links to your music online. Everything sent this way will receive a response. No guarantee of response to any links sent by email.

## House of Mythology
34 Trinity Crescent
London
SW17 7AE
*Email:* info@houseofmythology.com
*Website:* https://www. houseofmythology.com/
*Website:* https://www.facebook.com/ HOMlabel/

*Genres:* Electronic; Rock; Avant-Garde; Experimental

Independent record label specialising in qualitative boundary-bursting electronic, rock, avant-garde and experimental music.

## HQ Familia
38 Charles Street
Leicester
LE1 1FB
*Email:* yasin@hqrecording.co.uk
*Email:* yasinelashrafi1980@live.co.uk
*Website:* http://www.hqrecording.co.uk
*Website:* https://soundcloud.com/ hqrecording

*Genres:* Electronic; Urban

*Contact:* Yasin El-Ashrafi

A record label and collective of like minded artists, producers and creatives with the focus on pushing the boundaries of art and music.

## Hudson Records
Sheffield
*Email:* hudson@hudsonrecords.co.uk
*Website:* https://www.hudsonrecords.co.uk
*Website:* https://soundcloud.com/ hudsonpodcast/sets

*Genres:* Folk

Independent record label based in Sheffield, dealing mainly in folk. Send query by email with links to music online.

## Hyperdub Records
*Email:* info@hyperdub.net
*Email:* Marcus@hyperdub.net
*Website:* https://hyperdub.net
*Website:* https://www.facebook.com/ Hyperdub.Records

*Genres:* Electronic; Leftfield

Record label based in London. Send query by email with links to music online (private soundcloud link preferred).

## IKonic Image
45 Staple Lodge Road
*Email:* shawndavis22@hotmail.com
*Website:* https://milwaukie2003.wixsite.com/

ikonicimage
*Website:* https://twitter.com/VinylLike

*Genres:* Ambient; Electronic; Modern
Glitch; Techno

Experimental music label specialising in
deep ambient and hypnotic electronica,
which goes into the realms of Modern glitch
and intelligent techno.

## In the Nursery (ITN) Corporation
PO Box 1795
Sheffield
S3 7FF
*Email:* itn@inthenursery.com
*Website:* https://www.inthenursery.com
*Website:* https://www.facebook.com/
INTHENURSERY

*Genres:* Soundtracks

Handles soundtracks and theme music for
TV and film.

## Incessant Records
2 Angel Square
London
EC1V 1NY
*Email:* contact@incessantrecords.co.uk
*Website:* http://incessantrecords.co.uk
*Website:* https://www.facebook.com/
incessantrecords

*Genres:* Dance; Pop; R&B; Rock

Record label with offices in London and LA.
Send query via online form with links to
music online and social media.

## Infectious Music
8th Floor
5 Merchant Square
London
W2 1AS
*Email:* demos.uk@bmg.com
*Email:* info@infectiousmusicuk.com
*Website:* http://www.infectiousmusicuk.com
*Website:* http://www.facebook.com/
infectiousmusicuk?ref=mf

*Genres:* Alternative; Guitar based; Indie;
Singer-Songwriter

Record label based in London. Send demos
digitally by email, using specific subject line
provided on website.

## Invisiblegirl Records
Manchester
*Email:* julia@invisiblegirl.co.uk
*Website:* http://www.invisiblegirl.co.uk
*Website:* http://www.facebook.com/pages/
Invisiblegirl-Records/281793848983

*Genres:* All types of music

Independent record label, based in
Manchester, and founded in 2006. Send
demos by email as MP3 attachments.

## ISHQ Records
*Email:* viveck@dnhartists.com
*Website:* http://www.ishqrecords.com
*Website:* https://www.facebook.com/
ballysagoomusic

*Genres:* Regional

Interested in Indian music with a Western
crossover. S

## Jazz re:freshed
*Email:* sam@jazzrefreshed.com
*Website:* https://www.jazzrefreshed.com
*Website:* https://twitter.com/jazzrefreshed

*Genres:* Jazz

*Contact:* Sam Campbell

Record label with the intention to "challenge
the elitism and prejudice within the jazz
community that had kept jazz on the
sidelines far too long, whilst bringing the
incredibly diverse, colourful, expressive and
creative world that is jazz to the people –
live, fun and affordable."

## Jeepers! Music
Brighton
*Email:* nick@jeepersmusic.co.uk
*Email:* info@jeepersmusic.co.uk
*Website:* http://jeepersmusic.com
*Website:* https://www.facebook.com/
jeepersmusic/

*Genres:* House

*Contact:* Nick Hook

House label based in Brighton.Send submissions by email with demos as MP3s or private Soundcloud links.

## Jost Music
*Email:* info@jostmusic.co.uk
*Website:* https://www.jostmusic.co.uk
*Website:* https://www.soundcloud.com/user-883894064

*Genres:* All types of music

Record label and artist management. Send query by email with links to music online.

## K Dragon Records
*Email:* submissions@kdragonrecords.com
*Email:* kdragonrecords@gmail.com
*Website:* https://www.kdragonrecords.com
*Website:* https://www.facebook.com/KDragonRecords/

*Genres:* All types of music

Send demo by email with completed submission questionnaire (available on website).

## Kaneda Records
Newcastle
*Email:* kanedarecords@hotmail.com
*Website:* http://www.kanedarecords.com
*Website:* https://soundcloud.com/kanedarecords

*Genres:* Electronic; Dance; Hip-Hop

Record label based in Newcastle. Send demos by email.

## Keep Me Young (KMY)
*Email:* Dan@keepmeyoung.uk
*Website:* https://www.keepmeyoung.uk
*Website:* https://www.facebook.com/KeepMeYoungUK

*Genres:* All types of music

Mainly a music management company, but also run an indie label. Open to all genres, but particularly interested in acoustic and pop. Send query by email with links to music online.

## KFM Records
Edinburgh
*Email:* info@kfmrecords.com
*Website:* http://www.kfmrecords.com

*Genres:* Electronic; Experimental; IDM; Post Rock; Shoegaze; Hip-Hop; Avant-Garde Rock; Experimental Rock

An Edinburgh-based label whose output ranges from hip-hop to art rock.

## Kokeshi
London
*Email:* kokeshi@iheartkokeshi.com
*Website:* http://iheartkokeshi.com
*Website:* https://www.facebook.com/iheartkokeshi

*Genres:* Electronic; Dubstep; Garage; Grime; Chill

Record label based in London. Send query by email with links to music online.

## Lapsang House
*Email:* hello@lapsanghouse.com
*Website:* https://lapsanghouse.com
*Website:* https://www.facebook.com/LapsangHouse/

*Genres:* All types of music

Record label based in South East London. Send query by email with links to music online.

## Last Night From Glasgow
*Email:* ian@lastnightfromglasgow.com
*Website:* http://www.lastnightfromglasgow.com
*Website:* https://www.facebook.com/LastNightFromGlasgow

*Genres:* All types of music

Describes itself as the world's first crowd funded not-for-profit record label. Send query by email with soundcloud / dropbox links.

## Leisure Recordings
*Email:* leisurerecs@gmail.com
*Website:* https://www.facebook.com/

leisurerecs
*Website:* https://soundcloud.com/leisurerecs

*Genres:* Garage; Pop; Shoegaze

Send submissions by email, preferably as links.

## Less is More Music Ltd
Unit 36, 88-90
Hatton Garden
London
EC1N 8PN
*Email:* info@lessismoremusic.co.uk
*Website:* http://lessismoremusic.co.uk
*Website:* http://soundcloud.com/limm_uk/dropbox

*Genres:* Grime; Hip-Hop; Jazz; R&B; Soul

Independent, soul-orientated record company based in London. Send demos via soundcloud dropbox.

## Let Me Understand Records
*Email:* infolmurec@gmail.com
*Website:* https://www.facebook.com/lmurecords
*Website:* https://soundcloud.com/lmurecords

*Genres:* Electronic; House; Techno

Record label founded in 2018 by music industry veteran with decades of experience.

## LGM Records
52 Tottenham Court Road
London
W1T 2EH
*Email:* info@lgmrecords.co.uk
*Website:* http://lgmrecords.co.uk
*Website:* https://www.facebook.com/LGMRecordsUK/

*Genres:* All types of music

A record label and music publisher based in London.

The label have been featured in The Times and on BBC World News and their artists have been enjoyed widespread exposure on BBC Radio 1, Radio 2, 6Music, Radio X, Amazing Radio and Manchester XS, as well as, articles and excellent reviews in The

NME, The Times, The Metro, The Guardian, Mojo, UNCUT, the Evening Standard and many more.

## Libertino
*Email:* gruff.owen@libertinorecords.com
*Website:* https://www.libertinorecords.com
*Website:* https://www.facebook.com/Libertinorecords/

*Genres:* Alternative

Alternative label releasing both Welsh and English language bands. Send query by email with MP3s or links to music online.

## Lo Recordings
2(b) Swanfield Street
London
E2 7DS
*Email:* info@hub100.com
*Email:* jon@hub100.com
*Website:* https://www.lorecordings.com
*Website:* https://soundcloud.com/lo-recordings

*Genres:* Electronic

*Contact:* Jon Tye

Record label with offices in London and Millbrook, Cornwall. Send demo by email as links or MP3 attachment.

## Lockjaw Records
29 Ardmore Avenue
Guildford
GU2 9NJ
*Email:* rob@lockjawrecords.co.uk
*Email:* lesley@lockjawrecords.co.uk
*Website:* https://www.lockjawrecords.co.uk
*Website:* https://www.facebook.com/lockjawrecords/

*Genres:* Hardcore; Punk

Independent record label based in Guildford. Send demo by post or by email.

## Loner Noise
*Email:* michael@lonernoise.com
*Website:* https://www.lonernoise.com
*Website:* https://soundcloud.com/lonernoise

*Genres:* Rock; Alternative

*Contact:* Michael Edward

Send demos as streams by email or through online form. No files.

## Long Records
Reading
*Email:* studio@longrecords.com
*Website:* http://longrecords.com
*Website:* https://www.facebook.com/longrecords.official/

*Genres:* All types of music, except: Heavy Metal; Extreme Noise Core

*Contact:* Claude Rajchert

Record label originally based in Poland, now based in Reading, UK.

## Lost in the Manor
*Email:* chris@lostinthemanor.co.uk
*Email:* nick@lostinthemanor.co.uk
*Website:* http://www.lostinthemanor.co.uk

*Genres:* Acoustic; Alternative; Dance; Folk; Hip-Hop; Jazz; Pop; Reggae; Rock

Always seeking new bands and artists. See website for details on how to approach.

## Lucky Number Music Limited
Suite 3 Second Floor
344 Kingsland Road
London
E8 4DA
*Email:* contact@luckynumbermusic.com
*Website:* https://www.luckynumbermusic.com
*Website:* https://soundcloud.com/luckynumbermusic

*Genres:* Dance; Electronic; Indie; Pop; Singer-Songwriter

Independent music company based in London.

## M1 Music Limited
*Email:* info@m1music.com
*Website:* http://www.m1music.com
*Website:* https://www.facebook.com/M1Music2001/
*Website:* https://myspace.com/m1musicltd

*Genres:* Hip-Hop; R&B; Reggae; Funk; Rap; Soul

No cover bands, just original acts. Send demo and any relevant links by email.

## Make-That-A-Take Records
Dundee
*Email:* info@makethatatakerecords.com
*Website:* http://makethatatakerecords.com
*Website:* https://www.facebook.com/makethatatakerecords

*Genres:* Punk

DIY punk rock record label/collective based on the east coast of Scotland. Puts on punk shows and releases music. Send query by email with links to music online.

## Malicious Damage
*Email:* info@maliciousdamage.co.uk
*Website:* http://www.maliciousdamage.biz
*Website:* https://www.facebook.com/groups/123103610446/
*Website:* https://myspace.com/maliciousdamage79

*Genres:* All types of music

*Contact:* Mike Coles

A totally independent record label releasing new and original music, without the commercial pressures and deadlines associated with a lot of bigger labels.

## Manhaton Records
9 School Road
Twyford
Hampshire
SO21 1QQ
*Email:* arm@manhatonrecords.com
*Website:* https://www.manhatonrecords.com
*Website:* https://www.facebook.com/manhatonrecords2/

*Genres:* Blues; Jazz; Singer-Songwriter

Describes itself as one of Britain's leading record labels for contemporary blues, rock and roots music.

## Mayfield Records
2A Down End Road
Drayton
Hampshire
PO6 1HT
*Email:* info@mayfieldrecords.com
*Website:* https://mayfieldrecords.com
*Website:* https://www.facebook.com/
mayfieldrecordsltd

*Genres:* All types of music

Recording studio, record label, and video
production. Send query by email with links
to music online.

## Me & You Music
*Email:* meandyoumusic@yahoo.co.uk
*Website:* https://www.facebook.com/
meandyoumusic1

*Genres:* All types of music

Artist management, record label, promotions,
and online PR. Send query by email with
MP3s or links to music online.

## Melee Recording Group
Birmingham
*Email:* info@mrg-group.co.uk
*Website:* http://mrg-group.co.uk

*Genres:* Hip-Hop; Urban

*Contact:* Chris Brown; Nathaniel Thompson

Hip hop label based in Birmingham.
Specialises in urban music but willing to
consider music from any genre.

## Mellowtone Records
Static Gallery
23 Roscoe Lane
Liverpool
L1 9JD
*Email:* info@mellowtonerecords.com
*Website:* http://mellowtonerecords.com/
*Website:* https://www.facebook.com/
mellowtoneclub

*Genres:* Acoustic; Roots; Singer-Songwriter;
Country; Folk; Blues

*Contact:* David McTague

Record label based in Liverpool. Send query
by email with links to music online or MP3
attachments.

## MHM
*Email:* hq@mhmmusic.com
*Website:* http://www.mhmmusic.com
*Website:* https://www.facebook.com/
mhmmusichq/

*Genres:* All types of music

Records, publishing, distribution and
management.

## Midhir Records
Northern Ireland
*Email:* info@midhirrecords.com
*Website:* http://www.midhirrecords.com
*Website:* https://twitter.com/midhir

*Genres:* Black Metal; Metal; Folk; Ambient;
Experimental; Avant-Garde

*Contact:* Jon Hope

Record label of dark music.

## Mighty Atom
*Email:* label@mightyatom.co.uk
*Website:* http://www.mightyatom.co.uk
*Website:* https://www.facebook.com/Mighty-
Atom-Records-158656654146720/

*Genres:* Metal; Rock

Independent Record label based in South
Wales that was at forefront of the Emo/
Hardcore music scene in early 2000s.

## Modern Sky
*Email:* info@modernsky.uk
*Website:* http://modernsky.uk
*Website:* https://soundcloud.com/modernsky-
uk

*Genres:* All types of music

Music entertainment and events company
based in the North of England.

## Monomyth Records
Leeds
*Email:* Bob@monomythrecords.info

*Website:* https://www.monomythrecords.com
*Website:* https://www.facebook.com/
Monomythrecords

*Genres:* All types of music

Record label / artist collective based in
Leeds. Send query by email with links to
music online.

## Multiverse Music
*Email:* info@multiverse-music.com
*Website:* http://www.multiverse-music.com
*Website:* https://soundcloud.com/multiverse

*Genres:* Experimental; Electronic; Modern
Classical; Soundtracks

A boutique music publisher and label house
with a focus on experimental, electronic and
modern classical music, as well as scores for
feature films and trailers.

## Musical Bear Records
*Email:* info@musicalbearrecords.co.uk
*Website:* http://www.
musicalbearrecords.co.uk

*Genres:* All types of music

Provides artists with a platform to further
their careers by offering digital / CD / Vinyl
distribution across the globe. Send query by
email or through contact form on website,
with links to music online.

## musicXart
*Email:* info@musicxart.co.uk
*Website:* http://www.musicxart.co.uk

*Genres:* Acoustic; Experimental

*Contact:* Francis

Willing to consider all genres but
particularly interested in acoustic and
experimental material. Send query by email
with MP3 attachments.

## My Little Empire
London
*Email:* hello@mylittleempirerecords.com
*Website:* http://www.
mylittleempirerecords.com
*Website:* https://twitter.com/MLE_Records

*Genres:* Americana; Country; Guitar based;
Indie; Roots

DIY indie label based in London. Send query
by email with links to music online. No MP3
attachments or submissions by post.

## Navigator Records
*Website:* http://www.navigatorrecords.co.uk
*Website:* https://www.facebook.com/
navigatorrecords

*Genres:* Acoustic; Folk; Singer-Songwriter;
Traditional

Releases albums by artists on the
contemporary folk scene.

## NB Audio
Manchester
*Email:* info@nbaudio.tv
*Email:* dance@nbaudio.tv
*Website:* http://nbaudio.tv
*Website:* https://soundcloud.com/nbaudio

*Genres:* Alternative; Electronic; Dance;
Drum and Bass; Dub; Dubstep; Hip-Hop;
Reggae

Record label based in Manchester, UK. Send
query by email with links to music online.

## Never Fade Records
London
*Email:* info@neverfaderecords.com
*Website:* http://neverfaderecords.com
*Website:* https://www.facebook.com/
NeverFadeRecordsUK/

*Genres:* All types of music

Independent record label based in London.
Send query by email with MP3s or links to
music online.

## New Street Records
*Email:* hello@newstreetrecords.com
*Website:* http://www.newstreetrecords.com
*Website:* https://www.facebook.com/
newstreetrecords/

*Genres:* All types of music

University record label run by students, for students. Send query by email with MP3s or links to music online.

## Nice Swan Records
*Email:* info@niceswanrecords.com
*Website:* http://www.niceswanrecords.com
*Website:* https://soundcloud.com/
NiceSwanRecords/

*Genres:* Garage; Indie; Rock

Independent record label specialising in vinyl releases, which are also made available via the usual online digital music outlets. Send query by email with links to music online.

## Nu:Generation Music
*Email:* nugenerationmusic83@gmail.com
*Website:* https://linktr.ee/nugenerationmusic
*Website:* https://www.facebook.com/
nugenerationmusic

*Genres:* Hip-Hop; Soul; Urban

Send query by email with EPK and links to music online.

## Of Paradise Records
London
*Email:* info@ofparadiserecords.com
*Website:* https://www.facebook.com/
OfParadiseRecords/
*Website:* https://soundcloud.com/
ofparadiserecords

*Genres:* Dance

Dance label based in London. Send demos by email.

## 1-2-3-4 Records
30A Redchurch Street
London
*Email:* sean@seanmclusky.com
*Email:* elliott@1234records.com
*Website:* https://www.1234records.com
*Website:* https://www.facebook.com/
1234records
*Website:* http://www.myspace.com/
1234records

*Genres:* Electronic; Indie; Rock; Garage; Guitar based; Punk

Send demos by post or by email as links to music online.

## 101BPM
*Email:* leon@101bpm.com
*Website:* https://www.facebook.com/
101BPM

*Genres:* Electronic; Urban

Music agency and record label. Send query by email with link to your latest music or showreel. Aims to respond within two weeks.

## Organ Records
*Email:* demo@organrecords.com
*Website:* http://www.organrecords.com
*Website:* https://www.facebook.com/
OrganRecords/?fref=ts

*Genres:* Alternative; Guitar based; Indie; Soul; Underground

A label for underground music. Send query by email with MP3s or links to music online.

## OXRecordings
*Email:* demos@oxrecordings.com
*Email:* info@oxrecordings.com
*Website:* https://oxrecordings.com
*Website:* https://soundcloud.com/
oxrecordings

*Genres:* Drum and Bass

Handles drum & bass and neurofunk only. No house. Send private soundcloud link by email. No attachments.

## Partisan Records
*Email:* info@partisanrecords.com
*Website:* https://www.partisanrecords.com
*Website:* https://www.facebook.com/
partisanrecords

*Genres:* Alternative

Record label based in Brooklyn and London. Send query by email with links to music online.

## Payne Records
*Email:* support@paynerecords.com
*Website:* https://www.facebook.com/
PayneRecords/
*Website:* https://twitter.com/paynerecords

*Genres:* All types of music

Record label launched in 2017. Send query
by email with links to music online.

## Peaceville Records
*Website:* https://peaceville.com
*Website:* https://soundcloud.com/peaceville
*Website:* http://www.myspace.com/
peacevillerecords

*Genres:* Metal; Rock

Rock and metal label. Send submissions as
links to music online via contact form on
website.

## Perfect Havoc Limited
Flat 7
46 De Beauvoir Crescent
London
N1 5RY
*Email:* info@perfecthavoc.com
*Website:* https://www.perfecthavoc.com

*Genres:* Disco; House

Submit demos via online form on website.

## Phantasy
PO Box 56972
London
N10 9BR
*Email:* demos@phantasysound.co.uk
*Email:* phantasyhq@gmail.com
*Website:* https://shop.phantasysound.co.uk/
*Website:* https://soundcloud.com/
phantasysound

*Genres:* Alternative Dance; Dance;
Electronic

Record label based in London. Send demo
by email. See website for full guidelines.

## Phono Sounds UK
London
*Email:* phonosounds@gmail.com
*Website:* https://soundcloud.com/
phonosounds
*Website:* https://www.facebook.com/
phonosounds

*Genres:* Electronic; Hip-Hop; Pop; R&B

Independent minded recording label based in
London. Send query by email with links to
music online.

## Pink Lane Records
Newcastle Upon Tyne
*Email:* pinklanerecords@gmail.com
*Website:* https://pinklanerecords.
bandcamp.com

*Genres:* All types of music

Record label based in Newcastle. Send query
by email with bio and links to music online
and social media presence.

## Planet Mu Records
*Email:* demo@planet.mu
*Email:* mike@planet.mu
*Website:* https://www.planet.mu

*Genres:* Dub; IDM; Dubstep; Experimental;
Downtempo

*Contact:* Mike Paradinas

Send links to streaming music online by
email (no download links, MP3s or
attachments). Do not contact for feedback or
to ask if your demo has been listened to.

## Planet Records
Pendle Hawk Music
11 New Market Street
Colne
Lancashire
BB8 9BJ
*Email:* info@pendlehawkmusic.co.uk
*Website:* http://www.
pendlehawkmusic.co.uk/Planet_Records.htm

*Genres:* Blues; Folk; Roots

Record label based in Colne, Lancashire.

## Polar Opposites Records
Sheffield
*Email:* polaroppositesdirect@gmail.com

*Website:* https://facebook.com/
PolarOppositesDirect
*Website:* https://soundcloud.com/
polaroppositesdirect

*Genres:* Hip-Hop; Soul; Urban

Independent record label based in Sheffield.
Send query by email with links to music
online.

## Pollytone Records

PO Box 124
Ruislip
Middlesex
HA4 9BB
*Email:* val@pollytone.com
*Website:* http://www.pollytone.com
*Website:* https://myspace.com/
pollytonerecords

*Genres:* Country; Rock and Roll;
Rockabilly; Swing

*Contact:* Val

Record label based in Ruislip, Middlesex.

## Portfolio Music

*Email:* info@theportfoliomusic.com
*Website:* http://www.theportfoliomusic.com
*Website:* https://www.facebook.com/
theportfoliomusic

*Genres:* Electronic; Grime; Hip-Hop; House;
R&B; Rap; Urban

London-based record and publishing label.

## Project Allout Records

Sheffield
*Email:* projectalloutinfo@gmail.com
*Website:* https://www.facebook.com/
projectalloutrecords
*Website:* https://soundcloud.com/
projectalloutrecords

*Genres:* Garage; Grime; Underground;
Dubstep

Record label based in Sheffield. Send
submissions by email.

## Project Melody

*Email:* info@projectmelodymusic.com
*Website:* https://www.
projectmelodymusic.com
*Website:* https://www.facebook.com/
projectmelodypm/

*Genres:* All types of music

A creative hub that provides expertise,
resource and global content management in
order to produce dynamic multi genre music
and immersive content.

## Psymmetry Collective

*Email:* psymmetryrecords@gmail.com
*Website:* https://www.facebook.com/
psymmetrycollective/

*Genres:* Garage; Psychedelic Rock; Punk;
Punk Rock

Record label working with acts across the
North West of England. Send query by email
with MP3s, WAVs, or links to music online.

## Push & Run

*Email:* bub@pushandrun.co.uk
*Website:* https://www.pushandrun.co.uk
*Website:* https://soundcloud.com/pushandrun

*Genres:* All types of music

Record label based in London. Send
submissions by email.

## QM Records

*Email:* contact@qmrecords.com
*Email:* bookings@qmrecords.com
*Website:* https://www.qmrecords.com

*Genres:* Acoustic; Funk; Jazz; Grime; Hip-
Hop; Soul

Send demos by email as links to music
online.

## Ramajam Recordings

*Website:* http://ramajamrecordings.com
*Website:* https://soundcloud.com/ramajam-
recordings

*Genres:* Drum and Bass

Record label founded in Bristol in 2011. Send query by email with MP3 links.

## Reckless Yes
*Email:* pete@recklessyes.com
*Email:* sarah@recklessyes.com
*Website:* http://recklessyes.com
*Website:* https://www.facebook.com/ RecklessYes/

*Genres:* All types of music

*Contact:* Pete Darrington; Sarah Lay

An independent record label, artist management, live music agency and publishing house. Send demos by email to both addresses. See website for full details and specific subject line to include to prove you have read the submission guidelines.

## Recoverworld Label Group
*Email:* demos@recoverworld.com
*Website:* http://www.recoverworld.com
*Website:* https://www.facebook.com/ Recoverworld

*Genres:* Dance; Pop

An established and continually expanding collection of record labels, a publishing company, online record store and recording studio/mastering suite.

## Regent Street Records
71-75 Shelton Street
Covent Garden
London
*Email:* admin@regentstreetrecords.com
*Website:* https://regentstreetrecords.com
*Website:* https://www.facebook.com/ regentstreetrecords/

*Genres:* Grime; Punk; Rock

UK Based Record Label, Publisher and Sync Rep. See website for submission guidelines.

## Restless Bear
Chester
*Email:* info@restlessbear.com
*Website:* https://restlessbear.com
*Website:* https://soundcloud.com/user-804547797

*Genres:* Garage; Punk

Record label based in Chester. Send query by email with links to music online.

## Rhythmic Records
*Email:* info@rhythmic-records.co.uk
*Website:* https://www.rhythmic-records.co.uk
*Website:* https://www.facebook.com/ RhythmicRecordsUK

*Genres:* Dance; Hip-Hop; House; Soul; Urban

Submit demos via online form.

## Riff Rock Records
*Email:* leigh@riffrockrecords.co.uk
*Website:* https://www.riffrockrecords.co.uk
*Website:* https://www.facebook.com/pg/ RiffRockMusic/about/?ref=page_internal

*Genres:* Psychedelic Rock; Rock; Doom

Rock label launched in 2015. Send query by email or Facebook message with links to music online.

## Right Recordings Ltd
177 High Street
Harlesden
London
NW10 4TE
*Email:* contact@rightrecordings.com
*Email:* info@rightrecordings.com
*Website:* http://www.rightrecordings.com
*Website:* https://www.facebook.com/ RightRecordings

*Genres:* All types of music

Record label based in Harlesden, London. Send demos by post, or send links and MP3s by email.

## RIP Records
*Email:* pete@ripmanagement.com
*Website:* https://www.recordinpeace.com
*Website:* https://soundcloud.com/pete-heywoode

*Genres:* Indie; Rock; Psychedelic Rock; Singer-Songwriter Rhythm and Blues Rock and Roll

*Contact:* Pete Heywoode

Record label based in London. Send demos by email as links to music on Soundcloud or Bandcamp.

## Robot Needs Home
*Email:* info@robotneedshome.com
*Website:* http://www.robotneedshome.com

*Genres:* All types of music

DIY collective involved in promoting shows, releasing records, and providing assistance to bands.

## Rocket Recordings
*Website:* https://rocketrecordings.blogspot.com
*Website:* https://www.facebook.com/rocket.recordings.uk

*Genres:* Psychedelic; Space Doom; Kraut Rock; Acid Rock

Independent, UK based record label.

## Rooftop Records
Liverpool
*Email:* emily@parrstreetstudios.com
*Website:* http://www.rooftoprecs.com
*Website:* https://www.facebook.com/RooftopRecordsLimited

*Genres:* All types of music

Independent label based in Liverpool, set on developing emerging artists.

## RU:Listening
*Email:* matt@ru-listening.com
*Email:* T@ru-listening.com
*Website:* https://ru-listening.com
*Website:* https://www.facebook.com/RUlisteningLtd/

*Genres:* All types of music

Record label and international talent management company based in the UK and

UAE. Formed in 2014. Send query by email with Soundcloud links.

## Run Tingz Recordings
*Email:* bookings@runtingzrecordings.co.uk
*Website:* https://www.facebook.com/runtingzrecordings
*Website:* https://soundcloud.com/runtingzrecordings

*Genres:* Drum and Bass; Jungle

Send query by email with MP3 attachments or links to music online.

## Sad Club Records
London / Leeds
*Email:* sadclubrecords@gmail.com
*Website:* https://www.sadclubrecords.com
*Website:* https://www.facebook.com/sadclubrecords

*Genres:* All types of music

*Contact:* Tallulah Webb

Independent cassette label founded in 2016, based in Leeds and London. Send demos by email.

## Safe Suburban Home
79 Alness Drive
York
*Email:* safesuburbanhome@gmail.com
*Website:* https://www.facebook.com/safesuburbanhome
*Website:* https://safesuburbanhomerecords.bandcamp.com

*Genres:* Alternative; Indie; Psychedelic Rock; Shoegaze

Small independent record label specialising in physical limited edition singles for up and coming artists around the UK and Europe. Contact by email.

## Saffron Records
*Email:* info@saffronrecords.co.uk
*Website:* https://saffronrecords.co.uk
*Website:* https://www.facebook.com/Saffronrecords/

*Genres:* Electronic; Jazz; R&B

Artist development platform and record label.

## Sain

Canolfan Sain
Llandwrog
Caenarfon
Gwynedd
LL54 5TG
*Email:* sain@sainwales.com
*Email:* dmr@sainwales.com
*Website:* https://www.sainwales.com
*Website:* https://www.facebook.com/ SainRecordiau

*Genres:* All types of music

*Contact:* Dafydd Roberts; Ellen Davies

Record label based in Caenarfon. Send demo with bio by post or by email.

## Salute the Sun

*Email:* info@salutethesunrecords.com
*Website:* https://www. salutethesunrecords.com
*Website:* https://soundcloud.com/ wesalutethesun

*Genres:* Electronic; Hip-Hop; Pop; R&B; Soul

Send query by email with links to music online.

## Scottish Fiction

Glasgow
*Email:* scottishfiction@mail.com
*Website:* http://scottishfiction.co.uk
*Website:* https://scottishfiction. bandcamp.com

*Genres:* Alternative Rock; Electronic; Folk; Pop; Hip-Hop

DIY independent record label based in Glasgow. Send query by email with links to music online.

## Serotone Recordings

*Website:* http://serotonednb.co.uk
*Website:* https://www.facebook.com/ SerotoneRecordings

*Genres:* Drum and Bass

Send query by email with links to your music online.

## Shock Records

*Email:* shockrecords@gmail.com
*Website:* https://shockrecords.wixsite.com/ shock

*Genres:* Commercial Dance; Funky House; House; Trance

Send demos by email.

## Shogun Audio Ltd

29 Kensington Gardens
Brighton
East Sussex
BN1 4AL
*Email:* shogunaudio@label-engine.com
*Email:* info@shogunaudio.co.uk
*Website:* http://www.shogunaudio.co.uk
*Website:* http://shogunaudio.label-engine.com/demos

*Genres:* Electronic; Drum and Bass

Record label based in Brighton. Send demos via online submission system.

## Silverwood Music Group

*Website:* https://www.silverword.co.uk

*Genres:* All types of music

Independent record label based in Wales. Has over 15 record labels in its catalogue, covering most genres of music.

## Sister 9 Recordings

*Email:* demos@sister9.com
*Website:* https://sister9.com
*Website:* https://www.facebook.com/ Sister9Recordings

*Genres:* Alternative; Lo-fi; Post Punk Rock; Psychedelic Rock

Specialise in Alternative and Lo-Fi recordings and sessions.

The label also puts on gig nights and is home to a label set up to release previously recorded material by artists from anywhere in the world.

Interested in sourcing new artists to work with. Make contact via the website with links to music online.

## Sliced Note Recordings
*Email:* silentcodeuk@gmail.com
*Website:* http://www.
slicednoterecordings.com
*Website:* https://soundcloud.com/
slicednoterecordings

*Genres:* Drum and Bass; Jungle

Send query by email with private SoundCloud links.

## Snatch! Records
7 Bourne Court
Southend Road
Woodford Green
London
IG8 8HD
*Email:* contact@snatchrecords.com
*Website:* http://www.snatchrecords.com
*Website:* https://soundcloud.com/
snatchrecords

*Genres:* House

Record label dealing in House music, based in London. "Expect slamming fresh house cuts from some of the most exciting talent in the scene." Send query via form on website with links to music online (wetransfer, dropbox, or soundcloud with active download).

## Solar Distance
*Email:* demos@solardistance.com
*Email:* michele@solardistance.com
*Website:* http://www.solardistance.com
*Website:* https://soundcloud.com/
solardistance

*Genres:* Electronic; Techno

Submit demos by email.

## Some Bizzare Records
*Email:* info@somebizzare.com
*Website:* http://www.somebizarre.com

*Website:* https://www.facebook.com/Some-Bizzare-141551249228568/

*Genres:* Alternative

"Bold and adventurous label".

## Somewhere Records
*Email:* enquiry@somewhererecords.co.uk
*Website:* https://www.
somewhererecords.co.uk
*Website:* https://www.facebook.com/
somewhererecordsuk

*Genres:* All types of music

Independent record label based in Market Harborough, Leicestershire. Contact via form on website.

## Sonic Bear
*Email:* sonicbearlabel@gmail.com
*Website:* https://www.sonic-bear.com
*Website:* https://www.facebook.com/
sonicbearlabel

*Genres:* Electronic; House

Record label specialising in electronic house music / deep house. Send query by email with links to music online.

## Soulvent Records
London
*Email:* info@soulventrecords.co.uk
*Website:* http://soulventrecords.com
*Website:* http://soulventrecords.label-engine.com/demos

*Genres:* Drum and Bass

Independent East London record label. Send demo via online submission system.

## Sound-Hub Records
7 King Street
Belper
Derbyshire
DE56 1PS
*Email:* info@sound-hub.com
*Website:* http://www.sound-hub.com
*Website:* https://www.facebook.com/
SoundHubStudio

*Genres:* All types of music

Describe themselves as the "UK's leading independent label". Send details with YouTube or Soundcloud link via online web form, available on website. Only accepts submissions from the UK and Europe.

## Sounds Like Vinyl
*Email:* shawndavis22@hotmail.com
*Website:* https://milwaukie2003.wixsite.com/sounds-like-vinyl
*Website:* https://www.facebook.com/soundslikevinyl/

*Genres:* Electronic; Acid; Techno; Underground

Record label that seeks to capture the sound of vinyl in digital format.

## Sounds Of Meow
*Email:* contact@soundsofmeow.com
*Website:* https://soundsofmeow.com

*Genres:* Electronic Dance; Electronic Club; Commercial Dance; Melodic Techno; Underground House Techno; Melodic House Techno; Trance; Progressive House; Mainstream Dance

Deep/Tech/Club House, Trance and Melodic Techno music Label.
Was Estabilished in 2020 to bring more and more music to this world.

## Sour Grapes
Manchester
*Email:* info@sourgrapesrecords.co.uk
*Website:* http://www.sourgrapesrecords.co.uk
*Website:* https://www.facebook.com/sourgrapesmanchester/

*Genres:* Psychedelic; Garage; Punk; Rock; Rock and Roll

DIY record label and promoter based in Manchester. Send demos by email only.

## Speedy Enix Records
*Email:* info@se-records.co.uk
*Website:* http://www.se-records.co.uk
*Website:* https://www.facebook.com/speedyenixrecords

*Genres:* All types of music

Record label catering for raw, unsigned talent and independent musicians of all genres. Send links to music online via contact form on website.

## Speedy Wunderground
*Email:* info@speedywunderground.com
*Website:* http://speedywunderground.com
*Website:* https://www.facebook.com/speedywunder/

*Genres:* All types of music

*Contact:* Dan Carey

Record label focusing on speed to market. All recordings will be done on one day; all mixing the next. Records will be in the shops as soon as humanly possible. Send query by email with links to music online.

## Square Leg
*Email:* info@squarelegrecords.co.uk
*Website:* http://www.squarelegrecords.co.uk
*Website:* https://www.facebook.com/squarelegrecords/

*Genres:* All types of music

*Contact:* Charlie Andrew

Record label set up by award-winning record producer. Send query by email with links to music online.

## Standby
*Email:* demos@standbyrecords.co.uk
*Website:* https://www.standbyrecords.co.uk
*Website:* https://soundcloud.com/standby_records

*Genres:* Progressive House

Record label based in London, releasing Deep Tech Progressive House. Always looking to sign quality new music. Contact via Soundcloud with links to music online.

## State51 Conspiracy
*Email:* support@state51.com
*Website:* http://state51.com
*Website:* https://www.facebook.com/thestate51conspiracy/

*Genres:* All types of music

Ethical music company based in London. Send query by email with links to music online.

## Strawberry Moon Records

3B, 48 Comercial Road
Wolverhampton
*Email:* groundcontrol@
strawberrymoonrecords.co.uk
*Website:* https://www.facebook.com/
strawberrymoonrecordsltd

*Genres:* All types of music

Describes itself as one of the UK's most innovative independent record labels. Send query by email with links to your music online.

## Strong Island Recordings

*Email:* INFO@
STRONGISLANDRECORDINGS.com
*Website:* https://strongislandrecordings.
tumblr.com
*Website:* https://soundcloud.com/
strongislandrecordings

*Genres:* Psychedelic; Shoegaze; Garage Rock; Post Punk; Indie

Send query by email with link to music online.

## Stunted Records & Management

6 Cliff Gardens
Scunthorpe
North Lincolnshire
DN15 7PJ
*Fax:* +44 (0) 1724 358966
*Email:* john@stuntedrecords.co.uk
*Email:* jill@stuntedrecords.co.uk
*Website:* http://www.stuntedrecords.co.uk
*Website:* http://www.myspace.com/
stuntedrecords

*Genres:* Rock; Metal

*Contact:* John Clay

Send demos by post. Demos will not be returned. Include web address, contact phone

numbers, press / photos, and any gigs / tour dates. Will respond if interested.

## Subdust Music

Office 459
275 Deansgate
Manchester
M3 4EL
*Email:* admin(at)subdust.com
*Website:* https://www.subdust.com

*Genres:* Alternative; Electronic; Experimental; Mainstream; Urban; Commercial

*Contact:* Jason Holmes

An evolution of the normal record label model with collaborative production and artist releases with artist services including distribution and consultation. Send streaming links only by email.

## Sugar Shack Records Ltd

c/o Crystal WM
19 Portland Square
Bristol
BS2 8SJ
*Email:* info@sugarshackrecords.co.uk
*Email:* mike@sugarshackrecords.co.uk
*Website:* http://www.
sugarshackrecords.co.uk

*Genres:* Rock

*Contact:* Mike Darby

Always looking for great music. Send demos by post or by email.

## Supermarine Music

North Wiltshire
*Email:* hello@supermarinemusic.co.uk
*Email:* jon@supermarinemusic.co.uk
*Website:* https://www.
supermarinemusic.co.uk
*Website:* https://www.facebook.com/
supermarinemusic

*Genres:* Acoustic; Electronic; Alternative Rock; Folk

Start-up independent record label based in North Wiltshire, supporting new and original artists in the region and beyond. Send query by email with links to music online. No MP3 attachments.

## Survival Records
P.O. BOX 2502
DEVIZES
WILTS
SN10 3ZN
*Fax:* +44 (0) 1380 860596
*Email:* survivalrecords@globalnet.co.uk
*Website:* http://www.survivalrecords.co.uk

*Genres:* Celtic

*Contact:* Anne-Marie Heighway; David Rome

Record label based in Devizes, Wiltshire.

## These Bloody Thieves Records
Sheffield
*Email:* info@fansforbands.com
*Website:* https://www.thesebloodythievesrecords.com
*Website:* https://www.facebook.com/thesebloodythieves

*Genres:* Alternative; Acoustic; Indie; Folk; Metal; Rock

Indie label based in Sheffield. Send query by email with links to music online.

## 37 Adventures
London
*Email:* hello@37adventures.co.uk
*Website:* http://37adventures.co.uk
*Website:* https://soundcloud.com/37adventures

*Genres:* Electronic; Dance; Indie; Pop

Record label based in London. Send query by email with links to music online.

## This and That Lab
*Email:* info@thisandthatlab.com
*Website:* http://thisandthatlab.com/
*Website:* https://www.facebook.com/thisandthatlab

*Genres:* Electronic; House; Techno

Record label and think tank combining music, art, and culture.

## 3 Bar Fire
Arch 462, Kingsland Viaduct
83 Rivington Street
London
EC2A 3AY
*Email:* hi@outpostmedia.co.uk
*Website:* http://3barfire.com

*Genres:* All types of music

Record label based in London. Send query by email with links to music online.

## Tigertrap Records
14 Pixley Street
London
E14 7DF
*Email:* info@tigertrap.co.uk
*Website:* http://www.tigertrap.co.uk
*Website:* https://www.facebook.com/tigertraprecords

*Genres:* Alternative Electronic; Rock

Record label based in London. Send query by email with links to music online.

## Tight Lines
Leeds
*Email:* will@tightlinesmusic.co.uk
*Website:* https://www.tightlinesmusic.co.uk
*Website:* https://www.facebook.com/tightlinesmusic

*Genres:* Hip-Hop; Jazz; Leftfield; Punk; Soul

Independent record label presenting emerging bands from Leeds.

## Tip Top Recordings
London
*Email:* tiptoprecs@gmail.com
*Email:* ben@tiptoprecordings.com
*Website:* https://www.tiptoprecs.com/contact
*Website:* http://www.facebook.com/tiptoprecs

*Genres:* Alternative; Indie; Punk

Record label based in London, Chicago, and Cambridge. Send query by email with links to music online.

## TNS (That's Not Skanking) Records

Manchester
*Email:* info@tnsrecords.co.uk
*Email:* bev@tnsrecords.co.uk
*Website:* https://www.tnsrecords.co.uk
*Website:* https://www.facebook.com/group.php?gid=5735058846
*Website:* https://www.myspace.com/tnsrecords_uk

*Genres:* Punk; Ska; Underground

Not-for-profit label based in Manchester. Send query by email in first instance.

## ToneTrade Productions

70 Minet Avenue
London
NW10 8AP
*Email:* francescoaccurso@tonetrade.co.uk
*Website:* http://www.tonetrade.co.uk

*Genres:* Jazz; Urban Blues; Alternative Blues; Blues; Roots

Independent production company and management based in London. Send query by email with short bio and links to streaming music online.

## Trancespired Recordings

*Email:* demos@trancespired.com
*Email:* contact@trancespired.com
*Website:* https://trancespired.com
*Website:* https://soundcloud.com/trancespiredrecordings

*Genres:* Trance; Progressive

UK-based Trance Label, aspiring to release the best in Uplifting, Progressive, Tech and Vocal trance. Submit your demo by email as a link to your music online.

## Transgressive Records

London
*Email:* demos@transgressiverecords.com
*Website:* http://www.

transgressiverecords.co.uk
*Website:* https://soundcloud.com/transgressive-records
*Website:* http://www.myspace.com/transgressiverecords

*Genres:* All types of music

Record label based in London. Send query by email or through website contact form, with links to music online.

## Trashmouth Records

London
*Website:* https://trashmouthrecords.bandcamp.com
*Website:* https://www.facebook.com/trashmouthrecs

*Genres:* All types of music

Record label based in London. Prefers to hear demos rather than finished EPs / albums.

## Triassic Tusk

*Email:* Stephen@triassictuskrecords.com
*Website:* https://www.triassictuskrecords.com
*Website:* https://www.facebook.com/triassictuskrecords/

*Genres:* All types of music

*Contact:* Lucy Hine; Stephen Marshall

Small record label based in a brewery in the East Neuk of Fife. Send queries by email with links to music online.

## Tru Thoughts

PO Box 2818
Brighton
East Sussex
BN1 4RL
*Email:* demos@tru-thoughts.co.uk
*Email:* info@tru-thoughts.co.uk
*Website:* http://www.tru-thoughts.co.uk
*Website:* https://www.facebook.com/truthoughts

*Genres:* Funk; Hip-Hop; Break Beat; Jazz; Soul

*Contact:* Robert Luis

Contact by email.

## 21st Century Music
23 Collyer Road
London Colney
St Albans
Hertfordshire
AL2 1PD
*Email:* clifford.white@21newmedia.com
*Website:* https://www.21stcentury.co.uk
*Website:* http://www.21newmedia.com

*Genres:* Electronic Alternative Atmospheric
Downtempo Funky Melodic New Wave
Psychedelic

*Contact:* Clifford White

Incredible electronic music. That's what we
bring you. Our music will inspire you. Uplift
you. Enrich you. Top-quality, superbly
melodic, rich and full of originality. That's
21st Century Music. Electronic music for the
next generation...!

## Viking Promotions
*Email:* viking_promo_music.uk@aol.com
*Website:* https://www.facebook.com/
vikingpromotions

*Genres:* Acoustic; Blues; Country;
Americana; Folk

Independent record label, promoter, and
booking agency. Send query by email with
links to music online.

## Violette Records
Liverpool / Manchester / Paris
*Email:* matt@violetterecords.com
*Website:* http://violetterecords.com/
*Website:* https://www.facebook.com/
violetterecords

*Genres:* Acoustic; Country; Blues; Folk;
Indie; Lo-fi; Psychedelic Folk

Record label with offices in Liverpool,
Manchester, and Paris. Send query by email
with links to music online.

## Wall of Sound Recordings Ltd
*Email:* info@wallofsound.net
*Website:* https://www.facebook.com/
wallofsound.net
*Website:* https://www.twitter.com/
wallofsounduk

*Genres:* All types of music

Record label based in London. Send query
by email with links to music online.

## Warner Music Group UK
27 Wrights Lane
London
W8 5SW
*Website:* https://www.wmg.com

*Genres:* All types of music

UK arm of major international label. No
unsolicited submissions.

## What Came First
*Email:* demos@wcfrecordings.com
*Website:* https://www.egglondon.co.uk/label/
what-came-first

*Genres:* Electronic

Record label of electronic music. Send query
by email with demo tracks as downloadable
stream / wetransfer.

## When Planets Collide
*Email:* whenplanetscollide@hotmail.co.uk
*Website:* https://whenplanetscollide.
bigcartel.com
*Website:* https://www.facebook.com/
whenplanetscollideuk

*Genres:* Gothic; Heavy Metal; Underground

*Contact:* Gareth Kelly

Send query by email with links to music
online.

## Wobbly Music
Bakehouse Studio
52, Willows Lane
Accrington
Lancashire
BB5 0RT
*Email:* info@wobblymusic.net
*Email:* lynn@wobblymusic.net
*Website:* http://www.wobblymusic.net

*Website:* https://www.facebook.com/
WobblyMusic.net

*Genres:* Acoustic; Blues; Classic Dance;
Classical; Country; Dance; Ethnic; Folk;
Funk; Fusion; Pop; Reggae; Rock; Singer-
Songwriter

*Contact:* Lynn Monk

An independent music production, recording,
and internet marketing company dedicated to
the advancement of mature independent
musicians.

## Wobbly Records
Brighton
*Email:* mail@wobblyrecords.com
*Website:* https://wobblyrecords.
bandcamp.com
*Website:* https://www.facebook.com/
Wobbly-Records-118314701516905/

*Genres:* Electronic; Psychedelic

Always looking for new artists. Send query
by email.

## Wolf Tone
The Church Studios
145h Crouch Hill
N8 9QH
*Email:* info@wolf-tone.com
*Website:* http://www.wolf-tone.com
*Website:* https://www.facebook.com/
wolftoneHQ/

*Genres:* All types of music

London-based record label and publishing
company launched in 2012. Send query by
email with links to music online.

## A World Artists Love (AWAL)
*Website:* https://www.awal.com
*Website:* https://www.facebook.com/AWAL

*Genres:* All types of music

An alternative to the traditional music label,
offering artists and independent labels a
range of services without having to give up
ownership or control.

## Wrong Way Records
*Email:* info@wrongwayrecords.com
*Website:* http://wrongwayrecords.com
*Website:* https://www.facebook.com/
wrongwayrecords/

*Genres:* Psychedelic; Shoegaze; Space Rock;
Leftfield; Kraut Rock

Independent record label with a passion for
vinyl, specialising in psychedelia, shoegaze,
spacerock, leftfield and krautrock. Not taking
on bands for the foreseeable future.

## WW Records
London
*Email:* info@wwrecords.co.uk
*Website:* http://www.wwrecords.co.uk
*Website:* https://soundcloud.com/wwrecords

*Genres:* Alternative Dance

Record label based in London. Send query
by email with soundcloud links or MP3s.

## XL Recordings
UK OFFICE:
FAO A&R
1 Codrington Mews
London
W11 2EH

US OFFICE:
304 Hudson Street, 7th Floor
New York, 10013
*Fax:* +44 (0) 20 8871 4178
*Email:* xl@xlrecordings.com
*Website:* http://www.xlrecordings.com
*Website:* https://www.facebook.com/
xlrecordings

*Genres:* Alternative; Electronic

*Contact:* Matt Thornhill

Closed to submissions as at January 2018.
Approach via manager only.

## Xtra Mile Recordings
Y16 – Access House
207-211 The Vale
Acton
London
W3 7QS
*Email:* info@xtramilerecordings.com

*Website:* https://www.
xtramilerecordings.com
*Website:* https://soundcloud.com/
xtramilerecordings

*Genres:* All types of music

Record label based in Acton, London.

## XVII Music Group
Brighton
*Email:* info@xviimusic.com
*Website:* https://www.xviimusic.com
*Website:* https://soundcloud.com/
xviimusicgroup

*Genres:* All types of music

Artist development, record label, and recording studio based in Brighton.

## Yada Yada Records
London
*Email:* jc@yadayadauk.com
*Website:* http://www.yadayadauk.com
*Website:* http://facebook.com/yadayadauk

*Genres:* Alternative Pop

*Contact:* James Cattermole; Scott Verrill;
Luke Pettican

Alt-pop record label based in London. Send queries and demos by email.

## Yala! Records
London
*Email:* info@yalarecords.com
*Website:* http://www.yalarecords.com
*Website:* https://www.facebook.com/
yalarecords

*Genres:* Alternative; Electronic; Indie; Pop;
Punk; Punk Rock; Rock

London-based label/club night founded in 2016. Send queries by email with links to music online.

## ZTT Records
Sarm Studios
8-10 Basing Street
London
W11 1ET
*Email:* stephen@spz.com
*Website:* http://www.ztt.com
*Website:* https://www.facebook.com/
zttrecords

*Genres:* Alternative; Acoustic; Indie;
Electronic

Record label based in London. Send demo with contact details and SAE if return required, or send links to music online by email. Listens to every demo but responds only if interested.

## ZyNg Tapes
Newcastle Upon Tyne
*Email:* info@zyngtapes.co.uk
*Website:* http://www.zyngtapes.co.uk
*Website:* https://www.facebook.com/
zyngtapes

*Genres:* Indie; Lo-fi; Punk; Rock

Record label based in Newcastle. Send query through form on website with link to your music online.

# Canadian Record Labels

*For the most up-to-date listings of these and hundreds of other record labels, visit https://www.musicsocket.com/recordlabels*

*To claim your **free** access to the site, please see the back of this book.*

## Bonsound

160, Saint-Viateur Street East, suite 400
Montreal, QC
H2T 1A8
*Fax:* +1 (514) 700-1307
*Email:* nextbigthing@bonsound.com
*Email:* info@bonsound.com
*Website:* http://www.bonsound.com

*Genres:* Alternative; Rock

An artist management company, a record label, a booking agency, a concert producer and a promotion and publicity agency. Not actively looking to expand its roster, but willing to listen. Send query by email with links to music online. No physical submissions or MP3 attachments.

## Chacra Music

262 Rang 1
St. Etienne De Bolton
Quebec, J0E 2E0
*Fax:* +1 (450) 297-4616
*Email:* info@chacramusic.com
*Website:* http://www.chacramusic.com

*Genres:* New Age; Celtic; Guitar based; World

Record label based in St Etienne De Bolton, Quebec. Send demos by post on CD or cassette.

## Coalition Music

1731 Lawrence Avenue East
Toronto, ON M1R 2X7
*Email:* info@coalitionmusic.com
*Website:* http://coalitionmusic.com
*Website:* https://www.facebook.com/CoalitionMUS

*Genres:* All types of music

Record label based in Toronto, Ontario. Send demos by email.

## Constellation

PO Box 55012
CSP Fairmount
Montreal, Québec
H2T 3E2
*Fax:* +1 (253) 736-1966
*Email:* demos@cstrecords.com
*Email:* info@cstrecords.com
*Website:* http://cstrecords.com
*Website:* https://www.facebook.com/cstrecords

*Genres:* Alternative; Rock

Have released bands from the Canadian west coast, the United States, and Europe, but main artist focus remains predominantly regional, i.e. projects based in Montreal, the province of Quebec, or Central/Eastern Canada. Send query by email with links to music online. No attachments. Response not guaranteed.

## Curve Music
714 Gerrard Street East
Toronto, Ontario
*Email:* luckj@curvemusic.com
*Website:* http://curvemusic.com
*Website:* https://www.facebook.com/
curvemusiccanada

*Genres:* Alternative; Rock; Punk; Pop Rock

Record label based in Toronto, Ontario.

## Distort
1111 Privet Place
Oakville, ON
L6J 7J6
*Email:* demos@teamdistort.com
*Email:* info@teamdistort.com
*Website:* http://www.distortent.com
*Website:* https://www.facebook.com/Distort

*Genres:* Metal

Independent metal label based in Toronto.
Send query by email with links to music
online.

## Drip Out Music Records
*Email:* dripoutrecords@gmail.com
*Website:* https://dripoutmusicrecords.
bandzoogle.com/

*Genres:* All types of music

An Online independant Record Label and
Artist Management Agency, founded in
2019.

## Last Gang Records
134 Peter St, Suite 700
Toronto, Canada
M5V 2H2
*Email:* info@lastgang.com
*Website:* https://lastgang.com

*Genres:* Electronic; Rock

Entertainment company based in Toronto,
Ontario, including label, publishing,
licensing, management, and promotions.
Submit demos through Soundcloud.

## Mint Records
PO Box 3613
Vancouver, BC
V6B 3Y6
*Email:* info@mintrecs.com
*Website:* https://www.mintrecs.com
*Website:* https://www.facebook.com/
mintrecords

*Genres:* Indie

Record label based in Vancouver. Send
demo on CD by post with your contact
information. No fancy packaging required.
Response if interested.

## Open Road Recordings
Toronto, ON
*Email:* info@openroadrecordings.com
*Website:* http://www.
openroadrecordings.com
*Website:* https://www.facebook.com/
openroadrecordings

*Genres:* Country

A full service record company based in
Toronto, Ontario, dedicated to country
music. Offers marketing, promotion,
publicity, A&R and licensing services.

## Outside Music
7 Labatt Ave, Suite 210
Toronto, ON, M6K 1L4
*Email:* lloyd@outside-music.com
*Email:* evan@outside-music.com
*Website:* https://www.outside-music.com
*Website:* https://www.facebook.com/
OutsideMusic/

*Genres:* All types of music

*Contact:* Lloyd Nishimura; Evan Newman

Label and management company based in
Toronto.

## Paper Bag Records
955 Queen St. W. Suite 116
Toronto, ON M6J 3X5
*Email:* shop@paperbagrecords.com

*Website:* http://paperbagrecords.com

*Website:* https://www.facebook.com/
PaperBagRecords/

*Genres:* Alternative Rock

Alt rock label based in Toronto, Canada.

# Australian Record Labels

*For the most up-to-date listings of these and hundreds of other record labels, visit https://www.musicsocket.com/recordlabels*

*To claim your **free** access to the site, please see the back of this book.*

## Claudia eRecords
Brisbane
*Email:* claudia@claudiaerecords.com
*Website:* https://www.claudiaerecords.com

*Genres:* Alternative; Indie; Hip-Hop; Electronic; Pop; Rock; Dance; Punk; Rap; Soul

*Contact:* Claudia Ergenzinger

Record label also offering PR services, management, and digital music distribution. Approach via form on website.

## Cooking Vinyl Australia
Melbourne
*Email:* info@cookingvinylaustralia.com
*Website:* https://www.cookingvinylaustralia.com
*Website:* https://www.facebook.com/cookingvinylAU/

*Genres:* All types of music

Record label based in Melbourne, Australia, home to local and international acts.

## Inertia
*Email:* info@inertiamusic.com
*Website:* http://inertiamusic.com
*Website:* https://www.facebook.com/inertiamusic

*Genres:* All types of music

Describes itself as Australia's leading music company.

## Liberation Records
*Email:* info@liberationrecords.com.au
*Website:* http://www.liberationrecords.com.au
*Website:* https://soundcloud.com/liberationrecords

*Genres:* All types of music

Record label based in Albert Park, Australia.

## Secret Service
PO Box 401
Fortitude Valley
QLD, 4006
*Email:* stacey@secret-service.com.au
*Website:* http://www.secret-service.com.au
*Website:* https://www.facebook.com/secretservicePR

*Genres:* All types of music

*Contact:* Stacey Piggott; Shari Hindmarsh

Management company based in Fortitude Valley, Queensland.

# Record Labels Index

*This section lists record labels by their genres, with directions to the section of the book where the full listing can be found.*

*You can create your own customised lists of record labels using different combinations of these subject areas, plus over a dozen other criteria, instantly online at https://www.musicsocket.com.*

*To claim your **free** access to the site, please see the back of this book.*

**All types of music**
37 Degrees (*UK*)
3tone Records (*UK*)
Accidental Records Ltd (*UK*)
Acorn Records (*UK*)
Alya Records (*UK*)
Anchorage Records (*UK*)
Associated Music International (AMI) Media (*UK*)
Atlantic Records (*UK*)
Avenoir Records (*UK*)
Battle Worldwide (*UK*)
Bella Union (*UK*)
Bespoke Records (*UK*)
BFS Records (*UK*)
Bluesky Pie Records (*UK*)
BMG (*US*)
Brash Music (*US*)
Brushfire Records (*US*)
Bucks Music Group (*UK*)
Button Up Records (*UK*)
Canvasback Music (*US*)
Carved Records (*US*)
Catskills Records (*UK*)
Cheap Lullaby Records (*US*)
Chicago Kid Records (*US*)
Coalition Music (*Can*)
Collect Records (*US*)
Columbia Records (*UK*)
Columbia Records (*US*)

Come Play With Me (*UK*)
Communion Records US (*US*)
Cooking Vinyl Australia (*Aus*)
Crucial Records (*UK*)
Daptone Records (*US*)
Decca Records (*UK*)
Deek Recordings (*UK*)
Deltasonic Records (*UK*)
Denizen Recordings (*UK*)
DigSin (*US*)
Direct Management Group (*US*)
Discovering Arts Music Group (DAMG) (*UK*)
Disney Music Group (*US*)
DO IT Records (*US*)
Downtown Records (*US*)
Dr Johns Surgery Records (*UK*)
Drip Out Music Records (*Can*)
Droma Records (*UK*)
Eastzone Records (*UK*)
Electric Honey Music (*UK*)
Elektra Music Group (*US*)
Elliptic Records (*UK*)
Elm City Music (*US*)
Emblem Music Group (*US*)
End Of The Trail Records (*UK*)
Entertainment One (eOne) (*US*)
Epic Records Group (*US*)
Eromeda Records (*UK*)
Everloving (*US*)

Evil Genius Records (*UK*)
Fade To Silence (*US*)
Fame Throwa Records (*UK*)
Famous Records (*US*)
FatCat Records (*UK*)
Flowers in the Dustbin (*UK*)
Fool's Gold (*US*)
Frenchkiss Records (*US*)
Friendly Fire Recordings (*US*)
Fueled By Ramen (*US*)
Gameplan Records (*UK*)
Glassnote (*US*)
Hollywood Records (*US*)
Iamsound (*US*)
Inertia (*Aus*)
Infidel Records (*US*)
Innovative Leisure (*US*)
Inspired Studios Inc. (*US*)
Intelligent Noise (*US*)
Invisiblegirl Records (*UK*)
Jost Music (*UK*)
K Dragon Records (*UK*)
K Records (*US*)
Keep Me Young (KMY) (*UK*)
Killroom Records (*US*)
Lapsang House (*UK*)
Last Night From Glasgow (*UK*)
Lava Records (*US*)
LGM Records (*UK*)
Liberation Records (*Aus*)
Lightyear Entertainment (*US*)
Loma Vista (*US*)
Long Records (*UK*)
Loyalty Over Royalty Records (*US*)
Machin Entertainment (*US*)
Malicious Damage (*UK*)
Mandala Records (*US*)
Mascot Label Group (*US*)
Mayfield Records (*UK*)
Me & You Music (*UK*)
Metropolitan Groove Merchants (MGM) (*US*)
MHM (*UK*)
Middle West (*US*)
Mind of a Genius Records (*US*)
Mixpak (*US*)
Modern Sky (*UK*)
Mom + Pop (*US*)
Monomyth Records (*UK*)
Motown (*US*)
MPress Records (*US*)
Musical Bear Records (*UK*)
Neon Gold (*US*)
Never Fade Records (*UK*)
New Heights Entertainment (*US*)

New Street Records (*UK*)
No Quarter (*US*)
Not Not Fun (*US*)
Omnivore Recordings (*US*)
Outside Music (*Can*)
Paper Garden Records (*US*)
Partisan Records (*US*)
Payne Records (*UK*)
Phase One Network (*US*)
Photo Finish Records (*US*)
Pink Lane Records (*UK*)
Playing In Traffic Records (*US*)
+1 Records (*US*)
PPL Entertainment Group (*US*)
Project Melody (*UK*)
Pure Noise (*US*)
Push & Run (*UK*)
Rampage Records (*US*)
Reckless Yes (*UK*)
Red Bull Records (*US*)
Right Recordings Ltd (*UK*)
Rise Records, Inc. (*US*)
Robot Needs Home (*UK*)
Rooftop Records (*UK*)
RU:Listening (*UK*)
Sad Club Records (*UK*)
Sain (*UK*)
Secret Service (*Aus*)
Silverwood Music Group (*UK*)
Somewhere Records (*UK*)
Sound-Hub Records (*UK*)
Speedy Enix Records (*UK*)
Speedy Wunderground (*UK*)
Square Leg (*UK*)
State51 Conspiracy (*UK*)
Strawberry Moon Records (*UK*)
Sunset Music Supervision (*US*)
Sunset Recordings (*US*)
Sunset Special Markets (SSM) (*US*)
3 Bar Fire (*UK*)
Tonally Records (*US*)
Transgressive Records (*UK*)
Trashmouth Records (*UK*)
Triassic Tusk (*UK*)
Turkey Vulture Records (*US*)
Universal Music Group (*US*)
Wall of Sound Recordings Ltd (*UK*)
Warner Music Group UK (*UK*)
Wolf Tone (*UK*)
A World Artists Love (AWAL) (*UK*)
Xtra Mile Recordings (*UK*)
XVII Music Group (*UK*)
**Acid**
Brock Wild (*UK*)
Distinctive Records (*UK*)

Dorado Music (US) (*US*)
Futurist Recordings (*UK*)
Rocket Recordings (*UK*)
Sounds Like Vinyl (*UK*)

**Acoustic**
DJD Music Ltd (*UK*)
Everyday Records (*UK*)
Harbourtown Records (*UK*)
Haystack Records (*UK*)
Heist or Hit Records (*UK*)
Lost in the Manor (*UK*)
Maggie's Music (*US*)
Mellowtone Records (*UK*)
Moth Man Records (*US*)
musicXart (*UK*)
Navigator Records (*UK*)
QM Records (*UK*)
Red House Records (*US*)
Red Parlor Records (*US*)
Supermarine Music (*UK*)
Tama Industries Record Label (*US*)
These Bloody Thieves Records (*UK*)
Viking Promotions (*UK*)
Violette Records (*UK*)
Wobbly Music (*UK*)
ZTT Records (*UK*)

**Alternative**
0114 Records (*UK*)
Abattoir Blues (*UK*)
The Adult Teeth Recording Company (*UK*)
AnalogueTrash Ltd (*UK*)
Bad Bat Records (*UK*)
Bear Love Records (*UK*)
Black Bleach Records (*UK*)
Blak Hand Records (*UK*)
Bonsound (*Can*)
Box Records (*UK*)
Brightonsfinest (*UK*)
Bubblewrap Collective (*UK*)
Burnt Toast Vinyl (*US*)
Carpark Records (*US*)
Cascine (*US*)
CCT Records (*UK*)
Chalkpit Records Ltd (*UK*)
Claudia eRecords (*Aus*)
Compass Records (*US*)
Constellation (*Can*)
Curve Music (*Can*)
Dangerbird Records (*US*)
Dewey Dog Records (*US*)
Different Records (*UK*)
Dirty Bingo Records (*UK*)
Dirty Canvas Music (*US*)

DJD Music Ltd (*UK*)
Doghouse Records (*US*)
Doing Life Records (*UK*)
Don't Try (*UK*)
Drag City (*US*)
Easy Life Records (*UK*)
Eclipse Records, inc. (*US*)
The End Records (*US*)
Epitaph (*US*)
Equal Vision Records (*US*)
Everyday Records (*UK*)
Fearless Records (*US*)
Ferret Music (*US*)
4AD (*UK*)
Fox Records (*UK*)
Freaks R Us (*UK*)
Frontier Records (*US*)
Full Time Hobby (*UK*)
Ganbei Records (*UK*)
Graphite Records (*UK*)
Harmor Records (*UK*)
Headliner Records / George Tobin Music (*US*)
Heist or Hit Records (*UK*)
Highwheel Records (*US*)
Hit City USA (*US*)
Infectious Music (*UK*)
Jagjaguwar (*US*)
Kirtland Records (*US*)
Le Grand Magistery, LLC (*US*)
Libertino (*UK*)
Loner Noise (*UK*)
Lost in the Manor (*UK*)
Mad Dragon Music Group (*US*)
Metropolis Records (*US*)
Minty Fresh Records (*US*)
Moth Man Records (*US*)
Mute Records (*US*)
NB Audio (*UK*)
Nettwerk Records (*US*)
Nonesuch Records (*US*)
Oglio Entertainment (*US*)
Organ Records (*UK*)
Paper Bag Records (*Can*)
Parasol (*US*)
Park the Van Records (*US*)
Partisan Records (*US*)
Phantasy (*UK*)
Pinch Hit Records (*US*)
Pop Cautious Records (*US*)
Razor & Tie (*US*)
Righteous Babe Records (*US*)
Safe Suburban Home (*UK*)
Scottish Fiction (*UK*)
Sister 9 Recordings (*UK*)

Some Bizzare Records (*UK*)
Subdust Music (*UK*)
Supermarine Music (*UK*)
Swade Records (*US*)
These Bloody Thieves Records (*UK*)
Tigertrap Records (*UK*)
Tip Top Recordings (*UK*)
ToneTrade Productions (*UK*)
21st Century Music (*UK*)
WW Records (*UK*)
XL Recordings (*UK*)
Yada Yada Records (*UK*)
Yala! Records (*UK*)
ZTT Records (*UK*)
**Ambient**
The Adult Teeth Recording Company (*UK*)
Bad Bat Records (*UK*)
Canigou Records (*UK*)
CCT Records (*UK*)
Cold Spring (*UK*)
Delved in Dreams, inc. (*US*)
DJD Music Ltd (*UK*)
DOMO Records, Inc. (*US*)
IKonic Image (*UK*)
Midhir Records (*UK*)
Sequoia Records (*US*)
**Americana**
At the Helm Records (*UK*)
Aveline Records (*UK*)
Bear Love Records (*UK*)
Carnival Music (*US*)
Compass Records (*US*)
Dualtone Records (*US*)
Funzalo Records (*US*)
Idol Records (*US*)
Landslide Records (*US*)
Lightning Rod Records (*US*)
Little Fish Records (*US*)
Lost Highway Records (*US*)
Moth Man Records (*US*)
My Little Empire (*UK*)
Nettwerk Records (*US*)
New West Records LLC (*US*)
Nonesuch Records (*US*)
PS Classics (*US*)
R.O.A.D. (Riding on a Dream) Records (*US*)
Rainman Records (*US*)
Red Parlor Records (*US*)
SGNB Records (*US*)
Swade Records (*US*)
Viking Promotions (*UK*)
Yellow Dog Records (*US*)
**Atmospheric**

Beta Recordings (*UK*)
21st Century Music (*UK*)
**Avant-Garde**
Amulet Records, Inc. (*US*)
Dewey Dog Records (*US*)
DJD Music Ltd (*UK*)
Focused Silence (*UK*)
House of Mythology (*UK*)
KFM Records (*UK*)
Midhir Records (*UK*)
Moodswing Records (*US*)
**Black Metal**
Mad Decent (*US*)
Midhir Records (*UK*)
**Blues**
Abattoir Blues (*UK*)
Big Bear Records (*UK*)
Blues Matters Records (*UK*)
Compass Records (*US*)
Concord Music Group (*US*)
Delmark Records (*US*)
Delta Groove Music (*US*)
Dewey Dog Records (*US*)
Earache Records Inc. (*US*)
Earwig Music Company, Inc. (*US*)
East of Sideways Music (*US*)
Everyday Records (*UK*)
Fat Possum Records (*US*)
GNP Crescendo Records (*US*)
Lamon Records (*US*)
Landslide Records (*US*)
Little Fish Records (*US*)
Lovelane Music Group (*US*)
Manhaton Records (*UK*)
Mellowtone Records (*UK*)
Nettwerk Records (*US*)
New West Records LLC (*US*)
Orange Recordings (*US*)
Parliament Record Group (*US*)
Planet Records (*UK*)
Putumayo World Music (*US*)
R.O.A.D. (Riding on a Dream) Records (*US*)
Rainman Records (*US*)
Red House Records (*US*)
Red Parlor Records (*US*)
SGNB Records (*US*)
Swade Records (*US*)
Tama Industries Record Label (*US*)
ToneTrade Productions (*UK*)
Undertow Records (*US*)
Viking Promotions (*UK*)
Violette Records (*UK*)
Wobbly Music (*UK*)
Yellow Dog Records (*US*)

**Break Beat**
Distinctive Records (*UK*)
First Word Records (*UK*)
Forward Motion Records (UK) (*UK*)
Tru Thoughts (*UK*)

**Celtic**
Chacra Music (*Can*)
Compass Records (*US*)
Emerald Music (Ireland) Ltd (*UK*)
Green Linnet (*US*)
Maggie's Music (*US*)
Sequoia Records (*US*)
Survival Records (*UK*)

**Chill**
Kokeshi (*UK*)
Nervous Records NYC (*US*)
New Earth Records (*US*)
Quango Music Group (*US*)
Sequoia Records (*US*)

**Christian**
Capitol Christian Music Group (*US*)
Curb Records (*US*)
Delved in Dreams, inc. (*US*)
Dove Records (*UK*)
Fair Trade (*US*)
Lamon Records (*US*)
Maranatha Music (*US*)
Nettwerk Records (*US*)
Provident Label Group (*US*)
Tama Industries Record Label (*US*)

**Classic**
Delved in Dreams, inc. (*US*)
Everyday Records (*UK*)
Expansion Records (*UK*)
Frontier Records (*US*)
Heavy Metal Records Ltd (*UK*)
Rainman Records (*US*)
Tama Industries Record Label (*US*)
Wobbly Music (*UK*)

**Classical**
American Gramophone (*US*)
Cantaloupe Music (*US*)
Chesky Records (*US*)
Concord Music Group (*US*)
Curb Records (*US*)
Delos (*US*)
Delphian Records (*UK*)
Delved in Dreams, inc. (*US*)
DOMO Records, Inc. (*US*)
Everyday Records (*UK*)
Multiverse Music (*UK*)
Naxos Records (*US*)
Nonesuch Records (*US*)
Sony Masterworks (*US*)
Wobbly Music (*UK*)

**Club**
Alex King Records (*UK*)
Fine Chooned (*UK*)
Sounds Of Meow (*UK*)
Tama Industries Record Label (*US*)

**Commercial**
ChillnBass (*UK*)
Shock Records (*UK*)
Sounds Of Meow (*UK*)
Subdust Music (*UK*)
Tama Industries Record Label (*US*)

**Contemporary**
DOMO Records, Inc. (*US*)
Dove Records (*UK*)
Everyday Records (*UK*)
Fervor Records (*US*)
LML Music (*US*)
Nettwerk Records (*US*)
Nonesuch Records (*US*)
Pyramid Records (*US*)

**Country**
Arista Nashville (*US*)
Aveline Records (*UK*)
Big Machine Records (*US*)
Carnival Music (*US*)
Curb Records (*US*)
Delved in Dreams, inc. (*US*)
DM Music Group (*US*)
Dreamscope Media Group (DMG) (*UK*)
East of Sideways Music (*US*)
Emerald Music (Ireland) Ltd (*UK*)
GNP Crescendo Records (*US*)
Lamon Records (*US*)
Lost Highway Records (*US*)
Mellowtone Records (*UK*)
My Little Empire (*UK*)
New West Records LLC (*US*)
Open Road Recordings (*Can*)
Pollytone Records (*UK*)
Pyramid Records (*US*)
Quarterback Records (*US*)
SGNB Records (*US*)
Tama Industries Record Label (*US*)
Viking Promotions (*UK*)
Violette Records (*UK*)
Wobbly Music (*UK*)

**Cuban**
Delved in Dreams, inc. (*US*)

**Dance**
2020 Vision Recordings Ltd (*UK*)
Alex King Records (*UK*)
Axtone (*UK*)
Bad Bat Records (*UK*)
Beatphreak (*UK*)
Beta Recordings (*UK*)

*Claim your free access to www.musicsocket.com: See p.203*

Brightonsfinest (*UK*)
Capitol Music Group (*US*)
ChillnBass (*UK*)
Claudia eRecords (*Aus*)
Curb Records (*US*)
Dauman Music (*US*)
Defenders Ent (*UK*)
Delved in Dreams, inc. (*US*)
Dewey Dog Records (*US*)
Disruptor Records (*US*)
Distinctive Records (*UK*)
DJD Music Ltd (*UK*)
DM Music Group (*US*)
Eton Messy Records (*UK*)
Explosive Beatz Records (*UK*)
Fabyl (*UK*)
GNP Crescendo Records (*US*)
Gotham Records (*UK*)
Harmor Records (*UK*)
Incessant Records (*UK*)
Kaneda Records (*UK*)
King Street Sounds (*US*)
Lost in the Manor (*UK*)
LoveCat Music (*US*)
Lucky Number Music Limited (*UK*)
Music Plant Group (*US*)
NB Audio (*UK*)
Nervous Records NYC (*US*)
Of Paradise Records (*UK*)
Phantasy (*UK*)
Radikal Records (*US*)
Recoverworld Label Group (*UK*)
Rhythmic Records (*UK*)
Sequoia Records (*US*)
Shock Records (*UK*)
Sounds Of Meow (*UK*)
Tama Industries Record Label (*US*)
37 Adventures (*UK*)
Water Music Records (*US*)
Wobbly Music (*UK*)
WW Records (*UK*)
**Dancehall**
**Deep Funk**
Dewey Dog Records (*US*)
**Disco**
Alex King Records (*UK*)
Axtone (*UK*)
Coloursounds (*UK*)
DFA Records (*US*)
Perfect Havoc Limited (*UK*)
**Doom**
Black Tragick Records (*UK*)
Box Records (*UK*)
Cold Spring (*UK*)
Riff Rock Records (*UK*)

Rocket Recordings (*UK*)
**Downtempo**
Nervous Records NYC (*US*)
Planet Mu Records (*UK*)
21st Century Music (*UK*)
**Drum and Bass**
Alex King Records (*UK*)
Beta Recordings (*UK*)
BS1 Records (*UK*)
Dorado Music (US) (*US*)
Elevate Records (*UK*)
NB Audio (*UK*)
OXRecordings (*UK*)
Ramajam Recordings (*UK*)
Run Tingz Recordings (*UK*)
Serotone Recordings (*UK*)
Shogun Audio Ltd (*UK*)
Sliced Note Recordings (*UK*)
Soulvent Records (*UK*)
**Dub**
Alex King Records (*UK*)
NB Audio (*UK*)
Planet Mu Records (*UK*)
**Dubstep**
Alex King Records (*UK*)
Axtone (*UK*)
CCT Records (*UK*)
Kokeshi (*UK*)
NB Audio (*UK*)
Planet Mu Records (*UK*)
Project Allout Records (*UK*)
Tama Industries Record Label (*US*)
**Electronic**
!K7 Records (*UK*)
2020 Vision Recordings Ltd (*UK*)
Adapted Vinyl (*UK*)
The Adult Teeth Recording Company (*UK*)
Akira (*UK*)
Alex King Records (*UK*)
Axtone (*UK*)
Bad Bat Records (*UK*)
Beta Recordings (*UK*)
Bingo Records (*UK*)
Black Bleach Records (*UK*)
Brightonsfinest (*UK*)
Bubblewrap Collective (*UK*)
Canigou Records (*UK*)
Cantaloupe Music (*US*)
Cascine (*US*)
CCT Records (*UK*)
Claudia eRecords (*Aus*)
Cleopatra Records (*US*)
Cold Spring (*UK*)
Coloursounds (*UK*)

musicXart (*UK*)
No Sleep (*US*)
Planet Mu Records (*UK*)
Subdust Music (*UK*)
**Extreme**
Earache Records Inc. (*US*)
**Folk**
0114 Records (*UK*)
Acony Records (*US*)
Akira (*UK*)
Audio Vendor (*UK*)
Aveline Records (*UK*)
Bear Love Records (*UK*)
Bingo Records (*UK*)
Black Tragick Records (*UK*)
Box Records (*UK*)
Breakfast Records LLP (*UK*)
Brightonsfinest (*UK*)
Bubblewrap Collective (*UK*)
Canigou Records (*UK*)
Compass Records (*US*)
Delved in Dreams, inc. (*US*)
Dewey Dog Records (*US*)
DJD Music Ltd (*UK*)
DOMO Records, Inc. (*US*)
Dreamscope Media Group (DMG) (*UK*)
Dualtone Records (*US*)
Emerald Music (Ireland) Ltd (*UK*)
Everyday Records (*UK*)
Full Time Hobby (*UK*)
Funzalo Records (*US*)
Ganbei Records (*UK*)
Get Hip Recordings (*US*)
GNP Crescendo Records (*US*)
Green Linnet (*US*)
Harbourtown Records (*UK*)
Haystack Records (*UK*)
Hudson Records (*UK*)
Jagjaguwar (*US*)
Lamon Records (*US*)
Landslide Records (*US*)
Little Fish Records (*US*)
Lost Highway Records (*US*)
Lost in the Manor (*UK*)
Mellowtone Records (*UK*)
Midhir Records (*UK*)
The Militia Group (*US*)
Navigator Records (*UK*)
Nettwerk Records (*US*)
New West Records LLC (*US*)
One Little Independent Records US (*US*)
Orange Recordings (*US*)
Parasol (*US*)
Planet Records (*UK*)
Pop Cautious Records (*US*)

Putumayo World Music (*US*)
Razor & Tie (*US*)
Red House Records (*US*)
Righteous Babe Records (*US*)
Scottish Fiction (*UK*)
Sequoia Records (*US*)
Supermarine Music (*UK*)
These Bloody Thieves Records (*UK*)
Viking Promotions (*UK*)
Violette Records (*UK*)
Wobbly Music (*UK*)
Yellow Dog Records (*US*)
**Funk**
Bamboleo Records (*UK*)
Chalkpit Records Ltd (*UK*)
Dewey Dog Records (*US*)
Expansion Records (*UK*)
First Word Records (*UK*)
Lovelane Music Group (*US*)
M1 Music Limited (*UK*)
Moth Man Records (*US*)
QM Records (*UK*)
Tru Thoughts (*UK*)
Wobbly Music (*UK*)
**Funky**
Dewey Dog Records (*US*)
Fine Chooned (*UK*)
Forward Motion Records (UK) (*UK*)
Moth Man Records (*US*)
Shock Records (*UK*)
21st Century Music (*UK*)
**Fusion**
Delved in Dreams, inc. (*US*)
Wobbly Music (*UK*)
**Garage**
0114 Records (*UK*)
Abattoir Blues (*UK*)
Alex King Records (*UK*)
Black Bleach Records (*UK*)
Blak Hand Records (*UK*)
Breakfast Records LLP (*UK*)
Bush Bash Recordings (*UK*)
Epitaph (*US*)
From Concentrate (*UK*)
God Unknown Records (*UK*)
In the Red Records (*US*)
Kokeshi (*UK*)
Leisure Recordings (*UK*)
Moth Man Records (*US*)
Nice Swan Records (*UK*)
1-2-3-4 Records (*UK*)
Project Allout Records (*UK*)
Psymmetry Collective (*UK*)
Restless Bear (*UK*)
Sour Grapes (*UK*)

Strong Island Recordings (*UK*)
Swade Records (*US*)
**Glam**
Mad Decent (*US*)
**Glitch**
Alex King Records (*UK*)
IKonic Image (*UK*)
**Gospel**
Capitol Christian Music Group (*US*)
Delved in Dreams, inc. (*US*)
Dove Records (*UK*)
Emerald Music (Ireland) Ltd (*UK*)
Hacienda Records (*US*)
Hidden Beach Recordings (*US*)
Lamon Records (*US*)
Maranatha Music (*US*)
Motown Gospel (*US*)
Parliament Record Group (*US*)
Polo Grounds Music (*US*)
Provident Label Group (*US*)
Pyramid Records (*US*)
Razor & Tie (*US*)
Tama Industries Record Label (*US*)
**Gothic**
Cleopatra Records (*US*)
Tama Industries Record Label (*US*)
When Planets Collide (*UK*)
**Grime**
Alex King Records (*UK*)
Bush Bash Recordings (*UK*)
Fabyl (*UK*)
Kokeshi (*UK*)
Less is More Music Ltd (*UK*)
Portfolio Music (*UK*)
Project Allout Records (*UK*)
QM Records (*UK*)
Regent Street Records (*UK*)
**Guitar based**
Abattoir Blues (*UK*)
Blak Hand Records (*UK*)
Breakfast Records LLP (*UK*)
Chacra Music (*Can*)
Copro Productions (*UK*)
DJD Music Ltd (*UK*)
Everyday Records (*UK*)
Infectious Music (*UK*)
Moth Man Records (*US*)
My Little Empire (*UK*)
1-2-3-4 Records (*UK*)
Organ Records (*UK*)
SGNB Records (*US*)
Swade Records (*US*)
**Hard**
0114 Records (*UK*)
DJD Music Ltd (*UK*)

Drag City (*US*)
Ferret Music (*US*)
Forward Motion Records (UK) (*UK*)
Moth Man Records (*US*)
Prosthetic Records (*US*)
Tama Industries Record Label (*US*)
**Hardcore**
Alex King Records (*UK*)
Bridge Nine Records (*US*)
Bullet Tooth (*US*)
Disconnect Disconnect Records (*UK*)
Doghouse Records (*US*)
Epitaph (*US*)
Fearless Records (*US*)
Hopeless Records (*US*)
Hydra Head Records (*US*)
Lockjaw Records (*UK*)
Metal Blade Records, Inc. (*US*)
Moth Man Records (*US*)
No Sleep (*US*)
Tama Industries Record Label (*US*)
United Riot Records (*US*)
**Heavy**
Copro Productions (*UK*)
DJD Music Ltd (*UK*)
Heavy Metal Records Ltd (*UK*)
Hydra Head Records (*US*)
Moth Man Records (*US*)
Pavement Music (*US*)
Prosthetic Records (*US*)
When Planets Collide (*UK*)
**Hip-Hop**
Bush Bash Recordings (*UK*)
Cash Money Records (*US*)
CCT Records (*UK*)
Claudia eRecords (*Aus*)
Cleopatra Records (*US*)
Derrty Entertainment (*US*)
Dewey Dog Records (*US*)
Different Records (*UK*)
DJD Music Ltd (*UK*)
Dose Entertainment (*UK*)
Duck Down Music (*US*)
East of Sideways Music (*US*)
Epitaph (*US*)
Evil Twin Records (*UK*)
Explosive Beatz Records (*UK*)
Fabyl (*UK*)
First Word Records (*UK*)
Ghostly International (*US*)
Hidden Beach Recordings (*US*)
Idol Records (*US*)
Interscope Geffen A&M (*US*)
Jaggo Records, LLC (*US*)
Kaneda Records (*UK*)

KFM Records (*UK*)
Less is More Music Ltd (*UK*)
Lost in the Manor (*UK*)
LoveCat Music (*US*)
M1 Music Limited (*UK*)
Mass Appeal Records (*US*)
Maybach Music Group (*US*)
Melee Recording Group (*UK*)
Morphius Records (*US*)
Music Plant Group (*US*)
NB Audio (*UK*)
Nervous Records NYC (*US*)
No Sleep (*US*)
Nu:Generation Music (*UK*)
Oglio Entertainment (*US*)
One Little Independent Records US (*US*)
Parliament Record Group (*US*)
Penalty Entertainment (*US*)
Phono Sounds UK (*UK*)
Polar Opposites Records (*UK*)
Polo Grounds Music (*US*)
Portfolio Music (*UK*)
Pyramid Records (*US*)
QM Records (*UK*)
Quality Control (*US*)
RCA Records (*US*)
Rhythmic Records (*UK*)
Salute the Sun (*UK*)
Scottish Fiction (*UK*)
Six Lowa Records (*US*)
Tama Industries Record Label (*US*)
Tight Lines (*UK*)
Tru Thoughts (*UK*)
**House**
Alex King Records (*UK*)
Axtone (*UK*)
Bamboleo Records (*UK*)
Beta Recordings (*UK*)
Brock Wild (*UK*)
Bush Bash Recordings (*UK*)
Circus Recordings (*UK*)
Coloursounds (*UK*)
DFA Records (*US*)
Distinctive Records (*UK*)
F&G Dj Trade (*UK*)
Fine Chooned (*UK*)
Forward Motion Records (UK) (*UK*)
Futurist Recordings (*UK*)
Harmor Records (*UK*)
Jeepers! Music (*UK*)
Let Me Understand Records (*UK*)
Mad Decent (*US*)
Nervous Records NYC (*US*)
Perfect Havoc Limited (*UK*)
Portfolio Music (*UK*)

Rhythmic Records (*UK*)
Shock Records (*UK*)
Snatch! Records (*UK*)
Sonic Bear (*UK*)
Sounds Of Meow (*UK*)
Standby (*UK*)
This and That Lab (*UK*)
**House**
Alex King Records (*UK*)
Axtone (*UK*)
Bamboleo Records (*UK*)
Beta Recordings (*UK*)
Brock Wild (*UK*)
Bush Bash Recordings (*UK*)
Circus Recordings (*UK*)
Coloursounds (*UK*)
DFA Records (*US*)
Distinctive Records (*UK*)
F&G Dj Trade (*UK*)
Fine Chooned (*UK*)
Forward Motion Records (UK) (*UK*)
Futurist Recordings (*UK*)
Harmor Records (*UK*)
Jeepers! Music (*UK*)
Let Me Understand Records (*UK*)
Mad Decent (*US*)
Nervous Records NYC (*US*)
Perfect Havoc Limited (*UK*)
Portfolio Music (*UK*)
Rhythmic Records (*UK*)
Shock Records (*UK*)
Snatch! Records (*UK*)
Sonic Bear (*UK*)
Sounds Of Meow (*UK*)
Standby (*UK*)
This and That Lab (*UK*)
**IDM**
Alex King Records (*UK*)
Harmor Records (*UK*)
KFM Records (*UK*)
Planet Mu Records (*UK*)
**Indie**
0114 Records (*UK*)
The Adult Teeth Recording Company (*UK*)
Akira (*UK*)
Audio Vendor (*UK*)
Better Looking Records (*US*)
Bingo Records (*UK*)
Black Bleach Records (*UK*)
Breakfast Records LLP (*UK*)
Brightonsfinest (*UK*)
Bubblewrap Collective (*UK*)
Capitol Music Group (*US*)
Carnival Music (*US*)

Chalkpit Records Ltd (*UK*)
Claudia eRecords (*Aus*)
Coloursounds (*UK*)
Copro Productions (*UK*)
Dance To The Radio (*UK*)
Dangerbird Records (*US*)
Delved in Dreams, inc. (*US*)
Demon Music Group (*UK*)
Dewey Dog Records (*US*)
DFA Records (*US*)
Dipped in Gold Recordings (*UK*)
Dirty Bingo Records (*UK*)
DJD Music Ltd (*UK*)
Doing Life Records (*UK*)
Domino Record Co. Ltd (*US*)
DOMO Records, Inc. (*US*)
Don't Try (*UK*)
Donut Records (*UK*)
Dovecote Records (*US*)
Dualtone Records (*US*)
The End Records (*US*)
Endearment Records (*UK*)
Epitaph (*US*)
Equal Vision Records (*US*)
Everyday Records (*UK*)
Fabyl (*UK*)
Fat Possum Records (*US*)
Fearless Records (*US*)
Fervor Records (*US*)
Funzalo Records (*US*)
Geilston Records (*UK*)
Get Hip Recordings (*US*)
Ghostly International (*US*)
Heist or Hit Records (*UK*)
Hopeless Records (*US*)
Idol Records (*US*)
Infectious Music (*UK*)
Interscope Geffen A&M (*US*)
Jagjaguwar (*US*)
Kanine Records (*US*)
Kill Rock Stars (*US*)
Lovitt Records (*US*)
Lucky Number Music Limited (*UK*)
Matador Records (*US*)
Merge Records (*US*)
Metropolis Records (*US*)
The Militia Group (*US*)
Mint Records (*Can*)
Minty Fresh Records (*US*)
Moth Man Records (*US*)
My Little Empire (*UK*)
Nettwerk Records (*US*)
New West Records LLC (*US*)
Nice Swan Records (*UK*)
Nine Mile Records (NMR) (*US*)

No Sleep (*US*)
One Little Independent Records US (*US*)
1-2-3-4 Records (*UK*)
Orange Recordings (*US*)
Organ Records (*UK*)
Parasol (*US*)
Pinch Hit Records (*US*)
Plug Research (*US*)
Pop Cautious Records (*US*)
Q Division Records (*US*)
Razor & Tie (*US*)
RIP Records (*UK*)
Safe Suburban Home (*UK*)
Strong Island Recordings (*UK*)
Tama Industries Record Label (*US*)
These Bloody Thieves Records (*UK*)
37 Adventures (*UK*)
Tip Top Recordings (*UK*)
Undertow Records (*US*)
Violette Records (*UK*)
Yala! Records (*UK*)
ZTT Records (*UK*)
ZyNg Tapes (*UK*)
**Industrial**
Cleopatra Records (*US*)
Cold Spring (*UK*)
Delved in Dreams, inc. (*US*)
DJD Music Ltd (*UK*)
**Instrumental**
Curb Records (*US*)
Delved in Dreams, inc. (*US*)
DJD Music Ltd (*UK*)
Everyday Records (*UK*)
Idol Records (*US*)
Red House Records (*US*)
Tama Industries Record Label (*US*)
**Jazz**
Big Bear Records (*UK*)
Blue Note Label Group (*US*)
Bolero Records (*US*)
Cantaloupe Music (*US*)
Chesky Records (*US*)
Chiaroscuro Records (*US*)
Cleopatra Records (*US*)
Compass Records (*US*)
Concord Music Group (*US*)
Curb Records (*US*)
Delmark Records (*US*)
Delved in Dreams, inc. (*US*)
Dewey Dog Records (*US*)
Dorado Music (US) (*US*)
Earwig Music Company, Inc. (*US*)
East of Sideways Music (*US*)
Everyday Records (*UK*)
Expansion Records (*UK*)

First Word Records (*UK*)
Focused Silence (*UK*)
GNP Crescendo Records (*US*)
Hidden Beach Recordings (*US*)
HighNote Records (*US*)
Jaggo Records, LLC (*US*)
Jazz re:freshed (*UK*)
Landslide Records (*US*)
Less is More Music Ltd (*UK*)
Little Fish Records (*US*)
Lost in the Manor (*UK*)
LoveCat Music (*US*)
Manhaton Records (*UK*)
Marsalis Music (*US*)
Mosaic Records (*US*)
Newvelle Records (*US*)
Nonesuch Records (*US*)
PRA Records (*US*)
QM Records (*UK*)
Reservoir Music (*US*)
Righteous Babe Records (*US*)
Saffron Records (*UK*)
Sony Masterworks (*US*)
Tama Industries Record Label (*US*)
Tight Lines (*UK*)
ToneTrade Productions (*UK*)
Tru Thoughts (*UK*)
Yellow Dog Records (*US*)
**Jungle**
Run Tingz Recordings (*UK*)
Sliced Note Recordings (*UK*)
**Kraut**
Rocket Recordings (*UK*)
Wrong Way Records (*UK*)
**Latin**
Bolero Records (*US*)
Concord Music Group (*US*)
Dewey Dog Records (*US*)
East of Sideways Music (*US*)
GNP Crescendo Records (*US*)
Hacienda Records (*US*)
Lamon Records (*US*)
LoveCat Music (*US*)
Music Plant Group (*US*)
Nacional Records (*US*)
Nettwerk Records (*US*)
Putumayo World Music (*US*)
Righteous Babe Records (*US*)
Sony Music Latin (*US*)
Tama Industries Record Label (*US*)
Universal Music Latin Entertainment (*US*)
**Leftfield**
Hyperdub Records (*UK*)
Tight Lines (*UK*)
Wrong Way Records (*UK*)

**Lo-fi**
Canigou Records (*UK*)
Moth Man Records (*US*)
Sister 9 Recordings (*UK*)
Violette Records (*UK*)
ZyNg Tapes (*UK*)
**Lounge**
DJD Music Ltd (*UK*)
Sequoia Records (*US*)
**Mainstream**
Decca Records US (*US*)
Delved in Dreams, inc. (*US*)
Everyday Records (*UK*)
Nonesuch Records (*US*)
Sounds Of Meow (*UK*)
Subdust Music (*UK*)
Swade Records (*US*)
**Melodic**
Beta Recordings (*UK*)
Everyday Records (*UK*)
Moth Man Records (*US*)
Sounds Of Meow (*UK*)
21st Century Music (*UK*)
**Melodicore**
Alex King Records (*UK*)
Moth Man Records (*US*)
**Metal**
ALM Records (*UK*)
Black Tragick Records (*UK*)
Bullet Tooth (*US*)
Cleopatra Records (*US*)
Copro Productions (*UK*)
Distort (*Can*)
DJD Music Ltd (*UK*)
Earache Records Inc. (*US*)
The End Records (*US*)
Equal Vision Records (*US*)
Ferret Music (*US*)
Graphite Records (*UK*)
Heavy Metal Records Ltd (*UK*)
Hopeless Records (*US*)
Hydra Head Records (*US*)
Knife Fight Media (*US*)
Magna Carta Records (*US*)
Metal Blade Records, Inc. (*US*)
Midhir Records (*UK*)
Mighty Atom (*UK*)
Pavement Music (*US*)
Peaceville Records (*UK*)
Prosthetic Records (*US*)
Rainman Records (*US*)
Razor & Tie (*US*)
SGNB Records (*US*)
Stunted Records & Management (*UK*)
Tama Industries Record Label (*US*)

These Bloody Thieves Records (*UK*)
United Riot Records (*US*)
When Planets Collide (*UK*)
**Modern**
Ernest Jenning Record Co. (*US*)
Expansion Records (*UK*)
IKonic Image (*UK*)
Moth Man Records (*US*)
Multiverse Music (*UK*)
Swade Records (*US*)
Tama Industries Record Label (*US*)
**MOR**
Everyday Records (*UK*)
**New Age**
Bolero Records (*US*)
Cantaloupe Music (*US*)
Chacra Music (*Can*)
Delved in Dreams, inc. (*US*)
DOMO Records, Inc. (*US*)
Everyday Records (*UK*)
New Earth Records (*US*)
Sequoia Records (*US*)
Tama Industries Record Label (*US*)
**New Wave**
DJD Music Ltd (*UK*)
Fire Records (*UK*)
Tama Industries Record Label (*US*)
21st Century Music (*UK*)
**Noise Core**
Cold Spring (*UK*)
**Non-Commercial**
Tama Industries Record Label (*US*)
**Nostalgia**
Delved in Dreams, inc. (*US*)
**Pop**
The Adult Teeth Recording Company (*UK*)
Alex King Records (*UK*)
Bingo Records (*UK*)
Blue Note Label Group (*US*)
Blue Shell Music (*UK*)
Brightonsfinest (*UK*)
Cantora (*US*)
Capitol Music Group (*US*)
Carnival Music (*US*)
Cascine (*US*)
Cash Money Records (*US*)
Chalkpit Records Ltd (*UK*)
Claudia eRecords (*Aus*)
Cleopatra Records (*US*)
Coloursounds (*UK*)
Compass Records (*US*)
Compound Entertainment (*US*)
Concord Music Group (*US*)
Crush Music (*US*)

Curb Records (*US*)
Curve Music (*Can*)
Delved in Dreams, inc. (*US*)
Dirty Bingo Records (*UK*)
Dirty Canvas Music (*US*)
Disconnect Disconnect Records (*UK*)
Disruptor Records (*US*)
DJD Music Ltd (*UK*)
DM Music Group (*US*)
DOMO Records, Inc. (*US*)
Don Rubin Productions (*US*)
Don't Try (*UK*)
Double Denim Records (*UK*)
Drag City (*US*)
Dreamscope Media Group (DMG) (*UK*)
East of Sideways Music (*US*)
ECR Music Group (*US*)
Emerald Music (Ireland) Ltd (*UK*)
Ernest Jenning Record Co. (*US*)
Everyday Records (*UK*)
Fabyl (*UK*)
Fearless Records (*US*)
From Concentrate (*UK*)
Ghostly International (*US*)
GNP Crescendo Records (*US*)
Gotham Records (*UK*)
Harbour Records (*US*)
Headliner Records / George Tobin Music (*US*)
Hit City USA (*US*)
Hit World Records (*US*)
Idol Records (*US*)
Incessant Records (*UK*)
Interscope Geffen A&M (*US*)
Jaggo Records, LLC (*US*)
Kanine Records (*US*)
Kirtland Records (*US*)
Leisure Recordings (*UK*)
LML Music (*US*)
Lost in the Manor (*UK*)
LoveCat Music (*US*)
Lucky Number Music Limited (*UK*)
The Militia Group (*US*)
Minty Fresh Records (*US*)
Moth Man Records (*US*)
Nettwerk Records (*US*)
Nine Mile Records (NMR) (*US*)
Nonesuch Records (*US*)
One Little Independent Records US (*US*)
Parasol (*US*)
Park the Van Records (*US*)
Peek-A-Boo Records (*US*)
Phono Sounds UK (*UK*)
Pinch Hit Records (*US*)
Polo Grounds Music (*US*)

1-2-3-4 Records (*UK*)
Orange Recordings (*US*)
Psymmetry Collective (*UK*)
Radical Records (*US*)
Regent Street Records (*UK*)
Restless Bear (*UK*)
Righteous Babe Records (*US*)
Sister 9 Recordings (*UK*)
Sour Grapes (*UK*)
Strong Island Recordings (*UK*)
Tama Industries Record Label (*US*)
Tight Lines (*UK*)
Tip Top Recordings (*UK*)
TNS (That's Not Skanking) Records (*UK*)
United Riot Records (*US*)
Yala! Records (*UK*)
ZyNg Tapes (*UK*)
**Ragga**
Tama Industries Record Label (*US*)
**RampB**
Alex King Records (*UK*)
Blue Note Label Group (*US*)
Brunswick Record Corporation (*US*)
Bush Bash Recordings (*UK*)
Concord Music Group (*US*)
Curb Records (*US*)
Defenders Ent (*UK*)
Dewey Dog Records (*US*)
DJD Music Ltd (*UK*)
DM Music Group (*US*)
Dose Entertainment (*UK*)
Dreamscope Media Group (DMG) (*UK*)
Everyday Records (*UK*)
Explosive Beatz Records (*UK*)
Gotee Records (*US*)
Headliner Records / George Tobin Music (*US*)
Hidden Beach Recordings (*US*)
Hit City USA (*US*)
Incessant Records (*UK*)
Jaggo Records, LLC (*US*)
Less is More Music Ltd (*UK*)
LoveCat Music (*US*)
Lovelane Music Group (*US*)
M1 Music Limited (*UK*)
Music Plant Group (*US*)
Parliament Record Group (*US*)
Phono Sounds UK (*UK*)
Polo Grounds Music (*US*)
Portfolio Music (*UK*)
Pyramid Records (*US*)
RCA Records (*US*)
Region Liberty Records (*US*)
Saffron Records (*UK*)
Salute the Sun (*UK*)

Six Lowa Records (*US*)
Tama Industries Record Label (*US*)
**Rap**
Bush Bash Recordings (*UK*)
Claudia eRecords (*Aus*)
Cleopatra Records (*US*)
Crosscheck Records (*US*)
Defenders Ent (*UK*)
Dewey Dog Records (*US*)
DJD Music Ltd (*UK*)
DM Music Group (*US*)
Dose Entertainment (*UK*)
Dove Records (*UK*)
East of Sideways Music (*US*)
Ghostly International (*US*)
Gotee Records (*US*)
Hidden Beach Recordings (*US*)
Idol Records (*US*)
Interscope Geffen A&M (*US*)
LoveCat Music (*US*)
M1 Music Limited (*UK*)
Maybach Music Group (*US*)
Oglio Entertainment (*US*)
One Little Independent Records US (*US*)
Polo Grounds Music (*US*)
Portfolio Music (*UK*)
Pyramid Records (*US*)
Six Lowa Records (*US*)
Tama Industries Record Label (*US*)
**Reggae**
0114 Records (*UK*)
Defenders Ent (*UK*)
Delved in Dreams, inc. (*US*)
DJD Music Ltd (*UK*)
Dove Records (*UK*)
Evil Twin Records (*UK*)
First Word Records (*UK*)
Gotee Records (*US*)
Gotham Records (*UK*)
Little Fish Records (*US*)
Lost in the Manor (*UK*)
M1 Music Limited (*UK*)
NB Audio (*UK*)
Polo Grounds Music (*US*)
Pyramid Records (*US*)
Six Lowa Records (*US*)
Tama Industries Record Label (*US*)
Wobbly Music (*UK*)
**Reggaeton**
Cleopatra Records (*US*)
LoveCat Music (*US*)
Polo Grounds Music (*US*)
Tama Industries Record Label (*US*)
**Regional**
Audiorec Limited (*UK*)

Canyon (*US*)
Delved in Dreams, inc. (*US*)
Emerald Music (Ireland) Ltd (*UK*)
ISHQ Records (*UK*)
Little Fish Records (*US*)
NorthSide (*US*)
**Relaxation**
Tama Industries Record Label (*US*)
**Remix**
Alex King Records (*UK*)
Dewey Dog Records (*US*)
**Rhythm and Blues**
Blues Matters Records (*UK*)
Delved in Dreams, inc. (*US*)
Everyday Records (*UK*)
RIP Records (*UK*)
Tama Industries Record Label (*US*)
**Rock and Roll**
Donut Records (*UK*)
Everyday Records (*UK*)
In the Red Records (*US*)
Moth Man Records (*US*)
Pollytone Records (*UK*)
Rainman Records (*US*)
RIP Records (*UK*)
SGNB Records (*US*)
Sour Grapes (*UK*)
Swade Records (*US*)
Tama Industries Record Label (*US*)
United Riot Records (*US*)
**Rock**
0114 Records (*UK*)
Abattoir Blues (*UK*)
The Adult Teeth Recording Company (*UK*)
Akira (*UK*)
ALM Records (*UK*)
Audio Vendor (*UK*)
Beta Recordings (*UK*)
Better Looking Records (*US*)
Black Bleach Records (*UK*)
Blak Hand Records (*UK*)
Bonsound (*Can*)
Box Records (*UK*)
Breakfast Records LLP (*UK*)
Bright Antenna Records (*US*)
Brightonsfinest (*UK*)
Bullet Tooth (*US*)
Cantaloupe Music (*US*)
Capitol Music Group (*US*)
Carnival Music (*US*)
Carpark Records (*US*)
Claudia eRecords (*Aus*)
Concord Music Group (*US*)
Constellation (*Can*)

Copro Productions (*UK*)
Crush Music (*US*)
Curb Records (*US*)
Curve Music (*Can*)
Dangerbird Records (*US*)
Deep South Records (*US*)
Dirty Canvas Music (*US*)
Disconnect Disconnect Records (*UK*)
Doghouse Records (*US*)
Doing Life Records (*UK*)
Domino Record Co. Ltd (*US*)
DOMO Records, Inc. (*US*)
Don Rubin Productions (*US*)
Donut Records (*UK*)
Dovecote Records (*US*)
Drag City (*US*)
Dreamscope Media Group (DMG) (*UK*)
Dualtone Records (*US*)
Earache Records Inc. (*US*)
East of Sideways Music (*US*)
Eclipse Records, inc. (*US*)
ECR Music Group (*US*)
Emerald Music (Ireland) Ltd (*UK*)
The End Records (*US*)
Epitaph (*US*)
Equal Vision Records (*US*)
Ernest Jenning Record Co. (*US*)
Fabyl (*UK*)
Fearless Records (*US*)
Ferret Music (*US*)
Fervor Records (*US*)
Fire Records (*UK*)
Frontier Records (*US*)
Full Time Hobby (*UK*)
Funzalo Records (*US*)
Ganbei Records (*UK*)
Get Hip Recordings (*US*)
Ghostly International (*US*)
GNP Crescendo Records (*US*)
God Unknown Records (*UK*)
Gotee Records (*US*)
Gotham Records (*UK*)
Graphite Records (*UK*)
Harbour Records (*US*)
Heavy Metal Records Ltd (*UK*)
Highwheel Records (*US*)
Hopeless Records (*US*)
House of Mythology (*UK*)
Idol Records (*US*)
Incessant Records (*UK*)
Interscope Geffen A&M (*US*)
Ipecac Recordings (*US*)
Jaggo Records, LLC (*US*)
Kanine Records (*US*)
KFM Records (*UK*)

Kirtland Records (*US*)
Knife Fight Media (*US*)
Landslide Records (*US*)
Last Gang Records (*Can*)
Le Grand Magistery, LLC (*US*)
Lightning Rod Records (*US*)
Little Fish Records (*US*)
Loner Noise (*UK*)
Lookout! Records (*US*)
Lost Highway Records (*US*)
Lost in the Manor (*UK*)
LoveCat Music (*US*)
Mad Dragon Music Group (*US*)
Magna Carta Records (*US*)
Megaforce Records (*US*)
Merge Records (*US*)
Metal Blade Records, Inc. (*US*)
Mighty Atom (*UK*)
The Militia Group (*US*)
Minty Fresh Records (*US*)
Morphius Records (*US*)
Moth Man Records (*US*)
New West Records LLC (*US*)
Nice Swan Records (*UK*)
Nine Mile Records (NMR) (*US*)
Oglio Entertainment (*US*)
Omnium Records (*US*)
One Little Independent Records US (*US*)
1-2-3-4 Records (*UK*)
Orange Recordings (*US*)
Paper Bag Records (*Can*)
Parasol (*US*)
Park the Van Records (*US*)
Pavement Music (*US*)
Peaceville Records (*UK*)
Peek-A-Boo Records (*US*)
Plug Research (*US*)
Pop Cautious Records (*US*)
Poptown Records (*US*)
Prosthetic Records (*US*)
Psymmetry Collective (*UK*)
Pyramid Records (*US*)
Q Division Records (*US*)
Radical Records (*US*)
Rainman Records (*US*)
Razor & Tie (*US*)
RCA Records (*US*)
Red Parlor Records (*US*)
Regent Street Records (*UK*)
Riff Rock Records (*UK*)
Righteous Babe Records (*US*)
RIP Records (*UK*)
Rocket Recordings (*UK*)
Safe Suburban Home (*UK*)
Scottish Fiction (*UK*)

SGNB Records (*US*)
Sister 9 Recordings (*UK*)
Sour Grapes (*UK*)
Strong Island Recordings (*UK*)
Stunted Records & Management (*UK*)
Sugar Shack Records Ltd (*UK*)
Supermarine Music (*UK*)
Swade Records (*US*)
Tama Industries Record Label (*US*)
These Bloody Thieves Records (*UK*)
Tigertrap Records (*UK*)
Undertow Records (*US*)
Water Music Records (*US*)
Wobbly Music (*UK*)
Wrong Way Records (*UK*)
Yala! Records (*UK*)
ZyNg Tapes (*UK*)
**Rockabilly**
Everyday Records (*UK*)
Moth Man Records (*US*)
Pollytone Records (*UK*)
Rainman Records (*US*)
SGNB Records (*US*)
**Roots**
Acony Records (*US*)
Compass Records (*US*)
Delta Groove Music (*US*)
Delved in Dreams, inc. (*US*)
DJD Music Ltd (*UK*)
Everyday Records (*UK*)
Harbourtown Records (*UK*)
Lamon Records (*US*)
Lightning Rod Records (*US*)
Lost Highway Records (*US*)
Mellowtone Records (*UK*)
My Little Empire (*UK*)
New West Records LLC (*US*)
NorthSide (*US*)
Parasol (*US*)
Planet Records (*UK*)
R.O.A.D. (Riding on a Dream) Records (*US*)
RCA Records (*US*)
Red House Records (*US*)
SGNB Records (*US*)
ToneTrade Productions (*UK*)
Undertow Records (*US*)
Yellow Dog Records (*US*)
**Shoegaze**
Bingo Records (*UK*)
Black Bleach Records (*UK*)
Canigou Records (*UK*)
KFM Records (*UK*)
Leisure Recordings (*UK*)
Moth Man Records (*US*)

Safe Suburban Home (*UK*)
Strong Island Recordings (*UK*)
Wrong Way Records (*UK*)
**Singer-Songwriter**
0114 Records (*UK*)
Aveline Records (*UK*)
Birdland Records (*UK*)
Burnt Toast Vinyl (*US*)
Crush Music (*US*)
Delved in Dreams, inc. (*US*)
Dewey Dog Records (*US*)
DJD Music Ltd (*UK*)
Doing Life Records (*UK*)
DOMO Records, Inc. (*US*)
Dualtone Records (*US*)
Everyday Records (*UK*)
Fabyl (*UK*)
Full Time Hobby (*UK*)
Infectious Music (*UK*)
Lucky Number Music Limited (*UK*)
Manhaton Records (*UK*)
Mellowtone Records (*UK*)
Merge Records (*US*)
The Militia Group (*US*)
Navigator Records (*UK*)
Nettwerk Records (*US*)
Nonesuch Records (*US*)
One Little Independent Records US (*US*)
Parasol (*US*)
Razor & Tie (*US*)
Red House Records (*US*)
Red Parlor Records (*US*)
RIP Records (*UK*)
SGNB Records (*US*)
Tama Industries Record Label (*US*)
Wobbly Music (*UK*)
**Ska**
0114 Records (*UK*)
Heavy Metal Records Ltd (*UK*)
Hopeless Records (*US*)
Swade Records (*US*)
TNS (That's Not Skanking) Records (*UK*)
United Riot Records (*US*)
**Soul**
Chalkpit Records Ltd (*UK*)
Claudia eRecords (*Aus*)
Concord Music Group (*US*)
Delved in Dreams, inc. (*US*)
Dewey Dog Records (*US*)
DJD Music Ltd (*UK*)
Dreamscope Media Group (DMG) (*UK*)
Everyday Records (*UK*)
Evil Twin Records (*UK*)
Expansion Records (*UK*)
Fabyl (*UK*)

First Word Records (*UK*)
From Concentrate (*UK*)
Jaggo Records, LLC (*US*)
Less is More Music Ltd (*UK*)
M1 Music Limited (*UK*)
Nu:Generation Music (*UK*)
Organ Records (*UK*)
Parliament Record Group (*US*)
Polar Opposites Records (*UK*)
QM Records (*UK*)
R.O.A.D. (Riding on a Dream) Records (*US*)
Rhythmic Records (*UK*)
Salute the Sun (*UK*)
Tight Lines (*UK*)
Tru Thoughts (*UK*)
Yellow Dog Records (*US*)
**Soulful**
Delved in Dreams, inc. (*US*)
Dewey Dog Records (*US*)
Everyday Records (*UK*)
Fine Chooned (*UK*)
Red Parlor Records (*US*)
Tama Industries Record Label (*US*)
**Soundtracks**
Cold Spring (*UK*)
Curb Records (*US*)
DOMO Records, Inc. (*US*)
DRG Records Incorporated (*US*)
Everyday Records (*UK*)
GNP Crescendo Records (*US*)
In the Nursery (ITN) Corporation (*UK*)
Lakeshore Entertainment (*US*)
Milan Records (*US*)
Multiverse Music (*UK*)
PS Classics (*US*)
Varese Sarabande Records (*US*)
**Space**
Rocket Recordings (*UK*)
Wrong Way Records (*UK*)
**Spoken Word**
DJD Music Ltd (*UK*)
Tama Industries Record Label (*US*)
**Swing**
Big Bear Records (*UK*)
Delved in Dreams, inc. (*US*)
Everyday Records (*UK*)
Pollytone Records (*UK*)
**Synthpop**
DJD Music Ltd (*UK*)
**Techno**
Alex King Records (*UK*)
Axtone (*UK*)
Bamboleo Records (*UK*)
Beta Recordings (*UK*)

CCT Records (*UK*)
Circus Recordings (*UK*)
Delved in Dreams, inc. (*US*)
Dewey Dog Records (*US*)
Futurist Recordings (*UK*)
IKonic Image (*UK*)
Let Me Understand Records (*UK*)
Solar Distance (*UK*)
Sounds Like Vinyl (*UK*)
Sounds Of Meow (*UK*)
Tama Industries Record Label (*US*)
This and That Lab (*UK*)
**Thrash**
Heavy Metal Records Ltd (*UK*)
Moth Man Records (*US*)
**Traditional**
Delved in Dreams, inc. (*US*)
Emerald Music (Ireland) Ltd (*UK*)
Fervor Records (*US*)
Harbourtown Records (*UK*)
LML Music (*US*)
Navigator Records (*UK*)
Nonesuch Records (*US*)
Red House Records (*US*)
**Trance**
Alex King Records (*UK*)
Axtone (*UK*)
Keyframe Music (*US*)
New Earth Records (*US*)
Sequoia Records (*US*)
Shock Records (*UK*)
Sounds Of Meow (*UK*)
Trancespired Recordings (*UK*)
**Tribal**
Delved in Dreams, inc. (*US*)
Dewey Dog Records (*US*)
Fine Chooned (*UK*)
Forward Motion Records (UK) (*UK*)
**Trip Hop**
Tama Industries Record Label (*US*)
**Underground**
Box Records (*UK*)
Futurist Recordings (*UK*)
Mad Decent (*US*)
Nervous Records NYC (*US*)
Organ Records (*UK*)
Pavement Music (*US*)
Project Allout Records (*UK*)
Sounds Like Vinyl (*UK*)
Sounds Of Meow (*UK*)
Tama Industries Record Label (*US*)
TNS (That's Not Skanking) Records (*UK*)
When Planets Collide (*UK*)
**Uptempo**
Alex King Records (*UK*)

Nervous Records NYC (*US*)
**Urban**
Alex King Records (*UK*)
Bush Bash Recordings (*UK*)
Capitol Music Group (*US*)
Cash Money Records (*US*)
Compound Entertainment (*US*)
Curb Records (*US*)
Derrty Entertainment (*US*)
Dewey Dog Records (*US*)
Different Records (*UK*)
Disturbing Tha Peace Records (DTP) (*US*)
Duck Down Music (*US*)
East of Sideways Music (*US*)
Fabyl (*UK*)
Fine Chooned (*UK*)
Hit World Records (*US*)
HQ Familia (*UK*)
Javotti Media (*US*)
Mass Appeal Records (*US*)
Melee Recording Group (*UK*)
Nu:Generation Music (*UK*)
101BPM (*UK*)
Penalty Entertainment (*US*)
Polar Opposites Records (*UK*)
Polo Grounds Music (*US*)
Portfolio Music (*UK*)
Pyramid Records (*US*)
Quality Control (*US*)
Razor & Tie (*US*)
RCA Records (*US*)
Region Liberty Records (*US*)
Rhythmic Records (*UK*)
Spitslam (*US*)
Subdust Music (*UK*)
Tama Industries Record Label (*US*)
ToneTrade Productions (*UK*)
**World**
Bolero Records (*US*)
Cantaloupe Music (*US*)
Canyon (*US*)
Chacra Music (*Can*)
Chesky Records (*US*)
Compass Records (*US*)
Concord Music Group (*US*)
DOMO Records, Inc. (*US*)
Emerald Music (Ireland) Ltd (*UK*)
Everyday Records (*UK*)
GNP Crescendo Records (*US*)
Green Linnet (*US*)
Jaggo Records, LLC (*US*)
Little Fish Records (*US*)
LoveCat Music (*US*)
Milan Records (*US*)
Moodswing Records (*US*)

New Earth Records (*US*)
Nonesuch Records (*US*)
Omnium Records (*US*)
One Little Independent Records US (*US*)

Putumayo World Music (*US*)
Razor & Tie (*US*)
Sequoia Records (*US*)
Tama Industries Record Label (*US*)

# US Managers

*For the most up-to-date listings of these and hundreds of other managers, visit https://www.musicsocket.com/managers*

*To claim your **free** access to the site, please see the back of this book.*

## 21st Century Artists, Inc.

853 Broadway, Suite 1607
New York, NY 10003
*Email:* info@21stca.com
*Website:* http://21stca.com

*Represents:* Artists/Bands

*Genres:* Folk; Rock; Roots

New York based management company representing artists dealing in folk music, rock, and roots.

## 25 Artist Agency

25 Music Square West
Nashville, TN 37203
*Fax:* +1 (615) 687-6699
*Email:* david@25ent.com
*Email:* dara@25ent.com
*Website:* https://www.25ccm.com/

*Represents:* Artists/Bands

*Genres:* Christian

*Contact:* David Breen; Dara Easterday; Todd Thomas

Christian record label, based in Nashville, Tennessee.

## Abba-Tude Entertainment

311 North Robertson Avenue, Suite 505
Beverly Hills, CA 90211
*Email:* kingabba@aol.com

*Represents:* Artists/Bands

*Genres:* All types of music

*Contact:* Mark Abbattista

Management company based in California. Accepts unsolicited material.

## ACA Music & Entertainment

705 Larry Court
Waukesha, WI 53186
*Fax:* +1 (262) 790-9149
*Email:* info@acaentertainment.com
*Website:* http://acaentertainment.com
*Website:* https://www.facebook.com/AcaMusicEntertainment/

*Represents:* Artists/Bands; DJs

*Genres:* All types of music

Describes itself as the oldest and largest provider of live entertainment in the Midwest.

## Act 1 Entertainment

28 Price Street
Patchogue, NY 11772
*Email:* info@act1entertainment.net
*Email:* karl@act1entertainment.net
*Website:* http://act1entertainment.net
*Website:* https://www.facebook.com/Act1Inc/

*Represents:* Artists/Bands; Comedians; DJs; Tribute Acts

*Genres:* Jazz; R&B; Soul; Blues; Swing; Roots; Rockabilly; Country; Reggae; Classic Rock

*Contact:* Karl BD Reamer

Management company based in Patchogue, New York.

## Advanced Alternative Media (AAM)
270 Lafayette Street, Suite 605
New York, NY 10012

LOS ANGELES
5979 West 3rd Street, Suite 204
Los Angeles, CA 90036

NASHVILLE
1600 17th Avenue South
Nashville, TN 37212
*Email:* info@aaminc.com
*Website:* http://www.aaminc.com
*Website:* https://www.facebook.com/AdvancedAlternativeMedia

*Represents:* Artists/Bands; Producers; Songwriters; Sound Engineers

*Genres:* Alternative; Pop; Rock; Indie

*Contact:* Matthew Clayman

Management company with offices in New York, Nashville, London, and Los Angeles.

## American Artists Corporation
8500 Wilshire Boulevard, Suite 525
Beverly Hills, CA 90211
*Email:* mike@americanartists.net
*Email:* spencer@americanartists.net
*Website:* https://www.americanartists.net

*Represents:* Artists/Bands

*Genres:* Country; Classic Rock; Rock; R&B; Swing

*Contact:* Michael Weinstein; Spencer Zubrow

Exclusive music booking agency based in Beverly Hills, California.

## American Artists Entertainment Group
29 Royal Palm Pointe Suite 5
Vero Beach, Florida 32960

NEW YORK OFFICE
245 E 63rd St suite 1701
New York, NY 10065

*Fax:* +1 (954) 251-4602
*Email:* online@aaeg.com
*Website:* http://www.aaeg.com
*Website:* http://www.facebook.com/pages/American-Artists-Entertainment-Group/147738265237919?ref=info
*Website:* https://myspace.com/aaeg

*Represents:* Artists/Bands

*Genres:* Country; Pop; R&B; Rock

Management company with offices in Vero Beach, Florida, New York, and Hollywood. Has a 45-year history in the performing arts, and today serves over 16 countries and over 100 cities worldwide. Submit via form on website.

## AMW Group Inc.
12333 Sowden Rd Ste B #8295
Houston, TX 77080

LOS ANGELES:
8605 Santa Monica Blvd
West Hollywood, CA 90069

NEW YORK:
228 Park Ave. South
New York City, NY 10003
*Website:* https://www.amworldgroup.com
*Website:* https://facebook.com/amwgrp

*Represents:* Artists/Bands

*Genres:* All types of music

Company with offices in Texas, LA, and New York. No unsolicited submissions. Offers promotion service packages.

## Angelica Arts & Entertainment
Nashville, TN
*Fax:* +1 (615) 591-1463

*Email:* mgmt@angelica.org
*Website:* http://www.angelica.org

*Represents:* Artists/Bands

*Genres:* Ambient; Lounge; New Age; Pop; World

Management company based in Nashville, Tennessee.

## APA (Agency for the Performing Arts)
405 S. Beverly Drive
Beverly Hills, CA 90212
*Website:* http://apa-agency.com

*Represents:* Artists/Bands

*Genres:* All types of music

Management company with offices in Los Angeles, Nashville, New York, Atlanta, Toronto, and London.

## Apex Talent Group
8383 Wilshire Blvd., Suite 800
Beverly Hills, CA 90211

*Email:* music@apextalentgroup.com
*Email:* info@apextalentgroup.com
*Website:* https://apextalentgroup.com

*Represents:* Artists/Bands; DJs; Songwriters

*Genres:* Alternative; Dance; Indie; Pop; Rock; Singer-Songwriter; Electronic

*Contact:* Richard Makarewicz

Offers full-service artist development. Connections with major record labels, A&Rs, music publishing, playlist curators, and promoters help our clients achieve success in the music business.

## Arslanian & Associates, Inc.
6671 Sunset Boulevard, Suite 1502
Hollywood, CA 90028
*Email:* oscar@discoverhollywood.com
*Website:* http://www.arslanianassociates.com

*Represents:* Artists/Bands

*Genres:* Classic Rock

*Contact:* Oscar Arslanian; Nyla Arslanian

Management company based in Hollywood, California.

## Artist in Mind
14100 Dickens Street, Suite 1
Sherman Oaks, CA 91423
*Fax:* +1 (818) 924-1000
*Email:* info@artistinmind.com

*Represents:* Artists/Bands; Film / TV Composers; Producers; Songwriters

*Genres:* Contemporary; Indie; Pop; Rock; Singer-Songwriter; Alternative; Americana; Folk; Modern Rock

*Contact:* Doug Buttleman

Management company based in Sherman Oaks, California. Not currently accepting submissions as at March 2019.

## Artist Representation and Management (ARM) Entertainment
1257 Arcade Street
St Paul, MN 55106
*Fax:* +1 (651) 776-6338
*Email:* jd@armentertainment.com
*Website:* http://www.armentertainment.com

*Represents:* Artists/Bands

*Genres:* Blues; Country; Classic Rock; Metal

*Contact:* John Domagall, President

Entertainment business with a focus on 70s, 80s, and 90s rock. No unsolicited material.

## Azoff Music Management
1100 Glendon Ave., Ste. 2000
Los Angeles, CA 90024

*Represents:* Artists/Bands

*Genres:* All types of music

Management company based in Los Angeles, California.

## Backstage Entertainment
*Email:* staff@backstageentertainment.net
*Website:* https://backstageentertainment.net

*Website:* https://www.facebook.com/
BackstageEntertainment

*Represents:* Artists/Bands

*Genres:* All types of music

*Contact:* Paul Loggins

Artist management/marketing firm which specialises in working with independent artists, and aims to bridge the gap between radio, print and social media.

## Bandguru Management
PO Box 11192
Denver, CO 80211
*Fax:* +1 (303) 561-1496
*Email:* mark@bandguru.com
*Website:* http://www.bandguru.com

*Represents:* Artists/Bands

*Genres:* All types of music

*Contact:* Mark Bliesener

Management and consulting company.
Offers consultancy services at $100 an hour.

## BBA Management & Booking
*Email:* info@bbabooking.com
*Website:* http://www.bbabooking.com
*Website:* https://www.facebook.com/
bbabooking

*Represents:* Artists/Bands

*Genres:* Jazz; Classical; Rock; Latin

*Contact:* Michael Mordecai; Laura Mordecai

Management and booking for jazz, classical, and versatile party bands in Central Texas.

## Big Beat Productions, Inc.
1515 University Drive, Suite 106
Coral Springs, FL 33071
*Fax:* +1 (954) 755-8733
*Email:* talent@bigbeatproductions.com
*Website:* http://www.bigbeatproductions.com
*Website:* https://www.facebook.com/Big-
Beat-Productions-Inc-Worldwide-
Representation-146226482073192/?ref=ts

*Represents:* Artists/Bands; Comedians; DJs

*Genres:* Contemporary; Classic Rock; R&B;
Disco; Regional; Jazz; Country

*Contact:* Richard Lloyd; Gary Ladka; Elissa
Solomon

Management company based in Coral
Springs, Florida.

## Big Hassle Management
NEW YORK:
40 Exchange Pl, Ste. 1900
New York, NY 10005

LA:
3685 Motor Avenue, Suite 240
Los Angeles, CA 90034
*Email:* weinstein@bighassle.com
*Email:* jim@bighassle.com
*Website:* http://www.bighassle.com

*Represents:* Artists/Bands

*Genres:* Indie; Pop; Rock; Alternative

*Contact:* Ken Weinstein

Management company with offices in New
York and Los Angeles.

## Big Noise
11 South Angell Street, Suite 336
Providence, RI 02906
*Email:* algomes@bignoisenow.com
*Email:* al@bignoisenow.com
*Website:* http://www.bignoisenow.com

*Represents:* Artists/Bands

*Genres:* All types of music

*Contact:* Al Gomes; A. Michelle

Award-winning Music Firm specialising in artist development, project management, career strategies, and promotion and publicity. Based in Providence, Rhode Island. Looking for artists who are unique, talented, professional, and ready to launch. Considers all genres. Query by phone or email in first instance. Must be at least 18.

## Bill Hollingshead Productions, Inc. Talent Agency
1010 Anderson Road
Davis, California 95616

*Fax:* +1 (530) 758-9777
*Email:* bhptalent@aol.com
*Website:* http://www.bhptalent.com

*Represents:* Artists/Bands

*Genres:* Classic Rock; Surf

Handles California surf music and classic 50s/60s rock.

## Bill Silva Management
*Website:* https://www. billsilvaentertainment.com

*Represents:* Artists/Bands; Songwriters

*Genres:* All types of music

*Contact:* Bill Silva

Management company based in West Hollywood, California.

## Bitchin' Entertainment
1750 Collard Valley Road
Cedartown, GA 30125
*Email:* Ty@BitchinEntertainment.com
*Email:* Rodney@BitchinEntertainment.com
*Website:* http://www. bitchinentertainment.com

*Represents:* Artists/Bands; Tribute Acts

*Genres:* Rock; Pop; R&B; Funk; Urban; Hip-Hop; Rap; Instrumental; Jazz; Classical; Ambient; World; Experimental; House; Trance; Electronic; Techno; Alternative; Metal; Punk; Gothic; Country; Americana; Blues; Folk; Singer-Songwriter; Spoken Word

Management company based in Cedartown, Georgia. Send query by email with link to your music online. No MP3s or links to MP3s. See website for full submission guidelines, and details of who to approach regarding specific genres.

## Black Dot Management
6820 La Tijera Boulevard, Suite 117
Los Angeles, CA 90045
*Fax:* +1 (323) 777-8169
*Email:* info@blkdot.com
*Website:* http://www.blkdot.com

*Represents:* Artists/Bands; Producers; Songwriters; Sound Engineers; Studio Musicians; Studio Technicians

*Genres:* Jazz; R&B; Urban; Contemporary

*Contact:* Raymond A. Shields II; Patricia Shields

Management company based in Los Angeles, California. Handles jazz, R&B, and urban.

## Blackheart Records Group
*Fax:* +1 (212) 353-8300
*Email:* blackheart@blackheart.com
*Website:* http://www.blackheart.com
*Website:* https://www.facebook.com/ BlackheartRecordsGroup/

*Represents:* Artists/Bands; Film / TV Composers; Producers; Songwriters

*Genres:* Punk; Rock

Query by email in first instance.

## Booking Entertainment
275 Madison Avenue 6th Floor
New York, NY 10016
*Email:* agents@bookingentertainment.com
*Website:* https://www. bookingentertainment.com

*Represents:* Artists/Bands

*Genres:* Pop; Rock; Jazz; R&B; Contemporary

Books big name entertainment for private parties, public concerts, corporate events, and fundraisers.

## Brick Wall Management
39 West 32nd Street, Suite 1403
New York, NY 10001
*Fax:* +1 (212) 202-4582
*Email:* bwmgmt@brickwallmgmt.com
*Website:* http://www.brickwallmgmt.com

*Represents:* Artists/Bands; Producers

*Genres:* Country; Pop; Rock; Singer-Songwriter

*Contact:* Michael Solomon; Rishon Blumberg

Management company based in New York.

## Brilliant Productions
Decatur, GA 30030
*Email:* nancy@brilliant-productions.com
*Website:* http://brilliant-productions.com
*Website:* https://www.youtube.com/user/itsbrilliant

*Represents:* Artists/Bands

*Genres:* Blues; Regional; Roots; Americana

*Contact:* Nancy Lewis-Pegel

Boutique agency based in Decatur, Georgia.

## The Brokaw Company
4135 Bakman Avevenue
North Hollywood, CA 91602
*Email:* jobrok@aol.com
*Email:* db@brokawco.com
*Website:* http://brokawcompany.com

*Represents:* Artists/Bands

*Genres:* Country; Hip-Hop; Pop; Christian; Rock

*Contact:* Joel Brokaw; David Brokaw; Sanford Brokaw

Management company based in North Hollywood, California. As well as handling music artists, has also handled publicity for hit shows such as The Cosby Show and Roseanne.

## Bulletproof Artist Management
241 Main Street
Easthampton, MA 01027
*Email:* patty@bulletproofartists.com
*Website:* https://bulletproofartists.com

*Represents:* Artists/Bands; Producers

*Genres:* Country; Pop; Rock; Folk

*Contact:* Patty Romanoff

Management company based in Easthampton, Massachusetts.

## Burgess World Co.
PO Box 646
Mayo, MD 21106-0646
*Email:* info@burgessworldco.com
*Website:* http://www.burgessworldco.com

*Represents:* Artists/Bands; Producers; Sound Engineers

*Genres:* Alternative; Blues; Jazz; Rock; Singer-Songwriter

Management company based in Mayo, Maryland. Originally founded to manage producers and engineers, but in the nineties expanded into artist management.

## Cantaloupe Music Productions, Inc.
157 West 79 Street
New York, NY 10024-6415
*Email:* ellenazorin@gmail.com
*Website:* http://www.cantaloupeproductions.com

*Represents:* Artists/Bands

*Genres:* Regional; Latin; World; Jazz; Blues; Swing

*Contact:* Ellen Azorin, President

Handles Brazilian music, Argentine tango, and other Latin-American music.

## Career Artist Management (CAM)
Los Angeles, CA
*Fax:* +1 (424) 230-7839
*Website:* http://www.camanagement.com

*Represents:* Artists/Bands

*Genres:* Pop; Rock

Management company based in Los Angeles, California.

## Case Entertainment Group Inc.
102 E. Pikes Peak Ave., Ste. 200
Colorado Springs, CO 80903
*Fax:* +1 (719) 634-2274
*Email:* rac@crlr.net

*Website:* http://www.newpants.com
*Website:* http://www.oldpants.com

*Represents:* Artists/Bands

*Genres:* Rock; Pop; Country; Folk; R&B; Rap

*Contact:* Robert Case

Management company based in Colorado Springs, Colorado.

## Celebrity Talent Agency Inc.

111 East 14th Street Suite 249
New York, NY 10003
*Fax:* +1 (201) 837-9011
*Email:* markg@celebritytalentagency.com
*Email:* alinak@celebritytalentagency.com
*Website:* http://www.
celebritytalentagency.com
*Website:* https://www.facebook.com/
CelebrityTalentAgency/

*Represents:* Artists/Bands; Comedians; DJs

*Genres:* Dance; Hip-Hop; R&B; Latin; Reggae; Jazz; Gospel

*Contact:* Mark Green; Alina Kim

Talent agency with offices in New York and London.

## Century Artists Management Agency, LLC

711 West End Avenue, Suite 3CS
New York, New York 10025
*Email:* phorton@centuryartists.com
*Website:* https://www.camatalent.com
*Website:* https://twitter.com/centuryartists

*Represents:* Artists/Bands; Producers; Songwriters

*Genres:* All types of music

*Contact:* Paul E. Horton, President

Offers strategic brand management for artists in music, television, film, and the performing arts. Seeking established and new talent.

## Chapman & Co. Management

14011 Ventura Boulevard #405
Sherman Oaks, CA 91423

*Fax:* +1 (818) 788-9525
*Email:* info@chapmanmanagement.com
*Email:* steve@chapmanmanagement.com
*Website:* http://chapmanmanagement.com

*Represents:* Artists/Bands

*Genres:* Contemporary Jazz

*Contact:* Steve Chapman

Management company based in Sherman Oaks, California. Concentrates on smooth, contemporary jazz.

## Circle City Records USA

*Email:* circlecityrecordsusa@comcast.net
*Website:* https://www.circlecityrecords.com

*Represents:* Artists/Bands

*Genres:* Country; Gospel; Pop

*Contact:* Lincoln Plowman

A full service Musician Development and Artist Management company.

If you are just beginning your Music Career or are an established Artist, we can help.

## Collin Artists

1099 N. Mar Vista Ave
Pasadena, CA 91104
*Email:* collinartists@gmail.com
*Website:* http://www.collinartists.com

*Represents:* Artists/Bands

*Genres:* Instrumental Jazz; Latin; World; Blues; R&B; Swing; Contemporary Jazz

*Contact:* Barbara Collin

Management company based in Pasadena, California.

## Columbia Artists Management Inc. (CAMI)

5 Columbus Circle
@ 1790 Broadway
New York, NY 10019-1412
*Fax:* +1 (212) 841-9744
*Email:* info@columbia-artists.com
*Website:* http://www.cami.com

*Represents:* Artists/Bands; Film / TV Composers; Lyricists; Variety Artists

*Genres:* Contemporary; Blues; Classical; Country; Folk; Indie; Jazz; Latin; Pop; R&B; World; Instrumental; Celtic

*Contact:* Tim Fox

Represents classical, jazz, and popular musicians; orchestras, ensembles, etc. Offices in US and Europe.

## Concerted Efforts
PO Box 440326
Somerville MA, 02144
*Fax:* +1 (617) 209-1300
*Email:* concerted@concertedefforts.com
*Website:* https://concertedefforts.com

*Represents:* Artists/Bands

*Genres:* Blues; Folk; Jazz; Gospel; Soul; Singer-Songwriter; Rock; World

Music booking agency based in Somerville, Massachusetts.

## Creative Artists Agency (CAA)
2000 Avenue of the Stars
Los Angeles, CA 90067
*Fax:* +1 (424) 288-2900
*Website:* https://www.caa.com

*Represents:* Artists/Bands

*Genres:* All types of music

Talent agency with offices across the US, as well as in the UK, China, and Europe.

## Crush Music Media Management
*Email:* info@crushmusic.com
*Website:* https://www.crushmusic.com

*Represents:* Artists/Bands; Producers; Songwriters

*Genres:* All types of music

Management company based in New York.

## Culler Talent Management
48 Kelley Ave
Battle Creek, MI 49017

*Email:* chandlerculler@gmail.com
*Website:* https://www.linkedin.com/in/chandler-culler-913972a8

*Represents:* Variety Artists

*Genres:* All types of music

*Contact:* Chandler Culler

Provides talent management and event booking for all types of entertainers from all over.

## D. Bailey Management, Inc.
17815 Gunn Hwy Suite 5
Odessa, FL 33556
*Email:* info@dbaileymanagement.com
*Website:* https://www.
dbaileymanagement.com
*Website:* https://www.facebook.com/dbaileymanagement

*Represents:* Artists/Bands

*Genres:* Pop; R&B; Rock

*Contact:* Dennis Bailey

Live entertainment, event management, and artist management, based in Odessa, Florida.

## DAS Communications Ltd
83 Riverside Drive
New York, NY 10024-5713

*Represents:* Artists/Bands; Producers; Songwriters

*Genres:* Hip-Hop; Pop; Rock

Management company based in New York.

## Dave Kaplan Management
1126 South Coast Highway 101
Encinitas, CA 92024
*Fax:* +1 (760) 944-7808
*Email:* demo@surfdog.com
*Website:* http://www.surfdog.com
*Website:* https://www.facebook.com/surfdogrecords/

*Represents:* Artists/Bands

*Genres:* Rock

*Contact:* Dave Kaplan; Scott Seine

Management company based in Encinitas, California. Also runs associated record label. Accepts submissions by post marked for the attention of A&R, but prefers links by email (no MP3 attachments).

## David Belenzon Management, Inc.

PO Box 5000 PMB 67,
Rancho Santa Fe, CA 92067

*Fax:* +1 (858) 832-8381
*Email:* David@Belenzon.com
*Email:* INFO@BELENZON.com
*Website:* http://www.belenzon.com

*Represents:* Artists/Bands; Variety Artists

*Genres:* Contemporary; Pop; Rock; R&B

*Contact:* David Belenzon

Management company based in Rancho Santa Fe, California, representing artists, variety artists, plus theatrical and production shows.

## Dawn Elder Management

*Email:* deworldmusic@aol.com
*Website:* https://dawnelderworldentertainment.com
*Website:* https://www.facebook.com/DawnElderWorldEntertainment

*Represents:* Artists/Bands

*Genres:* Classical; Jazz; Pop; Rock; Roots; Traditional; World

Have managed, represented and organised international tours for some of the most highly regarded international artists today.

## DCA Productions

302A 12th Street, # 330
New York, NY 10014
*Fax:* +1 (609) 259-8260
*Email:* info@dcaproductions.com
*Website:* http://dcaproductions.com

*Represents:* Artists/Bands; Comedians; Variety Artists

*Genres:* Pop; Rock; Folk

*Contact:* Daniel C. Abrahmsen, President; Gerri Abrahamsen, Vice President

Management company founded in 1983, specialising in variety performers, comedians, musical performers, theatre productions, and producing live events.

## DDB Productions

*Email:* ddbprods@gmail.com
*Website:* https://www.ddbprods.com/
*Website:* http://www.deedeebridgewater.com

*Represents:* Artists/Bands; Lyricists; Producers; Songwriters; Studio Vocalists

*Genres:* Jazz; World; Alternative

*Contact:* Dee Dee Bridgewater

A boutique record label, music production company and talent management firm, based in Los Angeles, CA and New Orleans, LA. Founded by triple Grammy and Tony award winning Jazz artist.

## Deep South Artist Management

RALEIGH
PO Box 17737
Raleigh, NC 27619

NASHVILLE
PO Box 121975
Nashville, TN 37212
*Email:* Hello@DeepSouthEntertainment.com
*Website:* http://www.deepsouthentertainment.com
*Website:* https://www.facebook.com/deepsouthent

*Represents:* Artists/Bands

*Genres:* Alternative; Country; Pop; Rock; Americana; Christian

Record label, artist management firm, talent agency, and concert production company based in Raleigh, North Carolina, with offices in both Raleigh and Nashville, Tennessee.

## The Derek Power Company & Kahn Power Pictures

433 North Camden Drive, Suite 600 Beverly Hills, CA 90210
*Email:* Artists4Film@gmail.com
*Email:* iampower007@me.com
*Website:* https://www.artists4film.com

*Represents:* Artists/Bands; Film / TV Composers

*Genres:* All types of music

*Contact:* Derek Power; Ilene Kahn Power

Production and talent management company based in Beverly Hills, California.

## Direct Management Group (DMG)

8332 Melrose Ave, Top Floor
Los Angeles, CA 90069
*Email:* info@directmanagement.com
*Website:* http://directmanagement.com

*Represents:* Artists/Bands

*Genres:* Pop

*Contact:* Martin Kirkup; Bradford Cobb; Steven Jensen

Management company based in West Hollywood, California. Founded in April 1985. Describes itself as an internationally oriented entertainment company with broad-based success in the representation of musical artists.

## Dog & Pony Industries

*Email:* info@dogandponyindustries.com
*Website:* http://www.dogandponyindustries.com

*Represents:* Artists/Bands

*Genres:* All types of music

Specializing in talent management and the coordinating of concert tours and special projects in the Music, TV & Film industries. Contact by email.

## Domo Music Group Management

11340 West Olympic Boulevard, Suite 270
Los Angeles, CA 90064
*Fax:* +1 (310) 966-4420
*Email:* domo@domo.com
*Email:* dino@domo.com
*Website:* https://www.domomusicgroup.com/management/
*Website:* https://www.facebook.com/officialdomomusicgroup

*Represents:* Artists/Bands; DJs; Film / TV Composers; Producers; Songwriters; Studio Musicians

*Genres:* Contemporary; Classical; Folk; Indie; New Age; Pop; Rock; Singer-Songwriter; World; Ethnic

*Contact:* Eiichi Naito; Dino Malito (A&R)

Management company based in Los Angeles, California, handling Japanese artists. Prefers links to music online by email or via submission form on website, or send CD by post marked for the attention of A&R.

## East Coast Entertainment (ECE)

*Email:* info@bookece.com
*Website:* https://www.bookece.com
*Website:* https://www.facebook.com/EastCoastEntertainment/

*Represents:* Artists/Bands; Comedians; DJs

*Genres:* All types of music

Describes itself as the largest full-service entertainment agency in the country.

## East End Management

12441 Ventura Ct
Studio City, CA 91604
*Website:* https://www.linkedin.com/company/east-end-management

*Represents:* Artists/Bands

*Genres:* Rock; Pop

Management company based in Studio City, California.

---

## Emcee Artist Management
*Email:* liz@emceeartist.com
*Email:* mfair@emceeartist.com
*Website:* https://www.emceeartist.com

*Represents:* Artists/Bands

*Genres:* Jazz; Blues; Rock

*Contact:* Liz Penta; Meagan Fair

Management company representing jazz, blues, and rock artists. No hip-hop.

## Empire Artist Management
235 West 23rd Street, 6th Floor
New York, NY 10011
*Email:* info@empireartistmanagement.com
*Website:* http://www.
empireartistmanagement.com

*Genres:* Electronic; Club; Techno

Management company based in New York.

## Entertainment Services International
1819 South Harlan Circle
Lakewood, CO 80232
*Fax:* +1 (303) 936-0069
*Email:* randy@esientertainment.com
*Website:* http://www.esientertainment.com

*Represents:* Artists/Bands

*Genres:* Rock; Classic Rock

*Contact:* Randy Erwin

Manager based in Lakewood, Colorado.

## Entourage Talent Associates, Ltd
150 West 28th Street, Suite 1503
New York, NY 10001
*Fax:* +1 (212) 633-1818
*Email:* info@entouragetalent.com
*Website:* http://www.entouragetalent.com
*Website:* https://www.facebook.com/
EntourageTalentAssociates

*Represents:* Artists/Bands

*Genres:* Pop; Rock; Singer-Songwriter; Jazz

Not currently seeking new acts for representation. However, you can submit your music and information for consideration for support/packaging with one of the existing clients for an upcoming tour. Send submissions by post or by email, or via form on website.

## Fat City Artists
1906 Chet Atkins Place, Suite 502 Nashville, TN 37212
*Fax:* +1 (615) 321-5382
*Website:* http://fatcityartists.com

*Represents:* Artists/Bands

*Genres:* Acoustic; Blues; R&B; Celtic; Country; Folk; Funk; Gospel; Jazz; Pop; Reggae; Rockabilly; Rock and Roll; Ska; Swing; World

Artists management based in Nashville, Tennessee. Not signing new artists as at July 2020.

## First Access Entertainment
New York / Los Angeles
*Email:* music@firstaccessent.com
*Email:* la@firstaccessent.com
*Website:* https://www.firstaccessent.com
*Website:* https://www.facebook.com/
firstaccessent

*Represents:* Artists/Bands

*Genres:* Pop; Rap; R&B; Hip-Hop

Entertainment company with offices in New York, Los Angeles, and London, offering recorded music, management and publishing services as well as film, TV and tech development and acting and model management.

## 5B Artist Management
220 36th St, Suite B442
Brooklyn, NY 11232

LOS ANGELES:
12021 Jefferson Blvd,
Culver City, CA 90230
*Email:* hello@5bam.com
*Website:* http://5bam.com

*Represents:* Artists/Bands

*Genres:* Alternative; Metal; Rock

Management company with offices in New York, Los Angeles and Birmingham (UK). Not accepting submissions as at March 2019.

## Fleming Artists
PO Box 1568
Ann Arbor, MI 48106
*Fax:* +1 (734) 662-6502
*Email:* jim@flemingartists.com
*Email:* cynthia@flemingartists.com
*Website:* http://www.flemingartists.com

*Represents:* Artists/Bands

*Genres:* Contemporary Roots Rock; Blues; Folk; Pop; Rock

Management company with a mission to "represent high quality performing artists by providing them with a unique, thoughtful and individualized approach to concert booking."

## Fresh Flava Entertainment
2705 12th Street NE
Washington, DC 20018
*Email:* freshflava17@gmail.com
*Website:* http://www.freshflava.com

*Represents:* Artists/Bands

*Genres:* Hip-Hop; Jazz; Gospel; R&B; Rock

Management company based in Washington DC. Accepts unsolicited submissions.

## Funzalo Records
PO Box 571567
Tarzana, CA 91357
*Email:* funzalorecords@gmail.com
*Email:* dan@mikesmanagement.com
*Website:* https://funzalorecords.com
*Website:* https://www.facebook.com/funzalorecords

*Represents:* Artists/Bands; Producers

*Genres:* All types of music

*Contact:* Mike Lembo; Dan Agnew

Send submission through form on website, with short bio and links to songs online.

## Gary Stamler Management
PO Box 34575
Los Angeles, CA 90034
*Email:* garystamler@me.com
*Email:* nancysefton@gsmgmt.net
*Website:* https://www.gsmgmt.net

*Represents:* Artists/Bands; Producers

*Genres:* All types of music

*Contact:* Gary Stamler; Nancy Sefton

Management company based in Los Angeles.

## Gayle Enterprises, Inc.
51 Music Square East
Nashville, TN 37203
*Email:* info@crystalgayle.com
*Website:* https://crystalgayle.com
*Website:* https://www.facebook.com/236343614779

*Represents:* Artists/Bands

*Genres:* All types of music

*Contact:* Bill Gatzimos

Management company based in Nashville, Tennessee, dedicated to representing one artist only. No submissions or queries.

## The Gorfaine/Schwartz Agency, Inc.
4111 West Alameda Avenue, Suite 509
Burbank, CA 91505
*Email:* reception@gsamusic.com
*Website:* https://www.gsamusic.com

*Represents:* Artists/Bands; Producers

*Genres:* All types of music

Management agency based in Burbank, California.

## Hardin Entertainment
*Email:* info@hardinentertainment.com
*Website:* http://www.hardinentertainment.com
*Website:* https://www.facebook.com/hardinbourke/

*Represents:* Artists/Bands; Film / TV Composers; Lyricists; Producers; Songwriters; Studio Vocalists; Supervisors

*Genres:* Contemporary; Alternative; Americana; Blues; Christian; Country; Dance; Electronic; Folk; Hardcore; Indie; Latin; Pop; Rock; Roots; Singer-Songwriter; World

Management company with offices in Los Angeles and New York.

## Harmony Artists
3575 Cahuenga Blvd. W, #560
Los Angeles, CA 90068
*Fax:* +1 (323) 655-5154
*Email:* mdixon@harmonyartists.com
*Email:* jross@harmonyartists.com
*Website:* http://www.harmonyartists.com
*Website:* https://www.facebook.com/
HarmonyArtistsLA/

*Represents:* Artists/Bands; Tribute Acts

*Genres:* Blues; Latin; Jazz; Swing

Specialises in providing top national headline and regional entertainment for venues throughout the world.

## Heart & Soul Artist Management
St Paul, MN
*Email:* mvt@utrmusicgroup.com
*Website:* http://utrmusicgroup.com
*Website:* https://www.facebook.com/
MikiMulvehill

*Represents:* Artists/Bands

*Genres:* All types of music

*Contact:* Miki Mulvehill

Management company based in St Paul, Minnesota.

## Hello! Booking, Inc.
PO Box 18717
Minneapolis, MN 55418
*Fax:* +1 (763) 463-1264
*Email:* eric@hellobooking.com
*Website:* http://www.hellobooking.com

*Website:* https://www.facebook.com/
hellobookingusa

*Represents:* Artists/Bands

*Genres:* Country; Folk; Indie; Jazz; Hip-Hop; Acoustic; Rockabilly; Rock; Pop

*Contact:* Eric Roberts

Show booking company based in Minneapolis.

## Hornblow Group USA, Inc.
*Email:* info@hornblowgroup.com
*Website:* https://www.hornblowgroup.com
*Website:* https://www.facebook.com/
hornblowmusic/

*Represents:* Artists/Bands; Film / TV Composers; Lyricists; Producers; Songwriters; Studio Musicians

*Genres:* Indie; Pop; Rock; Alternative; Singer-Songwriter

Full-service artist management firm, independent record label, purveyors of cool t-shirts and bumper stickers.

## Howard Rosen Promotion, Inc.
1129 Maricopa Highway
Ojai, CA 93023
*Email:* info@howiewood.com
*Email:* Howie@howiewood.com
*Website:* http://howiewood.com
*Website:* https://myspace.com/howardrosen

*Represents:* Artists/Bands

*Genres:* All types of music

*Contact:* Howard Rosen; Alex Louton

Full service radio promotion company based in Ojai, California. Submit music using online submissions system on website.

## IMC Entertainment Group
19360 Rinaldi Street, Suite 217
Porter Ranch, CA 91326
*Fax:* +1 (206) 600-5534
*Email:* sr@imcentertainment.com
*Website:* http://www.imcentertainment.com

*Represents:* Artists/Bands

*Genres:* Pop; R&B

Management company based in Porter Ranch, California, providing entertainment and production services worldwide. Specialises in music performance, production, publishing and supervision services.

## IMG Artists
Pleiades House
7 West 54th Street
New York, NY 10019
*Fax:* +1 (212) 994-3550
*Email:* artistsny@imgartists.com
*Website:* https://imgartists.com

*Represents:* Artists/Bands

*Genres:* Classic; Folk; Gospel; Jazz; World; Latin; Singer-Songwriter

*Contact:* Elizabeth Sobol, Senior Vice President, Managing Director; Steve Linder, Senior Vice President and Director, Attractions Division

Describes itself as the global leader in the arts management business, with offices in New York, London, Paris, Hanover, and Seoul.

## Impact Artist Management
275 Fair Street, Suite 10
Kingston, NY 12401
*Website:* http://www.impactartist.com
*Website:* https://www.facebook.com/impactartistmanagement

*Represents:* Artists/Bands; Film / TV Composers; Songwriters; Supervisors

*Genres:* Contemporary; Blues; Folk; Indie; Jazz; Latin; R&B; Rock; Roots; Singer-Songwriter; World; Alternative; Alternative Country

Management company based in Kingston, New York.

## In De Goot Entertainment
119 West 23rd Street, Suite 609
New York, NY 10011
*Fax:* +1 (212) 924-3242

*Email:* miurato@indegoot.com
*Website:* https://www.indegoot.com
*Website:* https://www.facebook.com/Indegoot/
*Website:* https://myspace.com/indegootentertainment

*Represents:* Artists/Bands

*Genres:* Indie; Metal; Pop; Rock; Underground

*Contact:* Michael Iurato

Management company based in New York.

## Ina Dittke & Associates
770 N.E. 69th Street, Suite 7c
Miami, FL 33138
*Email:* ina@inadittke.com
*Email:* gina@inadittke.com
*Website:* https://inadittke.com
*Website:* https://www.facebook.com/inadittkeassociates/

*Represents:* Artists/Bands

*Genres:* Jazz; Latin; World

Music agency based in Miami, Florida, representing a varied and international roster of artists.

## International Creative Management (ICM) Partners
LOS ANGELES
10250 Constellation Boulevard
Los Angeles, CA 90067

NEW YORK
65 East 55th Street
New York, NY 10022
*Email:* careersla@icmpartners.com
*Website:* http://www.icmtalent.com

*Represents:* Artists/Bands; Comedians

*Genres:* All types of music

*Contact:* Steve Levine

Concerts and live appearances department represents artists in all musical genres, including pop, rock, R&B, hip-hop, indie and adult contemporary. Arranges global engagements and tours in a wide variety of settings and venues.

## Intrigue Music
New Haven, CT
*Email:* staff@intriguegroup.net
*Website:* http://intriguemusic.com
*Website:* https://www.facebook.com/
intriguemusic

*Represents:* Artists/Bands

*Genres:* Pop; Rock

Full-service entertainment company based in
New Haven, CT. Specialises in worldwide
artist management, music publishing, and
intellectual property rights management.

## Invasion Group, Ltd
1133 Broadway Suite 919
New York, NY 10010
*Fax:* +1 (212) 414-0525
*Email:* info@invasiongroup.com
*Website:* http://www.invasiongroup.com
*Website:* https://facebook.com/
invasiongroupltd

*Represents:* Artists/Bands; Film / TV
Composers; Lyricists; Producers;
Songwriters; Sound Engineers; Studio
Musicians; Studio Technicians; Studio
Vocalists; Supervisors

*Genres:* All types of music

*Contact:* Steven Saporta; Peter Casperson;
Steve Dalmer

Management company based in New York.

## Jampol Artist Management
*Email:* assistant@jamincla.com
*Website:* https://wemanagelegends.com
*Website:* https://www.facebook.com/jjampol

*Represents:* Artists/Bands

*Genres:* All types of music

Manages great legacy artists. Dedicated to
the re-introduction of timeless art through
modern means, and helps iconic artist
legacies make the transition to the digital age
with integrity. Does not manage new artists.
If you are a legacy artist looking to extend
your reach, use new technologies, or place
your legacy in a modern context, send query
by email.

## Jeff Roberts & Associates
174 Saundersville Road, Ste 702
Hendersonville, TN
*Website:* http://www.jeffroberts.com
*Website:* https://www.facebook.com/
jrabooking

*Represents:* Artists/Bands

*Genres:* Christian

Christina music booking agency, based in
Tennessee.

## Kari Estrin Management & Consulting
PO Box 60232
Nashville, TN 37206
*Email:* kari@kariestrin.com
*Website:* http://www.kariestrin.com
*Website:* https://www.facebook.com/Kari-
Estrin-Management-118090355921/

*Represents:* Artists/Bands

*Genres:* Americana; Folk; Roots; Acoustic

Based in Nashville, Tennessee. Offers artist
management and consulting.

## KBH Entertainment
Los Angeles, CA
*Email:* support@kbhentertainment.com
*Website:* https://kbhentertainment.com
*Website:* https://www.facebook.com/
KBHEntertainment

*Represents:* Artists/Bands; Film / TV
Composers; Producers; Studio Musicians;
Studio Vocalists

*Genres:* All types of music

*Contact:* Brent Harvey

A full service entertainment consulting,
booking, event production, management and
marketing company, based in Los Angeles,
California.

## KCA Artists
1025 17th Avenue South, 2nd Floor
Nashville, TN 37212
*Fax:* +1 (615) 327-4949
*Email:* keith@keithcase.com

*Website:* https://www.kcaartists.com
*Website:* https://www.facebook.com/
KeithCaseAndAssociates

*Represents:* Artists/Bands

*Genres:* Blues; Folk; Roots; Singer-Songwriter; Pop; Gospel; Americana

*Contact:* Keith Case

Artist representation agency based in Nashville, Tennessee.

## Kraft-Engel Management
15233 Ventura Boulevard, Suite 200
Sherman Oaks, CA 91403
*Email:* info@Kraft-Engel.com
*Website:* http://www.kraft-engel.com

*Represents:* Film / TV Composers; Songwriters; Supervisors

*Genres:* Soundtracks

*Contact:* Richard Kraft; Laura Engel; Sarah Kovacs; Jeff Jernigan; Jonathan Clark

Management company based in Sherman Oaks, California, specialising in representing film and theatre composers, songwriters and music supervisors.

## Kragen & Company
*Email:* info@kragenandcompany.com
*Website:* https://www.kenkragen.com

*Represents:* Artists/Bands; Comedians; Songwriters; Variety Artists

*Genres:* Contemporary; Country; Singer-Songwriter

*Contact:* Ken Kragen

Management company based in Beverly Hills, California. Also offers consultancy services.

## Kuper Personal Management
515 Bomar Street
Houston, TX 77006
*Email:* info@kupergroup.com
*Website:* http://www.kupergroup.com

*Represents:* Artists/Bands

*Genres:* Alternative; Americana; Folk; Roots Rock

Management company based in Houston, Texas. Accepts unsolicited submissions.

## The Kurland Agency
173 Brighton Avenue
Boston, MA 02134-2003
*Fax:* +1 (617) 254-7541
*Email:* agents@thekurlandagency.com
*Website:* https://www.thekurlandagency.com

*Represents:* Artists/Bands

*Genres:* Jazz; Blues

*Contact:* Ted Kurland

Management company based in Boston, best known for representing jazz artists.

## Len Weisman, Personal Manager
357 S. Fairfax Ave. #430
Los Angeles, Ca. 90036
*Fax:* +1 (323) 653-7670
*Email:* parlirec@aol.com
*Website:* http://www.parliamentrecords.com

*Represents:* Artists/Bands

*Genres:* Gospel; R&B; Hip-Hop; Rap; Soul; Blues

Manager based in Los Angeles.

## Lippman Entertainment
*Fax:* +1 (805) 686-5866
*Email:* music@lippmanent.com
*Email:* info@lippmanent.com
*Website:* http://www.lippmanent.com
*Website:* https://www.facebook.com/
lippmanent
*Website:* http://www.myspace.com/
lippmanentertainment

*Represents:* Artists/Bands; Film / TV Composers; Producers; Sound Engineers; Studio Technicians

*Genres:* Pop; R&B; Rap; Hip-Hop; Rock; Singer-Songwriter; Urban

*Contact:* Michael Lippman; Nick Lippman

Management company based in California. Not accepting submissions as at September 2019.

## Loggins Promotion
Nashville, TN
*Email:* staff@logginspromotion.com
*Website:* http://www.logginspromotion.com
*Website:* https://www.facebook.com/logginspromotion

*Represents:* Artists/Bands

*Genres:* R&B; Urban; Rap; Hip-Hop; Dance; Alternative; Rock; Americana; Jazz; Country; Pop

Full service promotion firm based in Nashville, Tennessee. Submit music using online form, or send email for permission to submit by post.

## Lupo Entertainment
725 River Road, Suite 32-388
Edgewater, NJ 07020
*Email:* steve@lupomusic.com
*Email:* nicklopiccolo@lupoentertainment.com
*Website:* http://www.lupomusic.com

*Represents:* Artists/Bands

*Genres:* Country; Pop; R&B; Rock; Hip-Hop

*Contact:* Steve Corbin; Nick LoPiccolo

Management company and consulting service founded in 2003, based in Edgewater, New Jersey. Query before making submission.

## M. Hitchcock Management
Nashville, TN
*Email:* info@mhmgmt.com
*Website:* http://www.mhmgmt.com

*Represents:* Artists/Bands

*Genres:* Alternative Country; Contemporary; Country; Folk; Rock

*Contact:* Monty Hitchcock

Management company based in Nashville, Tennessee.

## Maine Road Management
PO Box 1412
Woodstock, NY 12498
*Email:* mailbox@maineroadmanagement.com
*Website:* http://www.maineroadmanagement.com

*Represents:* Artists/Bands; Producers

*Genres:* Country; Folk; Indie; Jazz; Rock

*Contact:* David Whitehead

New York-based management company.

## Major Bob Music, Inc.
1111 17th Avenue South
Nashville, TN 37212
*Website:* https://www.majorbob.com
*Website:* https://www.facebook.com/majorbobmusic

*Represents:* Artists/Bands; Songwriters

*Genres:* Country; R&B; Soul; Pop

*Contact:* Bob Doyle; Tina Crawford

Management and publishing company based in Nashville, Tennessee.

## The Management Ark, Inc.
Edward C. Arrendell, II
3 Bethesda Metro Center, Suite 700
Bethesda, MD 20814

Vernon H. Hammond III, CFP
116 Villiage Boulevard, Suite 200
Princeton, NJ 08540
*Email:* manageareast@comcast.net
*Email:* rai@mngtark.com
*Website:* http://www.managementark.com

*Represents:* Artists/Bands

*Genres:* Jazz

*Contact:* Edward C. Arrendell, II; Vernon H. Hammond III, CFP

Jazz management company with offices in Bethesda, Maryland, and Princeton, New Jersey.

## Mars Jazz
1006 Ashby Place
Charlottesville, VA 22901-4006
*Fax:* +1 (434) 979-6179
*Email:* reggie@marsjazz.com
*Website:* http://www.marsjazz.com

*Represents:* Artists/Bands

*Genres:* Jazz

*Contact:* Reggie Marshall

Jazz booking agency. Not currently accepting new clients or press kits, but happy to receive CDs and contact details and may contact further down the line if interested.

## Mascioli Entertainment
319 Dillon Cir.
Orlando, FL 32822
*Website:* http://www.masciolientertainment.com

*Represents:* Artists/Bands

*Genres:* Country; Jazz; R&B; Swing; Rock

*Contact:* Paul Mascioli; Mike Mascioli

Full-service entertainment company based in Orlando, Florida, offering artists management and booking for conventions, casinos, arenas, theaters, night clubs, fairs, festivals, and special events.

## Mauldin Brand Agency
*Email:* info@mauldinbrand.com
*Website:* https://www.mauldinbrandinc.com

*Represents:* Artists/Bands; Producers; Songwriters

*Genres:* Hip-Hop; R&B; Rap; Pop

*Contact:* Michael Mauldin

Management company based in Atlanta, Georgia.

## Max Bernard Management
*Email:* myron@maxbernard.com
*Website:* http://www.maxbernard.com
*Website:* https://www.facebook.com/maxbernardmanagement/

*Represents:* Artists/Bands; Producers; Songwriters; Studio Musicians; Studio Vocalists

*Genres:* Urban Indie Jazz R&B Soul Singer-Songwriter; Soundtracks Blues Mainstream Soulful

*Contact:* Myron Bernard

We, pride ourselves on this blueprint that we specialize in creating a backdrop of musical ambiance featuring the world's finest and unique talent while servicing your entertainment needs.

We actively commit to find quality entertainment and entertainer's that suit your local and international demographic areas and taste.

Offers personal consulting services in all areas of artist development, live entertainment and social media and online network marketing.

Media/PR services are outsourced additions provided to clients. Special event(s) implementation and tour management services are available upon request.

## McDonough Management LLC
*Email:* frank@mcdman.com
*Website:* http://www.mcdman.com
*Website:* https://www.facebook.com/mcdmanagement

*Represents:* Producers; Songwriters; Sound Engineers

*Genres:* Rock

*Contact:* Frank McDonough

Management company representing record producers, engineers and mixers.

## McGhee Entertainment
8730 West Sunset Boulevard, Suite 200
West Hollywood, CA 90069

NASHVILLE OFFICE:
21 Music Square West
Nashville, TN 37203
*Fax:* +1 (310) 358-9299
*Email:* info@mcgheela.com

*Website:* http://www.mcgheela.com
*Website:* https://www.facebook.com/
McGheeEntertainment

*Represents:* Artists/Bands; Songwriters

*Genres:* Country; Metal; Rock; Singer-Songwriter; World

*Contact:* Don McGhee; Scott McGhee

Management company with offices in Los Angeles and Nashville.

## The MGMT Company
6906 Hollywood Blvd
Hollywood, CA 90028
*Email:* inquiries@themgmtcompany.com
*Website:* http://www.themgmtcompany.com

*Represents:* Artists/Bands

*Genres:* All types of music

Management company based in Hollywood, California.

## Michael Anthony's Electric Events
Post Office Box 280848
Lakewood, CO 80228
*Email:* info2@electricevents.com
*Website:* http://www.electricevents.com

*Represents:* Artists/Bands

*Genres:* Country; Pop; Dance; Classic Rock

*Contact:* Michael A Tolerico

Music entertainment booking agency based in Lakewood, Colorado.

## Michael Hausman Artist Management Inc.
17A Stuyvesant Oval
New York, NY 10009
*Fax:* +1 (212) 505-1127
*Email:* info@michaelhausman.com
*Website:* http://www.michaelhausman.com

*Represents:* Artists/Bands

*Genres:* Contemporary; Pop; Rock; Singer-Songwriter

*Contact:* Michael Hausman

Management company based in New York.

## Michael Kline Artists
PO Box 312
Cape May Point, NJ 08212
*Email:* info@michaelklineartists.com
*Email:* michael@michaelklineartists.com
*Website:* http://www.michaelklineartists.com
*Website:* https://www.facebook.com/
Michaelklineartists

*Represents:* Artists/Bands

*Genres:* All types of music

*Contact:* Michael Kline

International management and booking agency based in New Jersey.

## Mike's Artist Management
PO Box 571567
Tarzana, CA 91357
*Email:* mike@mikesmanagement.com
*Email:* dan@mikesmanagement.com
*Website:* http://funzalorecords.com/mikes-artist-management/
*Website:* https://www.facebook.com/
funzalorecords

*Represents:* Artists/Bands

*Genres:* Americana; Pop; Rock; Indie; Folk

*Contact:* Mike Lembo; Dan Agnew

Record label and artist management based in Tarzana, California. Send submissions via contact form on website.

## Million Dollar Artists
12 Lake Forest Court West
St. Charles, MO 63301-4540
*Fax:* +1 (636) 724-1325
*Email:* info@americaneaglerecordings.com
*Email:* americaneaglerecordings@
earthlink.net
*Website:* http://www.milliondollarartists.net
*Website:* http://americaneaglerecordings.com

*Represents:* Artists/Bands

*Genres:* All types of music

*Contact:* Dr. Charles Max E. Million

Management company based in St. Louis, Missouri. Send demos on CD only, with lyrics, bio, and photos / press coverage. Download and complete Preliminary Questionnaire from website. No submissions of MP3s or links by email – these will be ignored.

## MM Music Agency
11 Island Avenue,Suite 1711
Miami, FL 33139
*Fax:* +1 (305) 831-4472
*Email:* maurice@mmmusicagency.com
*Email:* info@mmmusicagency.com
*Website:* http://www.mmmusicagency.com
*Website:* https://www.facebook.com/
mmmusicagency

*Represents:* Artists/Bands

*Genres:* Jazz; Regional; Contemporary

*Contact:* Maurice Montoya

Music agency based in Florida, handling jazz, Afro-Caribbean, Brazilian and contemporary music.

## MOB Agency
Los Angeles, CA
*Fax:* +1 (323) 653-0428
*Email:* Mitch@mobagency.com
*Email:* joy@mobagency.com
*Website:* http://www.mobagency.com

*Represents:* Artists/Bands

*Genres:* Alternative; Rock

Agency based in Los Angeles.

## Monotone, Inc.
820 Seward Street
Los Angeles, CA 90038
*Fax:* +1 (323) 308-1819
*Email:* info@monotoneinc.com
*Website:* https://www.monotoneinc.com

*Represents:* Artists/Bands

*Genres:* All types of music

*Contact:* Ian Montone

Music management company based in Los Angeles, California.

## Monqui Presents
PO Box 5908
Portland, OR 97228
*Email:* monquipresents@gmail.com
*Email:* web@monqui.com
*Website:* http://www.monqui.com
*Website:* https://www.facebook.com/
monquipresents

*Represents:* Artists/Bands

*Genres:* Alternative; Indie; Rock; Country; Pop

"Importers of fine live music", serving the Northwest since 1983. Send questions or comments by email and press kits by post.

## MPL Music Publishing, Inc.
New York
*Website:* http://www.
mplcommunications.com
*Website:* https://www.facebook.com/pages/
category/Publisher/MPL-Music-Publishing-
173757699346528/

*Represents:* Artists/Bands; Film / TV Composers; Lyricists; Songwriters

*Genres:* All types of music

No material accepted by post, but willing to listen to music online (e.g. MySpace) if you email them a link.

## MSH Management
Studio City, CA
*Email:* mshmgmt@yahoo.com
*Website:* https://mshmgmt.wixsite.com/
music-management

*Represents:* Artists/Bands

*Genres:* All types of music

*Contact:* Marney Hansen

Management company based in Studio City, California.

## Murphy to Manteo (MTM) Music Management
*Email:* MarkZenow@MTMfirm.com
*Website:* http://www.mtmfirm.com

*Represents:* Artists/Bands; Producers; Songwriters

*Genres:* All types of music

Management company with its roots in Columbia, South Carolina. Contact by phone or by email.

## Music + Art Management
15 W. Walnut St. Suite 202
Asheville, NC
*Website:* https://musicandart.net
*Website:* https://www.facebook.com/Music-and-Art-Management-163558147005567/

*Represents:* Artists/Bands

*Genres:* Electronic; World; Experimental; Rock; Jazz

Full service management and production company specialising in the careers of performing and recording artists. Based in Asheville, North Carolina.

## Music City Artists
7104 Peach Ct.
Brentwood, TN 37027
*Fax:* +1 (615) 266-6223
*Email:* cray@musiccityartists.com
*Website:* http://musiccityartists.com
*Website:* https://www.facebook.com/MusicCityArtists/

*Represents:* Artists/Bands

*Genres:* All types of music

*Contact:* Charles Ray, President / Agent

Full service booking agency representing nationally known artists for performing arts centers, casinos, and corporate entertainment.

## Music Inc.
468 N. Camden Drive
Beverly Hills, CA 90210
*Email:* vince@musicinc.org
*Website:* http://www.musicinc.org

*Represents:* Artists/Bands

*Genres:* Pop

*Contact:* Vincent Pileggi

Management company based in Beverly Hills, California. No longer accepting unsolicited material as at November 2019. Check website for current status.

## Music World Entertainment
5120 Woodway Drive
Houston, Texas 77056
*Website:* http://musicworldent.com

*Represents:* Artists/Bands; Producers

*Genres:* Gospel; Pop; R&B; Urban

Management company based in Houston, Texas.

## Mustang Agency
6119 Greenville Ave, Ste 361
75206 Dallas, Texas
*Email:* booking@mustangagency.com
*Website:* https://www.facebook.com/MustangAgency

*Represents:* Artists/Bands

*Genres:* Alternative; Country; Classic Rock; Metal; Pop; Rock

Established in 2003 by two prominent Attorneys located in Dallas, Texas, the Agency was created from a need to book bands nationally, regionally and locally.

## Myriad Artists
PO BOX 550
Carrboro, NC 27510
*Email:* trish@myriadartists.com
*Email:* booking@myriadartists.com
*Website:* https://www.myriadartists.com
*Website:* https://www.facebook.com/myriadartists/

*Represents:* Artists/Bands

*Genres:* Blues; Folk; Jazz; Americana

*Contact:* Trish Galfano

Management company based in Carrboro, North Carolina.

## Nancy Fly Agency
*Email:* piano@nflyagency.com
*Website:* http://www.nflyagency.com

*Represents:* Artists/Bands

*Genres:* Americana; Traditional; Roots Rock; Blues; World

*Contact:* Nancy Fly

Now in semi-retirement, continues to represent just two long-term clients. No new acts considered.

## Nettwerk Management
3900 West Alameda Ave, Suite 850
Burbank, CA 91505

NEW YORK
33 Irving Place
New York, NY 10003

BOSTON
15 Richdale Ave., Unit 203
Cambridge, MA 02140
*Fax:* +1 (747) 477-1093
*Email:* info@nettwerk.com
*Website:* http://www.nettwerk.com

*Represents:* Artists/Bands; Film / TV Composers; Producers; Songwriters; Sound Engineers; Studio Technicians

*Genres:* Contemporary; Christian; Electronic; Folk; Indie; Latin; Pop; Punk; Rap; Rock; Hip-Hop; Dance; Singer-Songwriter; World

Media company with offices in New York, London, Vancouver, Boston, Nashville, and Germany. Also label and music publishing company.

## New Heights Entertainment
*Email:* info@newheightsent.com
*Website:* http://www.newheightsent.com

*Represents:* Artists/Bands; Producers; Songwriters

*Genres:* All types of music

*Contact:* Alan Melina

Privately held personal management and consulting firm, with its core business focusing on Music Producers, Songwriters, Record Label Management, Music Publishing, Brand Development and Strategic Guidance for Entertainment

Content and IP Creators. No unsolicited materials.

## Nightside Entertainment, Inc.
*Email:* alsalzillo@nightsideentertainment.com
*Website:* https://www.nightsideentertainment.com
*Website:* https://www.facebook.com/nightsideentertainment/

*Represents:* Artists/Bands

*Genres:* All types of music

Full service music booking agency.

## NSI Management
PO Box 959
Newburyport, MA 01950
*Email:* contact@newsoundmgmt.com
*Website:* https://www.newsoundmgmt.com
*Website:* http://facebook.com/danrussellmusic

*Represents:* Artists/Bands

*Genres:* Folk; Indie; Rock; Singer-Songwriter

*Contact:* Dan Russell

Management company based in Newburyport, Massachusetts.

## Opus 3 Artists
470 Park Avenue South
9th Floor North
New York, NY 10016

LA OFFICE:

5670 Wilshire Blvd,
Suite 1800
Los Angeles, CA 90036
T: 323.954.1776
*Email:* info@opus3artists.com
*Website:* http://www.opus3artists.com

*Represents:* Artists/Bands

*Genres:* Classical; Jazz

Represents classical and jazz performing artists. Offices in New York and Los Angeles. No unsolicited submissions.

## Ozark Talent
718 Schwarz Rd
Lawrence, KS 66049
*Email:* ozarktalent@gmail.com
*Website:* https://www.facebook.com/pages/
Ozark-Talent/833757923407465

*Represents:* Artists/Bands

*Genres:* All types of music

*Contact:* Steve Ozark

Management company based in Lawrence,
Kansas.

## Pacific Talent
*Email:* andy@pacifictalent.com
*Website:* http://www.pacifictalent.com
*Website:* https://www.instagram.com/
pacifictalentpdx/

*Represents:* Artists/Bands

*Genres:* All types of music

*Contact:* Andy Gilbert

Management company based in Oregon.

## Paradigm Talent Agency
8942 Wilshire Boulevard
Beverly Hills, CA 90211
*Fax:* +1 (310) 288-2000
*Website:* https://www.paradigmagency.com

*Represents:* Artists/Bands

*Genres:* All types of music

Talent agency with offices in Los Angeles,
New York, Monterey, Nashville, San Diego,
Austin, London, Berkeley, Chicago, and
Toronto.

## Paradise Artists
108 E Matilija St.
Ojai, CA 93023

5 Penn Plaza #2382
New York, NY 10001
*Email:* info@paradiseartists.com
*Email:* howie@paradiseartists.com
*Website:* http://www.paradiseartists.com

*Represents:* Artists/Bands

*Genres:* Rock; Rock and Roll; Pop

*Contact:* Howie Silverman; Bill Monot

Management company with offices in New
York and California.

## Persistent Management
Los Angeles, CA
*Email:* pm@persistentmanagement.com
*Website:* https://www.
persistentmanagement.com
*Website:* https://soundcloud.com/
persistentmanagement

*Represents:* Artists/Bands

*Genres:* All types of music

*Contact:* Eric Knight

Management company based in Los
Angeles. Submit your details through online
Artist Submissions form, including links to
music online. No postal submissions or
phone calls.

## Piedmont Talent
*Email:* info@piedmonttalent.com
*Website:* http://piedmonttalent.com
*Website:* https://www.facebook.com/
PiedmontTalent/?ref=br_rs

*Represents:* Artists/Bands

*Genres:* Blues; Roots; Soul

Talent agency with offices in Los Angeles,
New York, and Palm Beach, Florida.

## Position Music
P.O. Box 25907
Los Angeles, CA 90025
*Email:* management@positionmusic.com
*Email:* contact@positionmusic.com
*Website:* https://www.positionmusic.com
*Website:* https://soundcloud.com/
position_music

*Represents:* Artists/Bands; Film / TV
Composers

*Genres:* Rap; Hip-Hop; Rock; Alternative;
Dance; Electronic; Hardcore; Metal; Pop;
R&B; Singer-Songwriter; Urban; World

Send web links or elecronic press kits by email. Do not chase by phone. Follow up by email only.

## PRA [Patrick Rains & Associates]

*Email:* pra@prarecords.com
*Website:* https://www.prarecords.com
*Website:* https://twitter.com/prarecords

*Represents:* Artists/Bands

*Genres:* Jazz; Pop; Rock

*Contact:* Patrick Rains; Stephanie Pappas

Management company based in New York. No unsolicited material.

## Pretty Lights

*Email:* contact@prettylightsmusic.com
*Website:* http://prettylightsmusic.com
*Website:* https://soundcloud.com/prettylights

*Represents:* Artists/Bands

*Genres:* All types of music

Submit demos using online form, available via website.

## Prodigal Son Entertainment

Brentwood, TN
*Email:* prodigalsonent@gmail.com
*Website:* https://www.prodigalson-entertainment.com
*Website:* http://www.myspace.com/prodigalsonentertainment

*Represents:* Artists/Bands

*Genres:* Alternative; Country; Christian; Instrumental; Rock; Hard Rock

*Contact:* Scott Williams

Artist management and career consultancy services.

## Progressive Global Agency (PGA)

PO Box 50294
Nashville, TN 37205
*Fax:* +1 (615) 354-9101

*Email:* info@pgamusic.com
*Website:* http://www.pgamusic.com

*Represents:* Artists/Bands

*Genres:* Pop; Rock; World

*Contact:* Buck Williams

Management company based in Nashville, Tennessee.

## Purple Rhino Music

*Email:* contact@purplerhinomusic.com
*Website:* http://www.purplerhinomusic.com

*Represents:* Artists/Bands; Lyricists; Producers; Studio Musicians

*Genres:* Acoustic Alternative Celtic Contemporary Commercial Electronic Experimental Extreme Funky Hard Glam Heavy Horror Industrial Mainstream Modern Melodic New Wave Power Post Progressive Soulful Thrash Tribal Twisted Underground Urban Black Metal Americana Black Origin Blue Beat Chill Classical Club Country Dance Deep Funk Emo Ethnic Fusion Funk Garage Gothic Grime Grind Guitar based Hardcore Hip-Hop Indie Instrumental Jazz Metal Melodicore Noise Core Nostalgia Pop Psychebilly Punk R&B Ragga Rap Reggae Reggaeton Rock Rock and Roll Rockabilly Roots Rhythm and Blues Singer-Songwriter Ska Soundtracks Spoken Word Swing Surf Synthpop Techno Trip Hop World

An international music management and promotions company. We currently operate in Houston, TX, London and Dublin.

We began operations in 2000 and represent a number of artists from numerous different genres.

If you are interested in our services, please feel free to visit our website or contact us directly.

## Pyramid Entertainment Group

377 Rector Place
, Suite 21A
New York, NY 10280
*Fax:* +1 (212) 242-6932
*Email:* smichaels@pyramid-ent.com
*Website:* https://pyramid-ent.com

*Represents:* Artists/Bands

*Genres:* Gospel; Jazz; Funk; Hip-Hop; R&B; Urban

*Contact:* Sal Michaels

Management company based in New York.

## Q Prime Management, Inc.
*Fax:* +1 (212) 302-9589
*Email:* newyork@qprime.com
*Email:* nashville@qprime.com
*Website:* http://www.qprime.com

*Represents:* Artists/Bands; Producers

*Genres:* Blues; Folk; Metal; Pop; Rock; Alternative; Singer-Songwriter

Management company with offices in New York, Los Angeles, Nashville and London. Not accepting unsolicited materials or demos as at December 2019.

## Rainmaker Artists
PO Box 342229
Austin, TX 78734
*Fax:* +1 (512) 843-7500
*Email:* paul@rainmakerartists.com
*Website:* http://www.rainmakerartists.com
*Website:* https://www.facebook.com/rainmaker.artists

*Represents:* Artists/Bands

*Genres:* Pop; Rock

Management company based in Austin, Texas. Accepts unsolicited material.

## Red Entertainment Agency
505 8th Avenue Suite 1004
New York, NY 10018
*Fax:* +1 (212) 563-9393
*Email:* info@redentertainment.com
*Email:* carloskeyes@redentertainment.com
*Website:* http://www.redentertainment.com
*Website:* https://www.facebook.com/RedEntertainmentAgencyGroup

*Represents:* Artists/Bands

*Genres:* Funk; Jazz; Gospel; Latin; Hip-Hop; Pop; Rock; R&B; Urban

*Contact:* Carlos Keyes

Since its founding in 2002, has established itself as a leading entertainment talent agency, guiding the careers of an elite roster of musical artists. Under the leadership of agency President, has carved out a distinctive niche in the entertainment landscape and earned a reputation for putting artists' interests above all else. With a select group of professional agents working side by side, the agency credo is one of team work and availability that translates into successful relationships for all clients.

The select yet diverse client list allows it to effectively compete with other large agencies while guaranteeing personalized attention to every client. With offices in New York City, provides representation to clients across its music, motion picture, television and personal appearances worldwide.

## Red Light Management (RLM)
Charlottesville; New York; Nashville; Los Angeles; Atlanta; Seattle
*Email:* info@redlightmanagement.com
*Website:* https://www.redlightmanagement.com
*Website:* http://twitter.com/redlightmgmt

*Represents:* Artists/Bands; Film / TV Composers; Songwriters; Studio Musicians

*Genres:* Blues; Christian; Country; Dance; Electronic; Hardcore; Indie; Latin; Metal; Pop; Rap; Hip-Hop; Rock; Singer-Songwriter; World

Management company with offices in Charlottesville, New York, Nashville, Los Angeles, London, Bristol, Atlanta, and Seattle.

## Regime Seventy-Two
Malibu, CA
*Email:* info@regimeinc.com
*Website:* http://www.regime72.com

*Represents:* Artists/Bands

*Genres:* All types of music

Management company based in Malibu, California, that is home to a wide variety of artists including musicians and actors.

## Richard Varrasso Management

Copperopolis, CA
*Email:* richard@varrasso.com
*Website:* https://www.varrasso.com
*Website:* https://www.facebook.com/
richardvarrasso

*Represents:* Artists/Bands; Comedians; DJs;
Other Entertainers; Producers; Songwriters;
Studio Musicians

*Genres:* All types of music

*Contact:* Richard Varrasso

Management company based in
Copperopolis, California. Old school turned
digital business leader with a proven track
record of driving results. Skilled in the
development and launch of new ventures.
Highly regarded for ability to problem-solve
and execute in complex, fast-moving
environments, consistently exceeding
operating plans.

## Riot Artists

*Email:* staff@riotartists.com
*Website:* http://www.riotartists.com
*Website:* https://www.facebook.com/
RiotArtists

*Represents:* Artists/Bands

*Genres:* World; Traditional; Contemporary

Management company specialising in World
music reflecting traditional culture, and
incorporating contemporary sounds to
varying degrees. Books artists from around
the world, with an emphasis on Canada, the
US, Mexico, Brazil, and Europe.

## Riot Squad

*Email:* main@riotsquad.com
*Website:* http://riotsquad.com/

*Represents:* Artists/Bands

*Genres:* All types of music

An artist management company.

## Ron Rainey Management Inc.

8500 Wilshire Boulevard, Suite 525
Beverly Hills, CA 90211
*Fax:* +1 (310) 557-8421
*Email:* rrmgmt@aol.com
*Website:* http://www.ronrainey.com

*Represents:* Artists/Bands

*Genres:* Contemporary; Blues; Pop;
Country; Rock

*Contact:* Ron Rainey; Greg Lewerke

Management company based in Beverly
Hills, California.

## Rosen Music Corp.

*Email:* rosenmusiccorp@me.com
*Website:* http://www.rosenmusiccorp.com
*Website:* https://www.facebook.com/steven.
rosen.969

*Represents:* Artists/Bands; DJs; Lyricists;
Producers; Songwriters

*Genres:* All types of music

*Contact:* Steven Rosen

Consulting company based in Palisades,
California.

## RPM Music Productions

420 West 14th Street, Suite 6NW
New York, NY 10014
*Email:* info@rpm-productions.com
*Website:* http://rpm-productions.com

*Represents:* Artists/Bands

*Genres:* Jazz; Pop

*Contact:* Danny Bennett

Management company based in New York.

## Russell Carter Artist Management

567 Ralph McGill Boulevard, NE
Atlanta, GA 30312
*Email:* russell.rcam@gmail.com
*Website:* https://www.facebook.com/pages/
Russell-Carter-Artist-Management/
174050332290?pnref=about.overview

*Website:* https://twitter.com/RCAM_mgnt
*Website:* https://myspace.com/rcam

*Represents:* Artists/Bands

*Genres:* Contemporary; Alternative;
Americana; Blues; Folk; Indie; Jazz; Singer-
Songwriter; Pop; Rock

*Contact:* Russell Carter

Management company based in Atlanta,
Georgia.

## Selak Entertainment, Inc.
466 Foothill Blvd. #184
La Canada, CA 91011
*Fax:* +1 (626)584-8122
*Email:* steve@selakentertainment.com
*Website:* https://selakentertainment.com

*Represents:* Artists/Bands; Comedians;
Tribute Acts

*Genres:* All types of music

Management company based in La Canada,
California. Not accepting any original
material.

## September Management (US)
New York / Los Angeles
*Email:* info@septembermanagement.com
*Website:* https://septembermanagement.com

*Represents:* Artists/Bands; Producers; Sound
Engineers

*Genres:* All types of music

Represents a roster of internationally
renowned recording artists, producers and
mix engineers who have collectively
amassed 44 Grammys, 12 Brit Awards, 2
Oscars, 2 Golden Globes and sold over 100
million albums worldwide. The company has
offices in London, New York and Los
Angeles.

## Sharpe Entertainment Services, Inc.
683 Palmera Avenue
Pacific Palisades, CA 90272
*Fax:* +1 (310) 230-2109
*Email:* frances@ses-la.com
*Website:* http://www.ses-la.com/SES

*Represents:* Artists/Bands; Film / TV
Composers; Producers; Songwriters;
Supervisors

*Genres:* Contemporary; Indie; Pop; Rock;
Alternative; Singer-Songwriter

*Contact:* Wil Sharpe

Management company based in Pacific
Palisades, California. Not accepting
unsolicited material as at January 2020.

## Siren Music Company
PO Box 12110
Portland, OR 97212-0110
*Fax:* +1 (503) 238-4771
*Email:* december@sirenmusiccompany.com
*Website:* http://www.
sirenmusiccompany.com

*Represents:* Artists/Bands

*Genres:* Americana; Roots; Folk; Country;
Alternative; Pop; Regional; Singer-
Songwriter; Blues

*Contact:* December Carson

Management company based in Portland,
Oregon. Not accepting submissions as a
January 2020 due to workload. Check
website for current status.

## SKH Music
540 President Street
Brooklyn, NY 11215
*Email:* skaras@skhmusic.com
*Email:* khagan@skhmusic.com
*Website:* http://www.skhmusic.com
*Website:* https://twitter.com/skhmusic

*Represents:* Artists/Bands; Lyricists;
Producers

*Genres:* All types of music

*Contact:* Steve Karas; Keith Hagan

Management company formed in June 2009,
based in Brooklyn, New York.

## SMC Artists
1525 Aviation Boulevard, Suite 1000
Redondo Beach, CA 90278-2805

*Email:* ovavrin@smcartists.com
*Website:* https://www.smcartists.com

*Represents:* Film / TV Composers;
Songwriters

*Genres:* All types of music

Management company representing film and
TV composers and songwriters.

## So What Media & Management
890 West End Avenue, #1A
New York, NY 10025
*Fax:* +1 (212) 877-9735
*Email:* sowhatasst@me.com

*Represents:* Artists/Bands

*Genres:* Pop; Rock

*Contact:* Lisa Barbaris

Management company representing musical
artists in the areas of pop and rock.

## Solid Music Company
*Email:* david@solidmusic.net
*Website:* http://www.solidmusic.net

*Represents:* Artists/Bands; DJs; Film / TV
Composers; Lyricists; Producers;
Songwriters; Sound Engineers; Studio
Musicians; Studio Technicians

*Genres:* All types of music

*Contact:* David Surnow

A management company for artist, record
producers, song writers, engineers, mixers
and composers. We are located in Los
Angeles and have been in business since
1990.

## Soundtrack Music Associates (SMA)
4133 Redwood Avenue, Suite 3030
Los Angeles, CA 90066
*Email:* INFO@SOUNDTRK.com
*Website:* http://soundtrk.com

*Represents:* Film / TV Composers;
Supervisors

*Genres:* Soundtracks

*Contact:* John Tempereau; Koyo Sonae;
Isabel Pappani

Represents award-winning composers, music
supervisors and music editors for film,
television and all media.

## Sparks Entertainment Management Co.
PO Box 82510
Tampa, FL 33682
*Email:* sparksentertainment78@gmail.com
*Website:* http://bsparksent.com
*Website:* https://www.facebook.com/
BSparksEntertainment
*Website:* https://myspace.com/ballnfresh

*Represents:* Artists/Bands

*Genres:* All types of music

*Contact:* Brian Sparks

Management company based in Tampa,
Florida.

## Spectrum Talent Agency
*Email:* chris@spectrumtalentagency.com
*Email:* jan@spectrumtalentagency.com
*Website:* http://spectrumtalentagency.com

*Represents:* Artists/Bands

*Genres:* Dance; Hip-Hop; Pop; R&B; House

Full service global booking agency.

## Spot Light Entertainment, Inc.
PO Box 1949
Lawrenceville, GA 30046
*Email:* info@spotlightentertainment.com
*Website:* http://www.
spotlightentertainment.com

*Represents:* Artists/Bands; Comedians;
Producers; Songwriters

*Genres:* Contemporary; Gospel; Hip-Hop;
Pop; R&B; Rap

Management company based in
Lawrenceville, Georgia.

## Starkravin' Management
McLane & Wong
11135 Weddington Street, Suite #424
North Hollywood, CA 91601
*Fax:* +1 (818) 587-6802
*Email:* bcmclane@aol.com
*Website:* http://www.benmclane.com

*Represents:* Artists/Bands; Producers;
Songwriters

*Genres:* Pop; R&B; Rock

*Contact:* Ben McLane

Management and entertainment law
company based in North Hollywood.
Provides personal management and legal
services.

## Sterling Artist Management
11054 Ventura Boulevard, #285
Studio City, California 91604
*Email:* mark@sterlingartist.com
*Website:* http://www.sterlingartist.com

*Represents:* Artists/Bands; Producers;
Songwriters; Studio Musicians

*Genres:* Blues; Jazz; Singer-Songwriter

*Contact:* Mark Sterling

Do not send demos without first making a
written enquiry. Represents singer-
songwriters, blues and jazz artists. If you do
not fall into one of these categories, please
don't consider contacting us.

## Steve Stewart Entertainment
12400 Ventura Boulevard #900
Studio City, CA 91604
*Email:* stevestewart@stevestewart.com
*Website:* https://www.stevestewart.com

*Represents:* Artists/Bands; Film / TV
Composers; Producers

*Genres:* Pop; Rock; Alternative; Hardcore

*Contact:* Steve Stewart

Management company based in Studio City,
California. Boasts more than 20 years of
experience and sales of more than 25 million
records worldwide.

## Steven Scharf Entertainment (SSE)
126 East 38th Street
New York, NY 10016
*Email:* SSCHARF@carlinamerica.com
*Website:* http://www.stevenscharf.com

*Represents:* Artists/Bands; Film / TV
Composers; Producers; Songwriters;
Supervisors

*Genres:* Alternative; Americana; Blues;
Folk; Indie; Jazz; Metal; Pop; Rap; Hip-Hop;
Rock; Roots; Singer-Songwriter; World;
Soundtracks

*Contact:* Steven Scharf

Management company based in New York.

## Stiefel Entertainment
21650 Oxnard St # 1925
Woodland Hills, CA 91364
*Email:* contact@StiefelEnt.com
*Website:* http://www.stiefelent.com
*Website:* https://www.linkedin.com/
company/stiefel-entertainment

*Represents:* Artists/Bands

*Genres:* Contemporary; Dance; Indie; Pop;
Rock; Singer-Songwriter

*Contact:* Arnold Stiefel

Management company based in Woodland
Hills, California.

## Street Smart Management
Los Angeles, CA
*Website:* https://www.facebook.com/
streetsmartmanagement

*Represents:* Artists/Bands

*Genres:* Indie; Rock; Metal; Pop

Management company based in Los
Angeles, California.

## Strike up the Brand
*Email:* bradgelfond@strike-up-the-brand.com
*Website:* https://www.strike-up-the-brand.com

*Website:* https://www.linkedin.com/in/
bradgelfond

*Represents:* Artists/Bands

*Genres:* Alternative

*Contact:* Brad Gelfond

Management company based in Los
Angeles, California.

## Suncoast Music Management
*Fax:* +1 (888) 727-1698
*Email:* suncoastbooking@aol.com
*Email:* suncoastoh@hotmail.com
*Website:* http://www.suncoastentertainment.
biz

*Represents:* Artists/Bands; Tribute Acts

*Genres:* Disco; Classic Rock; Rock

*Contact:* Al Spohn; Quinton Coontz; Andy
Bowman; Troy Tipton

Management company with offices in
Florida, Kentucky, Ohio, and Indiana,
specialising in tribute acts.

## TAC Music Management
9971 E. Ida Place
Greenwood Village, CO 80111
*Email:* traceyann75@hotmail.com
*Email:* tachirhart75@gmail.com
*Website:* http://tacmusicmanagement.com

*Represents:* Artists/Bands; Songwriters;
Studio Musicians; Tribute Acts

*Genres:* Acoustic; Classic; Hard;
Traditional; Regional; Soulful; Heavy;
Funky; Commercial; Alternative;
Americana; Blues; Country; Folk; Fusion;
Funk; Guitar based; Indie; Jazz; Metal;
R&B; Rock; Rock and Roll; Roots; Rhythm
and Blues; Singer-Songwriter; Rockabilly

*Contact:* Tracey Chirhart

Services include artist management,
booking, promotion and marketing to both
local and national artists. Genres include
blues, rock, Americana, bluegrass, folk,
country, and tributes.

## Take Out Management
1129 Maricopa Hwy
Ojai, CA 93023
*Email:* AlexTakeOutManagement@
gmail.com
*Email:* info@howiewood.com
*Website:* https://howiewood.com/take-out-
management/
*Website:* https://www.facebook.com/
HowardRosenPromotion/
*Website:* https://www.facebook.com/
HowardRosenPromotion/

*Represents:* Artists/Bands; Producers

*Genres:* All types of music

*Contact:* Howard Rosen; Scotty G.;
Samantha Schipman; Alex Louton

Management company based in Ojai,
California. Submit music using form on
website.

## Talent Source
The Mill at Nyack
15 North Mill Street
Nyack, NY 10960
*Fax:* +1 (845) 359-4609
*Email:* info@talentsourcemanagement.com
*Website:* http://www.
talentsourcemanagement.com

*Represents:* Artists/Bands; Variety Artists

*Genres:* All types of music

*Contact:* Margo Lewis; Faith Fusillo

Management company based in Nyack, New
York.

## Tenth Street Entertainment
6420 Wilshire Blvd. #950
Los Angeles, CA 90048

38 West 21st Street, Suite 300
New York, NY 10010
*Email:* info@10thst.com
*Website:* http://www.10thst.com

*Represents:* Artists/Bands; Producers

*Genres:* All types of music

International company with offices in LA,
London, and New York.

## That's Entertainment International Inc. (TEI Entertainment)

3820 E. La Palma Ave
Anaheim, CA 92807
*Email:* thomas@teientertainment.com
*Email:* jmcentee@teientertainment.com
*Website:* http://www.teientertainment.com

*Represents:* Artists/Bands

*Genres:* All types of music

*Contact:* John D. McEntee, President

Celebrity Entertainment Resource Company with offices in Anaheim and Sacramento, California, and Las Vegas, Nevada.

## Third Coast Talent

PO Box 334
Kingston Springs, TN 37082
*Fax:* +1 (615) 685-3332
*Email:* carrie@thirdcoasttalent.com
*Website:* https://www.thirdcoasttalent.com

*Represents:* Artists/Bands

*Genres:* Country

*Contact:* Carrie Moore-Reed

Management company based in Kingston Springs, Tennessee.

## Threee

918 North Western Avenue,Suite A
Los Angeles, CA 90029
*Fax:* +1 (213) 381-5115
*Email:* info@threee.com
*Website:* https://www.threee.com

*Represents:* Film / TV Composers; Producers; Songwriters

*Genres:* All types of music

Management company based in Los Angeles, California, representing producers, mixers, songwriters, and composers.

## TKO Artist Management

2303 21st Avenue South, 3rd Floor
Nashville, TN 37212
*Website:* http://www.
tkoartistmanagement.com
*Website:* https://www.facebook.com/
TKOArtistMgmt/

*Represents:* Artists/Bands

*Genres:* Country

Management company based in Nashville Tennessee.

## Tom Callahan & Associates (TCA)

*Email:* tc@tomcallahan.com
*Website:* https://www.tomcallahan.com
*Website:* https://www.facebook.com/
worldbudoartsboulder/

*Represents:* Artists/Bands

*Genres:* All types of music

Full service music consulting company based in Boulder, Colorado, offering record promotion, publicity, internet marketing, production, and more.

## Tony Margherita Management

*Email:* info@tmmchi.com
*Website:* http://tmmchi.com
*Website:* https://www.facebook.com/
tmmchimgmt

*Represents:* Artists/Bands

*Genres:* Jazz; Rock

*Contact:* Tony Margherita

Management company specialising in the exclusive worldwide representation of recording artists.

## Tower Management Group

106 Shirley Drive
Hendersonville, TN 37075
*Email:* rufuswendy@live.com
*Website:* http://www.castlerecords.com

*Represents:* Artists/Bands

*Genres:* Country; Rock; Blues

Management company based in Hendersonville, Tennessee. Send demo by post with code from website on front of package. No MP3 submissions by email.

## Tractor Beam Managing & Consulting

*Website:* http://www.tractor-beam.com

*Represents:* Artists/Bands

*Genres:* Folk; Indie; Jazz; Pop; Punk; Rock; Roots

*Contact:* Dan Efram

Long term client roster is full, so only currently offering career coaching and advice services.

## True Talent Entertainment

*Email:* TRUETALENTENTER@ GMAIL.com
*Website:* http://www.truetalententer.com
*Website:* https://www.youtube.com/channel/ UCXh-_1hDdqY1y92TorFfu7A

*Represents:* Artists/Bands; Film / TV Composers; Lyricists; Producers

*Genres:* R&B

Management, promotion, and production company. No unsolicited submissions.

## True Talent Management

9663 Santa Monica Boulevard, Suite 320, Dept. HMI
Beverly Hills, CA 90210
*Email:* ineedpr@truetalentpr.com
*Website:* https://www.truetalentpr.com

*Represents:* Artists/Bands; Producers; Songwriters; Supervisors

*Genres:* All types of music

*Contact:* Jennifer Yeko

PR company based in Beverly Hills, also offering various music services, including artist management.

## Tsunami Entertainment

Los Angeles / Las Vegas
*Email:* Info@tsunamient.com
*Website:* http://www.tsunamient.com

*Represents:* Artists/Bands; Producers

*Genres:* All types of music

*Contact:* Bruce Kirkland; Toni Young; Pip Moore

A creative and business solutions Company operating in the music, entertainment and media space, providing brand strategy, business development, marketing services, operational support systems and financial management.

## Tuscan Sun Music

Nashville, TN
*Email:* mgmt@angelica.org
*Website:* http://www.tuscansunmusic.com
*Website:* http://www.angelica.org

*Represents:* Artists/Bands

*Genres:* Ambient; New Age; Pop

Management company based in Nashville, Tennessee.

## Two Chord Touring

*Fax:* +1 (512) 416-7531
*Email:* davis@atomicmusicgroup.com
*Email:* davismclarty@gmail.com
*Website:* https://www.twochordtouring.com
*Website:* https://www.facebook.com/Two-Chord-Touring-138801512850466/

*Represents:* Artists/Bands

*Genres:* Country; Folk; Rockabilly

*Contact:* Davis McLarty; Todd Gardner; Lacey Johnson

Management company focusing on booking live events.

## Uncle Booking

5438 Winding Way Drive
Houston, TX 77091
*Email:* erik@unclebooking.com
*Website:* http://www.unclebooking.com

*Represents:* Artists/Bands

*Genres:* All types of music

Booking agency based in Texas.

## Union Entertainment Group
*Email:* info@ueginc.com
*Website:* http://www.ueginc.com

*Represents:* Artists/Bands

*Genres:* Rock; Alternative; Blues; Country;
Pop; Rap; Hip-Hop

Music management company.

## United Talent Agency
9336 Civic Center Drive
Beverly Hills, CA 90210
*Fax:* +1 (310) 385-1220

*Represents:* Artists/Bands

*Genres:* All types of music

International talent agency with offices in the
US, UK, and Sweden.

## Universal Attractions Agency
NEW YORK
15 West 36th Street, 8th Floor
New York, NY 10018

LOS ANGELES
22025 Ventura Boulevard, #305
Los Angeles, CA 91364

*Fax:* +1 (212) 333-4508 / +1 (646) 304-5178
*Email:* info@universalattractions.com
*Website:* http://universalattractions.com
*Website:* https://www.facebook.com/
UAAtalent/

*Represents:* Artists/Bands

*Genres:* All types of music

Talent agency with offices in New York and
Los Angeles.

## Universal Tone Management
PO Box 10348
San Rafael, CA 94912
*Email:* fanclub@santana.com
*Email:* merch@santana.com
*Website:* http://www.santana.com

*Represents:* Artists/Bands; Songwriters

*Genres:* Blues; Latin; Pop; Rock

Management company based in San Rafael,
California.

## Val's Artist Management (VAM)
*Email:* info@vamnation.com
*Website:* http://www.vamnation.com
*Website:* https://www.facebook.com/
VAMNation-Entertainment-
108496975907793/

*Represents:* Artists/Bands

*Genres:* Contemporary; Blues; Classical;
Country; Dance; Folk; Indie; Jazz; Latin;
Pop; Punk; R&B; Rap; Hip-Hop; Rock;
Roots; Urban; World

*Contact:* Valerie Wilson Morris

Selects artists who exhibit exceptional talent
while maintaining a defined individuality.

## Variety Artists International
1924 Spring Street
Paso Robles, CA 93446
*Fax:* +1 (805) 545-5559
*Email:* Bob@varietyart.com
*Email:* John@varietyart.com
*Website:* http://www.varietyart.com

*Represents:* Artists/Bands

*Genres:* Folk; Jazz; Pop; Rap; Rock

Management company providing tour
booking services.

## Vector Management
PO Box 120479
Nashville, TN 37212

276 Fifth Avenue, Suite 604
New York, NY 10001

LOS ANGELES
9350 Civic Center Drive
Beverly Hills, CA 90210
*Email:* info@vectormgmt.com
*Website:* http://www.vectormgmt.com

*Represents:* Artists/Bands; Songwriters

*Genres:* Contemporary; Alternative; Americana; Country; Folk; Gospel; Metal; Pop; Rock; Singer-Songwriter

Management company with offices in Nashville, New York, Los Angeles, and London.

## Velvet Hammer Music & Management Group
*Website:* https://velvethammer.net
*Website:* https://www.facebook.com/velvethammermusicandmanagementgroup
*Website:* http://myspace.com/velvethammermusic

*Represents:* Artists/Bands

*Genres:* All types of music

*Contact:* David Benveniste (Beno); Mark Wakefield; Taylor Brooks; Samantha Waterman; Kristin Van Trieste; Taryn Mazza; Samantha Surtida; Ravand Rustin; Susan Silver

Prides itself on identifying quality talent. Submit demos through online submission system.

## Walker Entertainment Group
PO Box 7926
Houston, TX 77270
*Email:* info@walkerentertainmentgroup.com
*Website:* http://www.walkerentertainmentgroup.com
*Website:* https://www.facebook.com/walkerentertainmentgrouptx/

*Represents:* Artists/Bands

*Genres:* All types of music

Global provider of event management, production, and entertainment services.

## Waxploitation
*Email:* artists@waxploitation.com
*Website:* http://www.waxploitation.com
*Website:* https://www.facebook.com/WaxploitationRecords/

*Represents:* Artists/Bands

*Genres:* Electronic; Indie; Hip-Hop; Rap; Reggae; Rock

Management company based in Los Angeles, California.

## Wolfson Entertainment, Inc.
2659 Townsgate Road, Suite 119
Westlake Village, CA 91361
*Email:* info@wolfsonent.com
*Website:* https://www.wolfsonent.com/
*Website:* https://www.facebook.com/wolfsonentinc

*Represents:* Artists/Bands

*Genres:* All types of music

*Contact:* Jonathan Wolfson

Management company based in Westlake Village, California.

## Worlds End Management
*Fax:* +1 (323) 965-1547
*Email:* info@worldsend.com
*Website:* https://worldsend.com
*Website:* https://www.facebook.com/WorldsEndMgmt/

*Represents:* Artists/Bands; Film / TV Composers; Producers; Songwriters; Sound Engineers; Studio Technicians; Supervisors

*Genres:* All types of music

*Contact:* Sandy Roberton

Management company founded in London in 1980, before moving to the US in 1985.

## Worldsound, LLC
17837 1st Ave South
Seattle, WA 98148
*Email:* Warren@WorldSound.com
*Email:* morgan@WorldSound.com
*Website:* https://www.worldsound.com
*Website:* https://www.facebook.com/worldsoundllc

*Represents:* Artists/Bands

*Genres:* Celtic; Folk; Pop; Rock; World; Rock and Roll

*Contact:* Warren Wyatt; Morgan Eattock

Management company founded in Southern California in 1992, now based in Seattle, Washington.

# UK Managers

*For the most up-to-date listings of these and hundreds of other managers, visit https://www.musicsocket.com/managers*

*To claim your **free** access to the site, please see the back of this book.*

## !K7
217 Chester House
Kennington Park
1-3 Brixton Road
London
SW9 6DE
*Email:* artist-mgmt@k7.com
*Website:* http://k7.com
*Website:* https://twitter.com/K7MusicHQ

*Represents:* Artists/Bands

*Genres:* All types of music

Represents a varied roster of artists from a wide range of genres.

## 0114 Records
Sheffield
*Email:* 0114records.submissions@gmail.com
*Website:* http://0114records.com

*Represents:* Artists/Bands

*Genres:* Alternative; Folk; Garage; Indie; Rock; Punk; Hard Rock; Reggae; Singer-Songwriter; Ska

Independent record label and artist management company based in Sheffield. Send query by email with links to music online. Must be over 18, live in the UK, and play original music.

## 360 Artist Development
42 Western Avenue
Birstall
WF17 0PF
*Email:* info@360artistdevelopment.com
*Website:* https://www.360artistdevelopment.com
*Website:* https://www.facebook.com/360artistdevelopment

*Represents:* Artists/Bands

*Genres:* All types of music

Management / consultancy company based in Wakefield. Submit demos via contact form on website.

## 4 Tunes Ltd
8 Whitehall Park Road
London
W4 3NE
*Fax:* +44 (0) 20 8442 7561
*Email:* andy@4-tunes.com
*Website:* http://4-tunes.com

*Represents:* Artists/Bands

*Genres:* All types of music

*Contact:* Andy Murray

Management company based in London.

## A&R Factory

*Email:* info@anrfactory.com
*Website:* https://www.anrfactory.com/
*Website:* https://www.facebook.com/
anrfactory

*Represents:* Artists/Bands

*Genres:* All types of music

Independent music blog that also offers an artist development program. Send demos through online submission form on website.

## A2E – Artists 2 Events

PO Box 64
Ammanford
Carmarthenshire
SA18 9AB
*Email:* mike@artists2events.co.uk
*Email:* rob@artists2events.co.uk
*Website:* http://www.artists2events.co.uk

*Represents:* Artists/Bands

*Genres:* Acoustic; Blues; Celtic

*Contact:* Mike / Rob

Management company based in Ammanford, Carmarthenshire.

## ADSRecords

*Email:* music@adsrecords.co.uk
*Email:* podcast@adsrecords.co.uk
*Website:* https://www.adsrecords.co.uk
*Website:* https://soundcloud.com/
adsrecordsuk

*Represents:* Artists/Bands

*Genres:* Acoustic; Alternative; Indie; Pop; Singer-Songwriter

*Contact:* Alex Dale-Staples

Artist management and composition services. To be considered for Artist Management send query by email, with "Artist Management" in the subject line, links to your music, and a 50-word description.

## AEC Music Management

*Email:* adrian@aecmusicmanagement.com
*Website:* http://www.

aecmusicmanagement.com
*Website:* https://facebook.com/
aecmusicmanagement

*Represents:* Artists/Bands

*Genres:* Singer-Songwriter; Pop; Rock; Folk

*Contact:* Adrian

Artist management, A&R consultancy and live showcase events. Send query by email with MP3 attachments or links to music online.

## AirMTM

Shepherds Building West
Rockley Road
Shepherds Bush
London
W14 0DA
*Email:* info@airmtm.com
*Website:* http://www.airmtm.com

*Represents:* Artists/Bands

*Genres:* All types of music

Management company based in Shepherd's Bush, London.

## AJM

*Email:* amijay@ajmofficial.co.uk
*Website:* https://www.ajmofficial.co.uk
*Website:* https://twitter.com/ajm_mgmt

*Represents:* Artists/Bands

*Genres:* Electronic; Pop

Send query by email with links to music online.

## Amber Artists

*Email:* management@amberartists.com
*Email:* info@amberartists.com
*Website:* http://www.amberartists.com

*Represents:* Artists/Bands

*Genres:* All types of music

Provides PR and management.

## Amour:Music
*Email:* info@amourmusic.co.uk
*Website:* https://amourmusic.co.uk
*Website:* https://soundcloud.com/amourmusicuk

*Represents:* Artists/Bands

*Genres:* Contemporary; Singer-Songwriter

*Contact:* James Brister

Send query by email with links to streaming music online. No attachments or download links.

## Aneko Music
Bournemouth / London
*Email:* ed@anekomusic.com
*Website:* http://anekomusic.com
*Website:* https://www.facebook.com/AnekoMusic

*Represents:* Artists/Bands

*Genres:* All types of music

*Contact:* Ed Hill

A Bournemouth and London based artist management company, record label and radio promotions agency. Send query by email with links to music online. Response not guaranteed unless interested.

## Anger Management
4-7 Forewoods Common
Holt
Wiltshire
BA14 6PJ
*Email:* george@anger-management.co
*Website:* https://www.anger-management.co
*Website:* https://www.facebook.com/AngerManagement100

*Represents:* Artists/Bands

*Genres:* All types of music

Provides artist and tour management services.

## Anglo Management
Unit 435, The Metal Box Factory
30 Great Guildford Street
London

SE1 0HS
*Email:* info@anglomanagement.co.uk
*Website:* http://www.anglomanagement.co.uk

*Represents:* Artists/Bands

*Genres:* All types of music

Management company based in London. Send demo by post or by email.

## The Animal Farm
4th Floor, Block A
The Biscuit Factory
100 Clements Road
London
SE16 4DG
*Email:* info@theanimalfarm.co.uk
*Website:* http://www.theanimalfarm.co.uk
*Website:* https://www.facebook.com/theanimalfarmmusic

*Represents:* Artists/Bands

*Genres:* All types of music

Send query by email giving link to Facebook or other website where you can be seen and your music heard. Include reason for approach. No MP3 attachments by email. Do not expect feedback.

## Arlon Music
*Email:* info@arlonmusic.com
*Website:* http://www.arlonmusic.com

*Represents:* Artists/Bands

*Genres:* Alternative; Pop; Singer-Songwriter

*Contact:* Jamie Arlon

Management company based in London, including publishing company and independent record label. Send query by email with links to music online. No MP3s.

## Askonas Holt Ltd
15 Fetter Lane
London
EC4A 1BW
*Fax:* +44 (0) 20 7400 1799
*Email:* info@askonasholt.co.uk
*Website:* https://www.askonasholt.com

*Website:* https://www.facebook.com/askonasholt/

*Represents:* Artists/Bands

*Genres:* Classical

Formed in 1998 through an amalgamation of two long-established artist management companies, both based in London but with international connections.

## ASM Talent
4th Floor, 63/66 Hatton Garden
London
EC1N 8LE
*Email:* albert@missioncontrol.net
*Email:* albert@asmtalent.co.uk
*Website:* https://asmanagement.co.uk

*Represents:* Artists/Bands

*Genres:* All types of music

*Contact:* David Samuel; Jason Samuel; Albert Samuel

Management company with music and TV and press departments. Clients have appeared on numerous high profile TV entertainment shows. Send query by email with links to music online.

## Aspire Music Management
*Email:* mel@aspiremusicmanagement.co.uk
*Website:* http://www.aspiremusicmanagement.co.uk
*Website:* https://www.facebook.com/AspireMusicManagement.co.uk/

*Represents:* Artists/Bands; Songwriters

*Genres:* Melodic Rock; Pop Rock; Acoustic

*Contact:* Melanie Perrett

Management company based in northern England, representing unsigned and indie artists and songwriters. Handles a wide range of genres, but particularly interested in Melodic Rock, Pop Rock, and Acoustic. Will consider other genres, however.

## Associated London Management
London
*Email:* martin@associatedlondonmanagement.com
*Email:* jason@associatedlondonmanagement.com
*Website:* http://www.associatedlondonmanagement.com
*Website:* https://facebook.com/ALMgmt

*Represents:* Artists/Bands

*Genres:* Alternative

Management company based in London. Send demos as MP3 attachments by email.

## ATC Management
The Hat Factory
166-168 Camden Street
London
NW1 9PT, UK
*Email:* info@atcmanagement.com
*Website:* http://www.atcmanagement.com
*Website:* https://www.facebook.com/atcmanagement/

*Represents:* Artists/Bands

*Genres:* All types of music

London based management company willing to consider artists in all genres. Send demo via website.

## Atomic
Albert House
256-260 Old Street
EC1V 9DD
*Email:* info@atomic-london.com
*Website:* http://www.atomic-london.com

*Represents:* Artists/Bands

*Genres:* All types of music

*Contact:* Mick Newton; Ben Newton

Management company based in London with over 20 years of experience. Send demo by post or by email as MP3s or links to music online.

## Atum Management Ltd
*Email:* info@atummanagement.com
*Website:* http://www.atummanagement.com
*Website:* https://soundcloud.com/
atummanagement

*Represents:* Artists/Bands

*Genres:* All types of music

Management company based in London.
Send demos by email.

## Audio Bay Management
Bristol
*Email:* jon@audiobaymanagement.com
*Website:* http://audiobaymanagement.com

*Represents:* Artists/Bands

*Genres:* Acoustic; Classical; Electronic;
Folk; Indie; Pop

Music company offering management, sync
and licensing, and consultancy. Send query
by email with links to music online.

## Autonomy Music Group
6a Tileyard Studios
London
N7 9AH
*Email:* hi@autonomymusicgroup.com
*Website:* http://autonomymusicgroup.com
*Website:* http://autonomymusicgroup.com

*Represents:* Artists/Bands; DJs; Producers

*Genres:* All types of music

Provides bespoke artist and campaign
services to artists, bands, producers, record
labels and DJs. Send query via online form
on website.

## Avenoir
40 Hawkes Way
Maidstone
Kent
ME15 9ZL
*Email:* enquiries@avenoirrecords.com
*Website:* https://avenoirrecords.com
*Website:* https://twitter.com/AvenoirOfficial

*Represents:* Artists/Bands

*Genres:* All types of music

Artist management and consultancy firm
based in Maidstone, Kent. Send query via
form on website.

## B&H Management
PO Box 1162
Bovingdon
Hertfordshire
HP1 9DE
*Email:* simon@bandhmanagement.
demon.co.uk
*Website:* http://www.sessionmusicians.co.uk

*Represents:* Artists/Bands

*Genres:* Commercial; Pop; Urban

*Contact:* Simon Harrison

Seeks pop and urban material with
commercial potential. Send query by email
with CV, MP3, and link to your website.

## B.H. Hopper Management Ltd.
Shepherds Building – Unit G7
Rockley Road
London
W14 0DA
*Email:* hopper@hopper-management.com
*Website:* http://www.
hoppermanagement.com

*Represents:* Artists/Bands

*Genres:* Jazz

Management company based in London
handling Jazz artists only. Send demo by
post.

## Bandzmedia
*Email:* into@bandzmedia.com
*Website:* http://www.bandzmedia.com
*Website:* https://www.facebook.com/
Bandzmedia

*Represents:* Artists/Bands

*Genres:* Acoustic; Pop; Rock; Soul; R&B

*Contact:* Jude Bumby

Management company based in York. Send
introductory email with brief bio and link to
your music online in first instance. No MP3s.

No hip hop/rap/garage, thrash/death metal, or techno.

## Bear Music Management
Hampshire
*Email:* info@bearmusicmanagement.co.uk
*Website:* https://www.
bearmusicmanagement.co.uk
*Website:* https://www.facebook.com/
bearmusicmanagementuk/

*Represents:* Artists/Bands

*Genres:* Indie; Pop; Rock

Management company based in Hampshire.
Send query by email or through contact form
on website with bio and links to music
online.

## Bernie Nelson Artist Management
*Email:* bernnelson@yahoo.com
*Website:* https://www.twitter.com/
iambernienelson
*Website:* https://www.instagram.com/
bernie85/

*Represents:* Artists/Bands

*Genres:* Folk; Indie; Singer-Songwriter

Send query by email with links to music
online.

## Big Bear Music
PO BOX 944
EDGBASTON
BIRMINGHAM
B16 8UT
*Email:* admin@bigbearmusic.com
*Website:* http://www.bigbearmusic.com
*Website:* http://www.
birminghamjazzfestival.com

*Represents:* Artists/Bands

*Genres:* Blues; Jazz; Swing

*Contact:* Jim Simpson

Represents and tours jazz, blue and swing
attractions of the highest quality, mostly
those signed to the Record label. We also
oranise events and jazz festivals, including a
midlands jazz festival established in 1985.

Send query by email with MP3s, links, bio
and photo.

## Big Dipper Productions Ltd
41 Finsbury Park Road
London
N4 2JY
*Email:* contact@wearebigdipper.com
*Website:* http://www.wearebigdipper.com

*Represents:* Artists/Bands

*Genres:* Indie; Pop; Rock

Management company based in London.
Send query by email with links to music
online.

## Big Hug Management
*Email:* jeff@bighugmanagement.com
*Website:* http://www.
bighugmanagement.com
*Website:* https://www.facebook.com/
bighugmanagement

*Represents:* Artists/Bands

*Genres:* All types of music

*Contact:* Jeff Powell

Send query by email with links to music
online.

## Big Life Management
67-69 Chalton Street
London
NW1 1HY
*Email:* reception@biglifemanagement.com
*Website:* http://www.
biglifemanagement.com

*Represents:* Artists/Bands; Producers

*Genres:* All types of music

Management company based in London,
representing bands, solo artists, and
producers. Send query by email with links to
music online.

## BiGiAM Promotions & Management
Brighton
*Email:* info@bigiam.co.uk

---

*Website:* http://bigiam.co.uk
*Website:* http://www.facebook.com/
bigiammusic

*Represents:* Artists/Bands

*Genres:* All types of music

*Contact:* Alison Hildyard; Mark Ede;
Roderick Udo

We promote, advise and manage businesses,
events and personal creativity linked to
music and the arts. Our portfolio is relatively
wide and relatively varied; we play a
significant role in the development, project
management, marketing/promotions and
sponsorship of a number of Brighton area
based events.

If you think we can help your
company/band/event etc, please approach us
for a no obligation chat; we may well be less
expensive than you think. Our aim is to
provide unrivalled value and excellence in
everything we do.

## BK40 Productions
*Email:* info@bk40.com
*Website:* http://bk40.com
*Website:* https://www.facebook.com/BK40-
Productions-119627332567/

*Represents:* Artists/Bands

*Genres:* All types of music

Security, tour, event, and artist management
company based in London. Manages
established artists and specialises in
developing unsigned acts. Send MP3s by
email.

## Black Bleach Records
Manchester
*Email:* blackbleachrecords@gmail.com
*Website:* http://blackbleachrecords.com
*Website:* https://www.facebook.com/
blackbleachrecords

*Represents:* Artists/Bands

*Genres:* Alternative; Electronic; Garage;
Indie; Pop; Post Punk; Psychedelic Rock;
Punk; Punk Rock; Shoegaze

Record label based in Manchester. Send
query by email with links to music online.

## Black Fox Management
1 Blythe Road
London
W14 0HG
*Email:* generalenquiries@
blackfoxmanagement.com
*Website:* http://blackfoxmanagement.com
*Website:* https://twitter.com/pollyrocker5

*Represents:* Artists/Bands

*Genres:* All types of music

*Contact:* Polly Comber; Josh Smith

Management company based in London.
Send demos by email.

## Blue Raincoat Music
Unit G2
1 Leonard Circus
64 Paul Street
EC2A 4DQ
*Email:* info@blueraincoatmusic.com
*Email:* artists@blueraincoatmusic.com
*Website:* https://www.
blueraincoatmusic.com
*Website:* https://soundcloud.com/
WeAreBRM

*Represents:* Artists/Bands

*Genres:* All types of music

Management company based in London.
Send demos by email.

## Blue Shell Music
Derry
*Email:* jonny@blueshellmusic.com
*Website:* https://www.facebook.com/
BlueShellMusicManagement

*Represents:* Artists/Bands

*Genres:* Pop

Management company based in Derry,
Northern Ireland.

## Bold Management
85 Bold Street
Liverpool
L1 4HF
*Fax:* +44 (0) 1517 091895
*Email:* martin@bold-management.com
*Website:* http://www.bold-management.com
*Website:* https://www.facebook.com/boldmanagement

*Represents:* Artists/Bands; Producers; Songwriters

*Genres:* Pop; Rock; Indie

*Contact:* Martin O'Shea

Management company based in Liverpool. Send demo with bio and photos by email only.

## BORDR
One Central Square
Cardiff
*Email:* bordrmanagement@gmail.com
*Website:* https://www.bordrmanagement.com
*Website:* https://www.facebook.com/bordrmanagement/

*Represents:* Artists/Bands

*Genres:* All types of music

Management company based in Cardiff. Send query by email with MP3s or links to music online.

## Brian Yeates Associates Ltd
*Website:* http://www.brianyeates.co.uk
*Website:* https://www.facebook.com/yeatesentertainment

*Represents:* Artists/Bands; Comedians; DJs; Tribute Acts

*Genres:* All types of music

*Contact:* Ashley Yeates

Management company based in Sutton Coldfield in the West Midlands, with 30 years experience representing a variety of acts.

## Brighthelmstone Promotions
*Email:* brighthelmstonepromotions@gmail.com
*Email:* james@brighthelmstonepromotions.co.uk
*Website:* http://www.brighthelmstonepromotions.co.uk
*Website:* https://www.facebook.com/brighthelmstonepromotions/

*Represents:* Artists/Bands

*Genres:* Americana; Folk; Indie

Management company based in Brighton, specialising in Americana and Roots.

## BUT! Management
BUT! Music Group
Walsingham Cottage
7 Sussex Square
Brighton
BN2 1FJ
*Email:* jamesie@butgroup.com
*Email:* sue@butgroup.com
*Website:* http://www.butgroup.com
*Website:* https://www.facebook.com/The-BUT-Music-Group-1596947130561446/

*Represents:* Artists/Bands; Producers; Songwriters

*Genres:* Alternative; Pop; Rock; Singer-Songwriter

*Contact:* Allan James; Sue Flood

Management, label, and publishing company based in Brighton. Founded to promote and develop new UK talent both domestically and internationally. Has a policy of listening to and providing feedback on anything received. Send demos by post.

## Catalyst Management
*Website:* http://catalyst-music.com
*Website:* https://www.facebook.com/officalcatalystmanagment/

*Represents:* Artists/Bands; Producers

*Genres:* All types of music

Management and marketing for UK artists aiming for mainstream success.

## Chicken Grease Presents
Brighton
*Email:* lawrence@
chickengreasepresents.com
*Website:* https://www.
chickengreasepresents.com

*Represents:* Artists/Bands

*Genres:* Jazz; Hip-Hop; Soul

Artist development agency based in
Brighton. Send query by email with links to
music online or MP3 attachments.

## Claudia eRecords
Liverpool
*Email:* claudia@claudiaerecords.com
*Website:* https://www.claudiaerecords.com
*Website:* https://soundcloud.com/
claudiaerecords

*Represents:* Artists/Bands

*Genres:* Alternative; Indie; Pop; Rock;
Dance; Electronic; Hip-Hop; Rap; Soul

Management company with offices in
Liverpool, UK, and Brisbane, Australia.
Send demos via form on website.

## Closer Artists Management & Publishing
Matrix Complex
91 Peterborough Road
London
SW6 3BU
*Email:* info@closerartists.com
*Website:* http://www.closerartists.com
*Website:* https://soundcloud.com/closer-
artists

*Represents:* Artists/Bands

*Genres:* All types of music

*Contact:* Paul McDonald; Ryan Lofthouse

Management and publishing company based
in London. Send demos through Soundcloud.

## CMP Entertainment
Anchor Courtyard
Atlantic Pavilion
Albert Dock
Liverpool
L3 4AS
*Email:* info@cmpentertainment.com
*Website:* http://www.cmpentertainment.com
*Website:* https://www.facebook.com/
CMPEntertainment

*Represents:* Artists/Bands; Tribute Acts

*Genres:* All types of music

*Contact:* Chas Cole; Rob Stringer

Management company based in Liverpool.
Will consider all types of music, but works
mainly with pop acts. Send demos by post.

## Conchord
London
*Email:* cathy@conchordmanagement.com
*Website:* http://conchordmanagement.com
*Website:* https://twitter.com/conchordmgmt

*Represents:* Artists/Bands

*Genres:* All types of music

Management company based in London.

## Consolidated Artists
PO Box 87
Tarporley
CW6 9FN
*Fax:* +44 (0) 1829 730499
*Email:* alecconsol@aol.com
*Email:* ross@consolidatedartists.co.uk
*Website:* http://www.
consolidatedartists.co.uk

*Represents:* Artists/Bands

*Genres:* Pop; Rock

*Contact:* Alec Leslie

Management company based in Tarporley.
Send query by email with links to music
online.

## Covert Talent Management
*Email:* covertdemos@gmail.com
*Email:* simon@coverttalent.com
*Website:* http://www.coverttalent.com
*Website:* https://twitter.com/coverttalent

*Represents:* Artists/Bands; Producers;
Songwriters

*Genres:* All types of music

*Contact:* Simon King

Career management company, focused on creative, strategic, and brand development. Send demos by email.

## Craft Management
*Email:* enquiries@craftmgmt.com
*Website:* http://www.craftmgmt.com

*Represents:* Artists/Bands; Producers

*Genres:* Alternative

Represents alternative artists and producers. Send submissions by email.

## Create Management
*Email:* kyd@createmanagement.com
*Email:* info@createmanagement.com
*Website:* http://www.createmanagement.com
*Website:* http://www.thecreategroup.co.uk

*Represents:* Artists/Bands; Producers

*Genres:* Commercial; Pop; Singer-Songwriter

Record label based in Godalming, Surrey. Send soundcloud links or MP3s by email.

## Creating Monsters
*Email:* matthew@creatingmonsters.com
*Email:* T@creatingmonsters.com
*Website:* http://www.creatingmonsters.com
*Website:* https://soundcloud.com/creating-monsters-ltd

*Represents:* Artists/Bands

*Genres:* All types of music

*Contact:* Matthew Haynes

Music production, management and artist development label. Send query by email with soundcloud links.

## Creative International Artist Management
*Email:* info@cruisin.co.uk
*Website:* http://www.cruisin.co.uk

*Represents:* Artists/Bands

*Genres:* Metal; Pop; Rock

Management company set in 250 acres of countryside on the Wiltshire/Somerset border.

## Creeme Entertainments
First Floor
293 Darwen Road
Bromley Cross
Bolton
BL7 9BT
*Email:* anthony@creeme.co.uk
*Website:* https://creeme.co.uk
*Website:* https://www.facebook.com/creemeentertainmentsltd

*Represents:* Artists/Bands; Comedians; Other Entertainers; Tribute Acts

*Genres:* All types of music

*Contact:* Anthony Ivers

Manages acts including music, tribute acts, lookalikes, comedians, after-dinner speakers, etc. for corporate events, and the pub and club circuits.

## Crockford Management
*Email:* info@crockfordmanagement.com
*Website:* http://www.crockfordmanagement.com
*Website:* https://www.facebook.com/crockfordmgmt/

*Represents:* Artists/Bands

*Genres:* All types of music

*Contact:* Paul Crockford

Manager with over 35 years of experience. His clients have sold over 250 million albums worldwide. Send submissions by email.

## Crosstalk Management
*Email:* hello@crosstalkmgmt.com

*Represents:* Artists/Bands

*Genres:* Guitar based

Send query by email with links to music online.

## Culture City

17 Mann Island
Liverpool
*Email:* info@culturecity.co.uk
*Website:* https://www.culturecity.co.uk
*Website:* https://www.facebook.com/
CultureCityTV/

*Represents:* Artists/Bands

*Genres:* All types of music

Artist management company based in
Liverpool. Send query by email with details
of your act and links to music online.

## Darren Adam

*Email:* darren.adam@lbc.co.uk
*Website:* http://www.darrenadam.com
*Website:* https://twitter.com/darrenadam

*Represents:* Artists/Bands

*Genres:* All types of music

Radio broadcaster, writer, voiceover artist,
and music manager.

## Dawson Breed Music

*Email:* debra@dawsonbreedmusic.com
*Website:* http://www.dawsonbreedmusic.com
*Website:* https://www.facebook.com/
Dawsonbreed
*Website:* https://myspace.com/dawson_breed

*Represents:* Artists/Bands

*Genres:* Americana; Folk; Indie; Pop;
Acoustic

*Contact:* Debra Downes

Music agency and management company.
Send email with links to music online.

## DEF (Deutsch Englische Freundschaft)

51 Lonsdale Road
Queen's Park
London
NW6 6RA
*Email:* info@d-e-f.com
*Website:* http://www.d-e-f.com
*Website:* https://www.facebook.com/
DEFallesistgut

*Represents:* Artists/Bands

*Genres:* Dance; Electronic

Concentrates on electronic dance, but willing
to consider all types of music. Send demo by
post or send email with links to music online.

## Defenders Ent

Industrial Estate
3A Juno Way, London
SE14 5RW
*Email:* music@defendersent.com
*Email:* info@defendersent.com
*Website:* https://www.defendersent.com

*Represents:* Artists/Bands

*Genres:* Dance; Reggae; R&B; Rap

Send demos by email only with links to
music online (no MP3 attachments).

## Deltasonic Records

Liverpool
*Email:* annheston@live.com
*Website:* http://deltasonicrecords.co.uk
*Website:* https://soundcloud.com/deltasonic-
records

*Represents:* Artists/Bands

*Genres:* All types of music

Management company based in Liverpool.
Send query via online form on website, with
soundcloud links.

## Deluxxe Management

*Email:* info@deluxxe.co.uk
*Website:* http://www.deluxxe.co.uk
*Website:* https://twitter.com/Delilah8888
*Website:* http://www.myspace.com/
deluxxemanagement

*Represents:* Artists/Bands

*Genres:* All types of music

*Contact:* Diane Wagg

Love to hear new music and listen to all
submissions, but no posted demos or emailed
MP3s. Send links to website or webpage
where you have three or four tracks to listen
to, and info about you and your live work.
Response not guaranteed if not interested.

## Denizen Artist Management
Antenna
Beck Street
Nottingham
NG1 1EQ
*Email:* kristi@denizen.uk.com
*Website:* http://denizen.uk.com
*Website:* https://www.twitter.com/
denizenartists

*Represents:* Artists/Bands

*Genres:* All types of music

Artist management arm of a music company
based in Nottingham, also running label and
publishing services. Send demo by email as
MP3 up to 10MB maximum with short bio
and links to any online content.

## Deuce Management & Promotion
*Email:* rob@deucemusic.com
*Website:* https://www.deucemusic.com
*Website:* https://www.facebook.com/
deucepr/

*Represents:* Artists/Bands

*Genres:* All types of music

*Contact:* Rob Saunders

Has established itself as one of the leading
companies to offer services to
unsigned/newly signed bands and artists
worldwide. With a growing reputation of
being at the forefront of the best new music
on the scene and with its idyllically placed
office in London, they aim to ensure bands
and artists are offered ways and means to get
their music heard to a wider audience.

For a FREE evaluation on your music please
send a link to your material by email.

## DFJ Artists
Studio 114
17 Amhurst Terrace
London
E8 2BT
*Email:* nikki@dfjartists.com
*Website:* http://www.dfjartists.com

*Represents:* Artists/Bands; Producers;
Songwriters

*Genres:* Jazz

Music management and consultancy services
across jazz and related music genres. Send
submissions by email.

## Disaster Artist Management
Walthamstow
London
*Email:* nick@
disasterartistmanagement.co.uk
*Email:* john.talbot@disasterartists.co.uk
*Website:* https://www.disasterartists.co.uk
*Website:* https://twitter.com/disasterarts

*Represents:* Artists/Bands

*Genres:* Indie; Pop; Rock

Management company based in
Walthamstow, London. Send submissions by
email.

## Discovering Arts Music Group (DAMG)
*Email:* discovering@damg.co.uk
*Website:* https://
discoveringartsmusicgroup.com
*Website:* https://www.facebook.com/
DAMGRECORDS

*Represents:* Artists/Bands

*Genres:* All types of music

A London-based company that believes in
business at the front and Music is at the
back, (whereby, we protect the artists and
their music). Providing a single home for
Artists, which is comprised of 8 core
businesses: *Record Company, *Publishing,
*Management, *Booking
*Studios/Production, *Events,
*Fashion/Merchandise, and *Distribution.
We promote, develop and support the visions
of our artists, nurturing their growth from
zero to hero. We are determined not to be
tied to one style or preconceived ideas, but
instead to embrace exceptional music from
across the spectrum.

Always on the lookout for new talents, so if
you have the talent and the confidence don't

hesitate to send your music through the online demo submission form on the website.

## Dissention Records + Artist Management

Wye Valley Barn
Brockweir Common
Chepstow
NP16 7NU
*Email:* matthew@dissentionrecords.com
*Email:* dissentionrecords@gmail.com
*Website:* https://www.dissentionrecords.com

*Represents:* Artists/Bands; Film / TV Composers; Other Entertainers

*Genres:* Alternative; Punk

*Contact:* Matthew Harris

Record label and artist management company originally founded in the States but now based in the UK. Send query by email with files or links to music online.

## DMF Music Ltd

51 Queen Street
Exeter
Devon
EX4 3SR
*Email:* info@dmfmusic.co.uk
*Website:* https://dmfmusic.co.uk
*Website:* https://www.facebook.com/
DMFMusicTeam

*Represents:* Artists/Bands

*Genres:* All types of music

*Contact:* David & Laura Farrow

Independent agency, artist management, promoter, and festival organiser based in Exeter. Send query by email with links to music online.

## Don't Try

Suffolk
*Email:* ben@donttryrecords.com
*Website:* https://www.donttrymusic.com
*Website:* https://www.facebook.com/
donttryuk

*Represents:* Artists/Bands; Producers

*Genres:* Alternative; Indie; Rock

Music company based in Suffolk, managing artists and producers.

## Dreamboat Management

*Email:* contact@dreamboatmanagement.com
*Email:* ben.baldwin@
dreamboatmanagement.com
*Website:* https://www.
dreamboatmanagement.com
*Website:* https://www.facebook.com/
dreamboatmanagement

*Represents:* Artists/Bands

*Genres:* Alternative; Indie

*Contact:* Ben Baldwin; Dean Christesen

International artist management company with staff in Bristol, UK, and Richmond, Virginia.

## Dusty Studio Productions

Brighton
*Email:* press@dustystudios.co.uk
*Email:* info@dustystudios.co.uk
*Website:* https://www.
dustystudioproductions.co.uk
*Website:* https://www.facebook.com/
DustyStudioProductions/

*Genres:* Electronic; Indie; Pop

Music Management, Blog and Events Company based in Brighton. Send query by email.

## East City

London
*Email:* demo@eastcitymanagement.com
*Website:* https://www.facebook.com/
eastcitymanagement
*Website:* https://twitter.com/eastcityMGMT

*Represents:* Artists/Bands

*Genres:* Alternative; Dance; Indie

Manager based in London. Send query by email with links to streaming music online.

## Electric Pineapple Music

Tileyard Studios
Tileyard Road
Kings Cross

London
N7 9AH
*Email:* info@electricpineapplemusic.co.uk
*Website:* http://www.
electricpineapplemusic.co.uk
*Website:* https://www.facebook.com/
ElectricPineappleClub

*Represents:* Artists/Bands

*Genres:* All types of music

Management company based in London.
Describes itself as "management with
morals". Send query by email with links to
your music online.

## Elephant Management
Manchester
*Email:* elephantmgmt@outlook.com
*Website:* https://elephantmanagement.
site123.me
*Website:* https://www.facebook.com/
elephantmanagement/

*Represents:* Artists/Bands

*Genres:* Alternative; Psychedelic Rock;
Shoegaze

Music management and promotion company
based in Manchester. Send query by email
with links to music online.

## End of the Trail Creative
*Email:* kelly@endofthetrailcreative.co.uk
*Website:* https://www.
endofthetrailcreative.co.uk

*Represents:* Artists/Bands

*Genres:* All types of music

Management company and record label.

## Enso Music Management
*Email:* rachaelh@ensomgmt.com
*Email:* elliott@ensomgmt.com
*Website:* http://ensomgmt.com
*Website:* https://www.facebook.com/
ensomanagement/

*Represents:* Artists/Bands

*Genres:* Metal

Southwest based band management, booking
and PR company. Specialises in Metal. Send
query by email with links to music online.

## Epic Venom
*Email:* sarah@epicVenom.com
*Website:* http://www.epicvenom.com
*Website:* https://www.facebook.com/
EpicVenom/

*Represents:* Artists/Bands

*Genres:* Rock

*Contact:* Sarah Furbey

Rock band management including PR,
bookings, travel management, event
scheduling, and financial record keeping.
Submit demos by email.

## Equator Music
London
*Website:* http://www.equatormusic.com

*Represents:* Artists/Bands

*Genres:* Indie; Pop; Rock

London-based management company which
has been managing the affairs of major
artists and writers for over 35 years.

## F&G Management
Unit D
63 Salusbury Road
London
NW6 6NJ
*Email:* gavino@fgmusica.com
*Website:* http://www.fgmusica.com
*Website:* https://www.facebook.com/
fgdjtrade

*Represents:* Artists/Bands; DJs

*Genres:* Alternative; Dance; Electronic;
Experimental; House; Techno

*Contact:* Gavino Prunas

Started as a DJ booking agency in the late
eighties. Interested in music which is
eclectic, different, or quirky. Send demo by
email.

## Fat Penguin Management
Leamington Spa
Warwickshire
Midlands
*Email:* chris@fatpenguinmanagement.co.uk
*Website:* http://fatpenguinmanagement.co.uk
*Website:* https://www.facebook.com/
fatpenguinmgt

*Represents:* Artists/Bands; Producers

*Genres:* Acoustic; Alternative; Folk; Indie;
Rock; Singer-Songwriter; Acoustic
Alternative Americana

*Contact:* Chris Rogers

Already working with a number of notable
artists and producers.

We offer three different levels of services to
artists, music businesses and music
producers alike. Ranging from basic music
consultancy and booking support all the way
up to the full treatment with full music
management services.

## Fave Sounds
*Email:* hello@favesounds.com
*Website:* https://www.favesounds.com
*Website:* https://www.facebook.com/
favesounds/

*Represents:* Artists/Bands

*Genres:* All types of music

Send submissions via contact form on
website.

## Feed Your Head
*Email:* fyhpresents@gmail.com
*Website:* http://www.fyhpresents.com

*Represents:* Artists/Bands

*Genres:* Alternative; Electronic; Dance;
Indie

Send query by email with links to 2 or 3
tracks online.

## Ferocious Talent
*Email:* ferociousmaura@gmail.com
*Email:* ferociousjonny1@gmail.com
*Website:* http://www.ferocioustalent.com

*Represents:* Artists/Bands

*Genres:* All types of music

Artist service company offering artist
management, music consultancy, music
business development, agency and rights
management, label services, and in-house
production. Send query by email with links
to music online. No file attachments.

## Finger Lickin' Management
6 Windmill Street
London
W1T 2JB
*Email:* info@fingerlickin.co.uk
*Email:* amie@fingerlickin.co.uk
*Website:* http://www.
fingerlickinmanagement.co.uk
*Website:* https://soundcloud.com/
fingerlickinmanagement
*Website:* http://www.myspace.com/
FingerLickinRecords

*Represents:* Artists/Bands

*Genres:* Dance; Electronic; Hip-Hop; Break
Beat

Management company based in London.
Send query by email with links to music
online.

## Flat50
Stratford
London
*Email:* artists@flat50.co.uk
*Email:* info@flat50.co.uk
*Website:* http://www.flat50.co.uk
*Website:* https://www.facebook.com/
Flat50Arts

*Represents:* Artists/Bands

*Genres:* Pop; Rock; Rap

Artist representation, promotion, and
management company based in London.
Send demos or queries by email.

## Flow State Music
2 Commercial Street
Edinburgh
EH6 6JA
*Email:* kyle@flowstatemusic.co.uk

*Website:* https://flowstatemusic.co.uk
*Website:* https://www.facebook.com/flowstateedinburgh/

*Represents:* Artists/Bands; DJs

*Genres:* Alternative Dance; Electronic

Music company based in Edinburgh, offering Event Production; Artist & Tour Management; Live Music Promotion; Music Programming; Digital Communications (Social Media / Direct Marketing). Send query by email with links to music online.

## Formidable Music Management

*Email:* carl@formidable-mgmt.com
*Email:* c.marcantonio@hotmail.com
*Website:* https://soundcloud.com/formidable-management
*Website:* https://twitter.com/carlmarcantonio

*Represents:* Artists/Bands

*Genres:* All types of music

*Contact:* Carl Marcantonio

Send demos by email.

## Freaks R Us

*Email:* freaks@freaksrus.net
*Website:* https://www.facebook.com/freakartists
*Website:* https://twitter.com/freakartists

*Represents:* Artists/Bands

*Genres:* Alternative; Electronic; Experimental; Post Punk

Record label and management company. Send query by email with MP3 attachments or links to music online.

## Freedom Management

Unit 2, King Street Cloisters
Clifton Walk
London
W6 0GY
*Email:* freedom@frdm.co.uk
*Website:* http://www.frdm.co.uk

*Represents:* Artists/Bands; Producers; Songwriters

*Genres:* Indie; Pop; Commercial

Management company based in London. Send demos by post.

## Friends Vs Music Ltd

London
*Email:* pip@friendsvsmusic.com
*Website:* https://www.friendsvsmusic.com
*Website:* https://twitter.com/pipvsrecords

*Represents:* Artists/Bands; Producers

*Genres:* All types of music

Artist and producer management company and music consultancy based in London. Approach via form on website.

## Front Room Songs

*Email:* katie@frontroomsongs.com
*Website:* https://frontroomsongs.com
*Website:* https://twitter.com/Frontroomsongs

*Represents:* Artists/Bands

*Genres:* Folk; Pop; Roots; World

Provides artist and project management for a growing roster of emerging artists spanning the folk / roots / world and pop genres. Send query through online contact form with links to music online.

## Fruition Music

*Email:* rod@fruitionmusic.co.uk
*Website:* http://www.fruitionmusic.co.uk

*Represents:* Artists/Bands

*Genres:* Dance; Indie

Send query by email with MP3s or links to music online.

## Future Songs

8 Berwick Street
Soho
London
*Email:* michael@futuresongs.co.uk
*Website:* https://www.facebook.com/futuresongspublishing
*Website:* https://soundcloud.com/future-songs

*Represents:* Artists/Bands; Producers;
Songwriters

*Genres:* Pop; R&B; Singer-Songwriter

Independent music company specialising in
management and publishing. Send demos by
email as MP3s or soundcloud links.

## Ganbei Records
Shelton Street
London
*Email:* info@ganbeirecords.com
*Website:* https://ganbeirecords.com
*Website:* https://www.facebook.com/
ganbeirecords

*Represents:* Artists/Bands

*Genres:* Alternative; Folk; Post Punk;
Psychedelic Rock

Record label and artist management
company that aims to help musicians release
and promote their music. Send query by
email with links to music online.

## Golden Arm
Unit 18, Walters Workshops
249 Kensal Road
London
*Email:* info@goldenarm.me
*Website:* http://www.goldenarm.me

*Represents:* Artists/Bands

*Genres:* Alternative; Indie; Pop; Rock

Management company based in London.
Send query by email with links to music
online.

## Goo Music Management Ltd
*Email:* contact@goomusic.net
*Website:* https://www.goomusic.net
*Website:* https://www.facebook.com/
goomusic

*Represents:* Artists/Bands

*Genres:* Alternative; Indie; Rock

*Contact:* Ben Kirby

Send query by email, giving links to music
online on websites or MySpace etc. No
postal submissions.

## GR Management
974 Pollokshaws Road
Glasgow
G41 2HA
*Email:* info@grmanagement.co.uk

*Represents:* Artists/Bands

*Genres:* Commercial; Mainstream

*Contact:* Rab Andrew

Will consider anything with commercial
appeal. Send demo with one-page bio and
photo by post.

## Grizzly Management
70 Chiswick High Road
London
*Email:* info@grizzlymanagement.com
*Email:* andy@grizzlymanagement.com
*Website:* http://grizzlymanagement.com
*Website:* https://www.facebook.com/
grizzlymanagement

*Represents:* Artists/Bands

*Genres:* All types of music

*Contact:* Andrew Viitalahde-Pountain

Artist management company based in
London. Send query by email with links to
music online.

## Guild Productions
Liverpool
*Email:* guildproductions@hotmail.com
*Website:* http://guildproductions.webs.com
*Website:* https://www.facebook.com/
guildproductions

*Represents:* Artists/Bands

*Genres:* All types of music

A team of Engineers/Producers, Artist
Managers and Songwriters, based in
Liverpool. Offers artist management and
other services for which artists are charged.

## Guvnor Management
*Email:* info@guvnormanagement.co.uk
*Website:* https://www.
guvnormanagement.co.uk

*Website:* https://www.facebook.com/
GuvnorManagement/?ref=settings

*Represents:* Artists/Bands; Comedians;
Other Entertainers; Tribute Acts

*Genres:* Pop; Rock

Management company based in Swansea,
Wales. Send query by email with links to
music online.

## Hand in Hive Independent Records & Management
London
*Email:* contact@handinhive.com
*Email:* tristan@handinhive.com
*Website:* http://www.handinhive.com
*Website:* https://soundcloud.com/hand-in-hive

*Represents:* Artists/Bands

*Genres:* Indie; Pop; Rock

Independent record label and artist
management company based in London.
Send query by email with links to music
online.

## Handshake Ltd.
2 Holly House
Mill Street,
Uppermill
Greater Manchester
OL3 6LZ
*Fax:* +44 (0) 1457 810052
*Email:* info@handshakegroup.com
*Website:* http://www.Handshakegroup.com
*Website:* https://www.facebook.com/
handshakeltd/

*Represents:* Artists/Bands; Comedians; DJs;
Tribute Acts; Variety Artists

*Genres:* Pop; Rock and Roll; Commercial

*Contact:* Stuart Littlewood

Artistes Representation, and Concert
Promotion Company, touring shows and
events in the UK.

Also offering certain productions on a
worldwide basis.

## Hannah Management
Matix Studio
91 Peterborough Road
Fulham
London
SW6 3BU
*Email:* info@hannahmanagement.co.uk
*Website:* http://www.
hannahmanagement.co.uk
*Website:* https://soundcloud.com/
hannahmanagement
*Website:* https://myspace.com/barberahannah

*Represents:* Artists/Bands; Producers

*Genres:* All types of music

*Contact:* A&R

A London based artist and producer
management company.

The founder has been successfully managing
artists and working in music publishing since
1978. The management team manage record
producers as well as up and coming bands.

They have purposely kept their roster small
with the intention of working with the best
talent and helping them develop all aspects
of their career.

## Happy House Management & Marketing Services
*Email:* happyhousemanagement@gmail.com
*Website:* http://happyhousemanagement.
weebly.com
*Website:* https://www.facebook.com/
happyhousemgmt

*Represents:* Artists/Bands

*Genres:* All types of music

*Contact:* Danny Watson

Management, marketing and product
management company. Send query by email
with links to music online.

## Heard and Seen
Greens Court
West Street
Midhurst
West Sussex

GU29 9NQ
*Email:* enquiries@heardandseen.com
*Website:* http://www.heardandseen.com
*Website:* https://www.facebook.com/Heard-and-Seen-Ltd-197097010394361/

*Represents:* Artists/Bands

*Genres:* All types of music

Offers a range of services to artists, including management. See website for full details. Prefers to receive demos on CD by post. Include bio and photo.

## Heist or Hit
12 Hilton Street
Manchester
M1 1JF
*Email:* mgmt@heistorhit.com
*Email:* team@heistorhit.com
*Website:* http://www.heistorhit.com
*Website:* https://www.facebook.com/heistorhitrecords

*Represents:* Artists/Bands

*Genres:* Acoustic; Alternative; Indie

Management company based in Manchester. Send postcard with URL (such as a private Soundcloud playlist), an email address, and a few words on the back.

## Holier than Thou (HTT) Music
91 Masons Road
Stratford Upon Avon
Warwickshire
CV37 9NE
*Email:* David@httmusic.co.uk
*Website:* http://www.holierthanthou.co.uk
*Website:* http://www.httmusic.co.uk
*Website:* http://www.myspace.com/holierthanhourecords

*Represents:* Artists/Bands; Tribute Acts

*Genres:* Rock; Metal; Electronic; Alternative; Melodic Metal; Progressive Metal; Gothic Metal; Melodic Thrash

*Contact:* David Begg

Offers music management, digital distribution, new release promotions, and music publishing admin. Handles Rock, Metal, and sub-genres including Electronic

Crossovers. No CDs or MP3 attachments. Send query by email with links to music online.

## Holy-Toto
103 Gaunt Street
London
SE1 6DP
*Email:* josh@holy-toto.com
*Website:* https://holy-toto.com

*Represents:* Artists/Bands

*Genres:* Dance; Electronic; Hip-Hop; Pop; R&B

Management company based in London. Send query by email with links to music online.

## Hot Gem
Glasgow
*Email:* sync@hotgem.co.uk
*Email:* demos@hotgem.co.uk
*Website:* http://www.hotgem.co.uk
*Website:* https://soundcloud.com/hotgemtunes

*Represents:* Artists/Bands

*Genres:* Ambient; Dance; Electronic; Experimental; Pop

Musician management and label based in Glasgow. Accepts demos, but must have difference / unique sound. No indie guitar bands. Send demos by email as MP3 attachments, or via soundcloud.

On hiatus as per July 2020.

## Hot House Music Ltd
C/O Abbey Road Studios
3 Abbey Road
London
NW8 9AY
*Fax:* +44 (0) 20 7446 7448
*Email:* info@hot-house-music.com
*Website:* http://www.hot-house-music.com
*Website:* http://www.facebook.com/pages/HotHouse-Music/128423608511

*Represents:* Film / TV Composers; Supervisors

*Genres:* All types of music

Management company based in London, representing film and TV composers / music supervisors / score co-ordinators.

## Hot Vox
London
*Email:* info@hotvox.co.uk
*Email:* sam@hotvox.co.uk
*Website:* https://hotvox.co.uk
*Website:* https://www.facebook.com/hotvox

*Represents:* Artists/Bands

*Genres:* All types of music

Music management, promotion and production company based in London, helping the aspirations of both new and established artists. Send query using form on website.

## House of Us
London
*Email:* us@houseofus.co.uk
*Email:* caspar@houseofus.co.uk
*Website:* http://www.houseofus.co.uk
*Website:* https://www.facebook.com/houseofusmanagement/

*Represents:* Artists/Bands

*Genres:* Dance; House; Indie; Pop

London-based music management, consultancy, and PR company. Send query by email with links to music online.

## HQ Familia
38 Charles Street
Leicester
*Email:* yasin@hqrecording.co.uk
*Email:* yasinelashrafi1980@live.co.uk
*Website:* http://www.hqrecording.co.uk/hq-familia/
*Website:* http://soundcloud.com/hqrecording

*Represents:* Artists/Bands

*Genres:* Electronic; Urban

Collective of like minded artists with associated record label and recording studio. Submit demos by post or by email.

## Humans & Other Animals
*Email:* rich@humansandotheranimals.co.uk
*Website:* http://www.humansandotheranimals.co.uk

*Represents:* Artists/Bands

*Genres:* Indie; Rock; Folk; Electronic

Interested in hearing from alternative and/or experimental indie, rock, folk and electronic artists.

## ie:music
111 Frithville Gardens
London
W12 7JQ
*Email:* info@iemusic.co.uk
*Website:* http://www.iemusic.co.uk
*Website:* https://www.facebook.com/iemusic-150700438296856

*Represents:* Artists/Bands

*Genres:* All types of music

Submit demos by post, or send web links by email. Include contact details with valid email address.

## Ignition Management
54 Linhope Street
London
NW1 6HL
*Fax:* +44 (0) 20 7258 0962
*Email:* chris@ignition.co.uk
*Website:* http://www.ignition.co.uk

*Represents:* Artists/Bands

*Genres:* Alternative; Indie; Pop; Rock

*Contact:* Marcus Russell, Managing Director

Management company based in London. Not accepting unsolicited demos as at March 2018. Check website for current status.

## Impact Management
*Website:* http://impactartist.com/#artist-management-banner
*Website:* https://www.facebook.com/impactartistmanagement

*Represents:* Artists/Bands

*Genres:* All types of music

Is a boutique music management company.

## Incendia Music
*Email:* info@incendiamusic.co.uk
*Website:* https://www.incendiamusic.co.uk
*Website:* https://soundcloud.com/incendia-music-management

*Represents:* Artists/Bands; Songwriters

*Genres:* Metal; Rock; Progressive

*Contact:* Lulu Davis

Artist Management, Publicity, and Consultancy services for Rock, Prog and Metal bands and artists.

## Indevine
*Email:* sean@indevine.com
*Website:* http://www.indevine.com

*Represents:* Artists/Bands

*Genres:* All types of music

Manager of a songwriter and several bands. Send query by email with links to music online.

## Innate – Music Ltd
*Email:* nathan@soundvault.tv
*Website:* https://www.innate-music.com/

*Represents:* Artists/Bands

*Genres:* All types of music

*Contact:* Nathan Graves

Creative strategy, project management, marketing and media consultancy established in 2003.

## Insomnia Music UK
*Email:* info@insomniamusic.co.uk
*Website:* http://insomniamusic.co.uk
*Website:* https://www.facebook.com/InsomniaMusicUK/

*Represents:* Artists/Bands

*Genres:* Commercial; Pop

Music management company specialising in pop and commercial. Query by email in first instance.

## Interlude Artists
London Borough of Wandsworth
London
SW12
*Email:* demos@interludeartists.co.uk
*Email:* ryan.walter@interludeartists.co.uk
*Website:* http://interludeartists.co.uk
*Website:* http://facebook.com/interludeartists

*Represents:* Artists/Bands; Songwriters

*Genres:* All types of music

*Contact:* Ryan Walter

A music and artist development agency based in London, established in 2010. Send query by email with links to music online.

## Intertalent Rights Group
Intertalent House
46 Charlotte Street
London
W1T 2GS
*Email:* info@intertalentgroup.com
*Website:* https://intertalentgroup.com

*Represents:* Artists/Bands

*Genres:* Classical; Pop

Accepts contact by post with CV and SAE, but prefers contact by email with links to music online.

## Intune Addicts
*Email:* info@intuneaddicts.com
*Website:* https://www.intuneaddicts.com
*Website:* https://www.facebook.com/intuneaddicts

*Represents:* Artists/Bands

*Genres:* All types of music

*Contact:* Bob James; Mark Smutz Smith; Graham Peacock; Holly Glanvill

Send query by email, describing achievements to date.

## Involved Management
London
*Email:* info@involvedmanagement.com
*Website:* http://www.
involvedmanagement.com

*Represents:* Artists/Bands

*Genres:* Chill; Electronic; House; Trance;
Progressive House

Management company with offices in
London and Los Angeles.

## Island Music Management
*Email:* info@islandmusicmanagement.com
*Website:* https://www.
islandmusicmanagement.com
*Website:* https://twitter.com/silkroybooth

*Represents:* Artists/Bands

*Genres:* Commercial; Indie

*Contact:* Andy Booth

Management company based on the Isle of
Wight. Send query by email with links to
music online.

## JA Artist Management
*Email:* info@jaartistmanagement.com
*Website:* https://www.
jaartistmanagement.com
*Website:* https://www.facebook.com/
JAArtistManagement

*Represents:* Artists/Bands

*Genres:* All types of music

Artist Management for South Coast UK
bands and solo artists. Send query by email
with links to music and other relevant
material online.

## James Joseph Music Management
85 Cicada Road
London
SW18 2PA
*Email:* jj3@jamesjoseph.co.uk
*Website:* http://www.jamesjoseph.co.uk

*Represents:* Artists/Bands

*Genres:* All types of music

*Contact:* James Joseph

Management company with offices in
London, UK, and Los Angeles, California.
Send demo by post.

## JBLS Management
Unit 13, The Tay Building
2A Wrentham Avenue
London
NW10 3HA
*Email:* louise@jblsmanagement.com
*Email:* jo@jblsmanagement.com
*Website:* http://www.jblsmanagement.com
*Website:* https://www.facebook.com/
JBLSManagement/

*Represents:* Artists/Bands; Producers;
Songwriters

*Genres:* Electronic; Alternative; Pop; Singer-
Songwriter

*Contact:* Louise Smith

London management company representing
artists, producers, remixers, mixers, and
writers.

## JD & Co.
*Email:* jdandco@mail.com
*Website:* http://www.jdandcomusic.com
*Website:* https://soundcloud.com/
jdandcomusic

*Represents:* Artists/Bands

*Genres:* All types of music

Manages artists, brands and creative
concepts, implementing them to ensure that
they can maximise all revenues and
opportunities through touring, production
and promotion. Send query by email with
links to music online.

## John Waller Management
The Old Truman Brewery
91 Brick Lane
London
E1 6QL
*Email:* john@johnwaller.net
*Website:* https://www.facebook.com/john.
waller.777

*Website:* https://twitter.com/AAAJayboy
*Website:* https://myspace.com/
johnwallermanagement

*Represents:* Artists/Bands

*Genres:* All types of music

*Contact:* John Waller

Management company based in London. Takes on fee-paying clients only, so you must have proper funding to take an album project to market. If so, send demo by email.

## Jost Music
*Email:* info@jostmusic.co.uk
*Website:* https://www.jostmusic.co.uk
*Website:* https://soundcloud.com/user-883894064

*Represents:* Artists/Bands

*Genres:* All types of music

Record label providing various services, including management. Send query by email with links to music online.

## Jude Street Management
*Email:* info@judestreet.com
*Email:* paul@judest.com
*Website:* http://judestreet.com
*Website:* https://soundcloud.com/grandpastan

*Represents:* Artists/Bands; Film / TV Composers; Producers

*Genres:* Alternative; Pop; Indie; Classical

*Contact:* Paul Devaney; Jeff Fernandez

Music services and management company based in East London and established in 2005. Provides professional representation for bands, artists, producers and composers/arrangers in the fields of Alt/Pop/Indie, Classical, Games, Film and TV. Send query by email and follow up with demos upon request.

## Karma Artists Music LLP
Unit 31, Tileyard Studios
Tileyard Road
Kings Cross

London
N7 9AH
*Email:* info@karmaartists.co.uk
*Website:* http://www.karmaartists.co.uk
*Website:* https://www.facebook.com/karmaartistsuk

*Represents:* Artists/Bands; Producers; Songwriters

*Genres:* All types of music

*Contact:* Jordan Jay; Ross Gautreau; Jess Miller

Multi-faceted entertainment company based in London, representing a roster with combined sales of over 100 million units. Send query by email with soundcloud links to your three best songs.

## Key Music Management
1E Basil Chambers
65 High Street
Manchester
M4 1FS
*Email:* contact@keymusicmanagement.com
*Website:* http://www.keymusicmanagement.com
*Website:* https://www.facebook.com/keymusicmanagement

*Represents:* Artists/Bands

*Genres:* Alternative

*Contact:* Richard Jones; Adam Daly; Ryan Terpstra

Management company based in Manchester. Send query by email, including details of your act and links to your music online.

## KMY (Keep Me Young)
*Email:* Dan@keepmeyoung.uk
*Website:* https://www.keepmeyoung.uk
*Website:* https://www.instagram.com/KeepMeYoungUK/

*Represents:* Artists/Bands

*Genres:* Pop

Send query by email with links to music online.

## KRMB Management & Consultancy

Metropolis Studios
70 Chiswick High Road
London
W4 1SY
*Email:* kreynolds@krmbmanagement.com
*Email:* krmb@mac.com
*Website:* http://www.krmbmanagement.com
*Website:* https://www.facebook.com/krmbmanagement

*Represents:* Artists/Bands

*Genres:* All types of music

*Contact:* Kevin Reynolds

Management and consultancy company offering artist development, creative direction, talent management, corporate entertainment, and consultancy.

## Laissez Faire Club

*Email:* jeremy@laissezfaireclub.com
*Website:* https://laissezfaireclub.tumblr.com

*Represents:* Artists/Bands

*Genres:* All types of music

*Contact:* Jeremy Lloyd

Originally a live promotions company, now focuses solely on artist management. Send query by email with links to streaming music online. No MP3s.

## Landstar Management

7a Chapel Street
Lancaster
Lancashire
LA1 1NZ
*Fax:* +44 (0) 1524 843499
*Email:* turnbuis@hotmail.com
*Website:* http://www.myspace.com/landstarmanagement

*Represents:* Artists/Bands; Film / TV Composers; Producers; Sound Engineers

*Genres:* Heavy Metal; Thrash; Indie; New Age; Electronic; Rock; Alternative Atmospheric Celtic Electronic Experimental Hard Heavy Industrial; Ambient Garage

Gothic Guitar based Indie Metal Mystical New Age Punk Rock World

*Contact:* Stuart Turnbull; Sylvia Thomas

State that they have no preferrence on bands or styles, but specifically mention the genres above. Send query by email giving details of your act and your music, or send demo by post.

## Line-Up pmc

10 Matthew Close
Newcastle upon Tyne
NE6 1XD
*Email:* chrismurtagh@line-up.co.uk
*Website:* http://www.line-up.co.uk

*Represents:* Artists/Bands

*Genres:* World

*Contact:* Chris Murtagh

Promotions and marketing consultancy company with over 25 years of experience specialising in live arts performance, ethnic and World Music. May not necessarily offer representation, but may pass your demo on to relevant contacts if potential is seen.

## Liquid Management

*Email:* david@liquidmanagement.net
*Email:* steve@Liquidmanagement.net
*Website:* https://www.musicglue.com/liquidmanagement
*Website:* https://twitter.com/liquidmgmnt

*Represents:* Artists/Bands; DJs; Producers

*Genres:* All types of music

*Contact:* David Manders; Steve Dix

Management company with 20 years of managing artists through all levels of the music industry.

## Listen to This Management

*Email:* grant@lttmusicmanagement.com
*Email:* charl@lttmusicmanagement.com
*Website:* https://lttmusicmanagement.com
*Website:* https://www.facebook.com/listentothisuk

*Represents:* Artists/Bands

*Genres:* Alternative; Alternative Country; Rock; Indie

*Contact:* Grant Tilbury; Charlotte Final

Artist and tour management company. Send query by email with links to music online.

## Little White Bear Music
London
*Email:* james@littlewhitebearmusic.com
*Website:* https://twitter.com/mrjamesmatthews

*Represents:* Artists/Bands

*Genres:* Pop; R&B; Rock; Singer-Songwriter; Soul

*Contact:* James Matthews

Artist management based in London.

## Lokation
*Email:* lokationcreativeproduction@gmail.com
*Website:* https://www.lokationco.com
*Website:* https://www.facebook.com/LokationCo/

*Represents:* Artists/Bands

*Genres:* Heavy Metal; R&B; Urban

Offers creative production and management.

## The Lost Atlantis Records
*Email:* Thelostatlantisrecords@gmail.com
*Website:* https://www.thelostatlantisrecords.com
*Website:* https://twitter.com/crystalchild01

*Genres:* Hip-Hop; House; Rap; Soul; Techno; Urban

*Contact:* Charlene Jones

Artist development and management. Send query by email with up to three MP3 attachments.

## Lucky Number Music Limited
Suite 3
Second Floor
344 Kingsland Rd
London

E8 4DA
*Email:* contact@luckynumbermusic.com
*Website:* https://www.luckynumbermusic.com/
*Website:* https://soundcloud.com/luckynumbermusic

*Represents:* Artists/Bands

*Genres:* Indie; Pop; Electronic

Provide management and producer services, and also operate a record label.

## Lyricom
*Email:* james@lyricom.co.uk
*Website:* https://lyricom.co.uk

*Represents:* Artists/Bands

*Genres:* Indie; Singer-Songwriter; Urban

Management company representing singer songwriters, solo artists, and bands. Currently expanding its roster. Send query by email with Soundcloud or YouTube links to a maximum of two songs.

## M24 Management
*Email:* m24managementagency@gmail.com
*Website:* https://www.facebook.com/M24ManagementAgency

*Represents:* DJs

*Genres:* House

Management company representing House DJs.

## MaDa Music Entertainment
London
*Email:* Adam@Madamusic.com
*Website:* http://www.madamusic.com
*Website:* https://soundcloud.com/mada-music

*Represents:* Artists/Bands; Producers

*Genres:* All types of music

London based multi divisional entertainment company specialising in Artist and Producer Management, Events, PR and Consultancy. Particularly interested in pop, indie, and rock, but will consider most genres. Send query by email with bio and links to music online.

## Madrigal Music artist management
Guy Hall
Awre
Gloucestershire
GL14 1EL
*Email:* artists@madrigalmusic.co.uk
*Email:* nickf@madrigalmusic.co.uk
*Website:* http://www.madrigalmusic.co.uk
*Website:* https://www.facebook.com/
madrigalmusic

*Represents:* Artists/Bands

*Genres:* Indie; Rock; Singer-Songwriter

*Contact:* Nick Ford

Send demo by post, preferably quality finished masters. Include SAE if return required. No MP3 submissions by email. No hip-hop or manufactured pop.

## Major Labl
*Website:* https://www.majorlabl.com
*Website:* https://www.facebook.com/
MajorLabl/

*Represents:* Artists/Bands

*Genres:* All types of music

Offers marketing and management services for unsigned and independent artists.

## Manners McDade Artist Management
3rd floor, 12 Greenhill Rents
London
EC1M 6BN
*Email:* submissions@mannersmcdade.co.uk
*Email:* info@mannersmcdade.co.uk
*Website:* http://mannersmcdade.co.uk
*Website:* https://www.facebook.com/
mannersmcdademusic/

*Represents:* Film / TV Composers

*Genres:* All types of music

Management company based in London, representing composers for film and TV.

Send submissions by email. Response only if interested.

## Manta Ray Music
7-7c Snuff Street
Devizes
Wiltshire
SN10 1DU
*Website:* http://www.mantaraymusic.co.uk

*Represents:* Artists/Bands

*Genres:* All types of music

Management company focusing on early-stage A&R, "seeking out innate talent and potential". Offices in London and Berlin.

## MBM (Music Business Management Ltd)
Labrican
Healey Dell Nature Reserve
Rochdale
OL12 6BG
*Email:* info@mbmcorporate.co.uk
*Email:* anne@mbmcorporate.co.uk
*Website:* https://www.mbmcorporate.co.uk
*Website:* https://www.facebook.com/
MBMCorporate

*Represents:* Artists/Bands; DJs; Tribute Acts

*Genres:* All types of music

*Contact:* Phil Barrett

Entertainment consultancy and artiste management. Specialises in Tributes and Tribite shows. Make approach using form on website.

## Memphia Music Management
Bristol
*Email:* jp@memphia.com
*Website:* https://www.memphia.com
*Website:* https://www.facebook.com/
MemphiaMM/

*Represents:* Artists/Bands

*Genres:* Indie; Rock

Management company based in Bristol. Query by email or via contact us page on website.

## Metal Music Bookings
London
*Fax:* +44 (0) 20 7084 0323
*Email:* contact@metalmusicbookings.com
*Email:* denise@metalmusicbookings.com
*Website:* http://www.
metalmusicbookings.com
*Website:* https://www.facebook.com/
MetalMusicBookings

*Represents:* Artists/Bands

*Genres:* Alternative; Metal; Rock

*Contact:* Denise Dale

Independent Booking Agency based in
London, specialising in representing artists
in the Heavy Metal and Rock genres, but
willing to consider other genres. Send query
by email with bio and links to music online.

## Miller Music Management
*Fax:* +44 (0) 20 8964 4965
*Email:* info@m-music-m.com
*Website:* http://www.m-music-m.com

*Represents:* Artists/Bands

*Genres:* Indie; Rock; Singer-Songwriter

*Contact:* Carrie Hustler

Management company with offices in
London and Los Angeles. Send demo by
email with bio and Soundcloud link.

## MJM Agency
*Email:* demos@mjmagency.co.uk
*Email:* info@mjmagency.co.uk
*Website:* http://www.mjmagency.co.uk

*Represents:* Artists/Bands, DJs, Other
Entertainers

*Genres:* All types of music

*Contact:* Mike Jones

Management agency run on a part-time
basis. Handles musical entertainers and
performing acts. Send demos and/or band
details by email.

## Modest! Management
The Matrix Complex
91 Peterborough Road
London
SW6 3BU
*Email:* info@modestmanagement.com
*Website:* https://www.
modestmanagement.com
*Website:* https://www.facebook.com/
modestmanagement

*Represents:* Artists/Bands

*Genres:* Pop

*Contact:* Will Bloomfield; Richard Griffiths;
Harry Magee

Management company based in London,
handling several X-Factor winners/finalists.
Send demos by email.

## Moksha Management
PO Box 102
London
E15 2HH
*Fax:* +44 (0) 20 8519 6834
*Email:* recordings@moksha.co.uk
*Email:* info@moksha.co.uk
*Website:* http://www.moksha.co.uk
*Website:* https://twitter.com/mokshamgt

*Represents:* Artists/Bands

*Genres:* Alternative Electronic Fusion;
Contemporary; Dance

Demos preferred as streaming weblinks.

## Moneypenny
*Fax:* +44 (0) 7977 455882
*Email:* enquiry@moneypennymusic.co.uk
*Website:* https://moneypennymusic.co.uk

*Represents:* Artists/Bands

*Genres:* Acoustic; Americana; Country;
Classic Rock

*Contact:* Nigel Morton; Liz Lenten

A boutique, hands-on style booking agency
for acts of assorted genres, specializing in
Acoustic, Americana / Country and classic
rock.

## Mother Artist Management
*Email:* mark@motherartistmanagement.com
*Email:* lucy@motherartistmanagement.com
*Website:* http://www.
motherartistmanagement.com
*Website:* https://www.facebook.com/
motherartistmanagement/

*Represents:* Artists/Bands

*Genres:* All types of music

Send query by email with bio and links to music online.

## Music by Design
27 Lexington Street
Soho
London
W1F 9AQ
*Email:* info@musicbydesign.co.uk
*Website:* http://www.musicbydesign.co.uk
*Website:* https://twitter.com/i/events/
1281585300804755458

*Represents:* Artists/Bands

*Genres:* All types of music

*Contact:* Sarah Edwards

"Innovative out of the box thinkers required. Send us your idea, receive a song. Let's create something good together".

## Musicarchy Media
3 Gower Street
1 Floor
London
*Email:* info@musicarchymedia.com
*Website:* https://www.musicarchymedia.com

*Represents:* Artists/Bands

*Genres:* Alternative; Gothic; Indie; Metal; Rock; Hard; Heavy

*Contact:* Kiara

Rock and Metal management and record label based in London since 2014. Founded by chart topping vocalist.

## musicmedia
788-790 Finchley Road
London

NW11 7TJ
*Email:* info@musicmediaartists.com
*Website:* http://www.musicmediaevents.com
*Website:* https://www.facebook.com/pages/
musicmedia-events/110527535666030

*Represents:* Artists/Bands

*Genres:* Pop; Acoustic; Alternative; Folk

Management company with parent company registered offices in London. Send links to your music online in first instance.

## N.O.W. Music Management
1st Floor
25 Commercial Street
Brighouse
HD6 1AF
*Email:* info@now-music.com
*Website:* https://www.now-music.com

*Represents:* Artists/Bands; Tribute Acts

*Genres:* Pop; Rock

A management company based in Brighouse, West Yorkshire, with strong connections in Europe and with a small independent record company.

## Nettwerk Management UK
15 Adeline Place, Ground Floor
London
WC1B 3AJ
*Fax:* +44 (0) 20 7456 9501
*Email:* info@nettwerk.com
*Website:* http://www.nettwerk.com
*Website:* https://www.facebook.com/
nettwerkmusicgroup

*Represents:* Artists/Bands

*Genres:* All types of music

Management company headquartered in Vancouver, with offices in London, Hamburg, LA, New York, and Boston. Send query by email with links to streaming music online.

## New Level Music Management
Oxford
*Email:* newlevelmgmt@gmail.com
*Website:* https://www.facebook.com/

NewLevelMgmt
*Website:* https://twitter.com/NewLevelMgmt

*Represents:* Artists/Bands

*Genres:* All types of music

Music management based in Oxford, with contacts with UK and international record labels, publishers, promoters, and booking agents. Provides artist management, tour booking / management, professional guidance, PR, release campaigns, and contract negotiation, but does not accept unsolicited artists.

## New Outlaw
*Email:* clare@newoutlaw.co.uk
*Website:* https://www.outlaw-pr.co.uk
*Website:* https://www.facebook.com/newoutlawmusic/

*Represents:* Artists/Bands

*Genres:* All types of music

Specialises in album release management, PR, graphics and merchandise development for music artists. Send query by email with links / social media.

## No Half Measures Ltd
1st Floor
5 Eagle Street
Glasgow
G4 9XA
*Email:* info@nohalfmeasures.com
*Website:* http://nohalfmeasures.com
*Website:* https://www.facebook.com/nohalfmeasures

*Represents:* Artists/Bands

*Genres:* All types of music

Based in Glasgow, Scotland, working in the areas of artist management; intellectual property & rights management; music publishing; recording, manufacturing, distribution, marketing & promotion; live performance, presentation & touring; event management and logistics; sponsorship & branding; merchandise; and more. Send demo by post, or by email as links or MP3s.

## North Central Music (NCM)
*Email:* sed@northcentralmusic.co.uk
*Website:* https://facebook.com/northcentralmusic

*Represents:* Artists/Bands

*Genres:* Alternative; Underground

Northern artist management company. Represents alternative / underground, but no heavy metal. Send submissions by email.

## Northern Music Co. Ltd
5A Victoria Road
Saltaire
Shipley
West Yorkshire
BD18 3LA
*Fax:* +44 (0) 1274 593546
*Email:* demos@northernmusic.co.uk
*Email:* info@northernmusic.co.uk
*Website:* http://www.northernmusic.co.uk
*Website:* https://www.facebook.com/NMCLtd

*Represents:* Artists/Bands

*Genres:* Metal; Rock

*Contact:* Andy Farrow

Send query by email with your band/act's name in the subject line, with details on what you are looking for; links to stream your music; a brief bio of your band/act; links to your website / social media / videos; and any details of existing industry partners / releases / live dates, etc.

## NSB Artist Management
*Email:* nsbartistmanagement@gmail.com
*Website:* https://www.facebook.com/nsbartistmanagement
*Website:* https://linktr.ee/nsbartistmanagement

*Represents:* Artists/Bands

*Genres:* Hip-Hop; Soul; Urban

Send query by email with EPK and links to music online.

## Off the Chart Promotions

17 Spitfire Road
Upper Cambourne
Cambridgeshire
CB23 6FL
*Email:* tim@offthechart.co.uk
*Website:* https://www.offthechart.co.uk

*Represents:* Artists/Bands

*Genres:* Folk; Pop; Rock; Indie; Singer-Songwriter

Management company based in Cambridge. Works with artists from the East of England and London.

## Offbeat Management

*Fax:* +44 (0) 1912 640601
*Email:* info@offbeat-management.co.uk
*Website:* http://www.offbeat-management.co.uk

*Represents:* Artists/Bands

*Genres:* Acoustic Alternative Heavy Power Progressive Psychedelic Thrash; Ambient Black Metal Blues Chill Doom Garage Guitar based Instrumental Metal R&B Rock Rhythm and Blues Singer-Songwriter; Hard

Management company representing one band.

## OnDaBeat Talent Management

West London Art Factory
153 Dukes Road
London
W3 0SL
*Email:* mgmt@odbentltd.com
*Website:* https://ondabeat.co.uk
*Website:* https://soundcloud.com/ondabeatmgmt

*Represents:* Artists/Bands

*Genres:* Drum and Bass; Electronic; House; Hip-Hop; Rap; Techno

Management company and record studios based in London. Send query by email with links to music online.

## One Fifteen

A&R
One Fifteen
1 Globe House
Middle Lane Mews
London
N8 8PN
*Fax:* +44 (0) 20 8442 7561
*Email:* demos@onefifteen.com
*Email:* enquiries@onefifteen.com
*Website:* http://www.onefifteen.com

*Represents:* Artists/Bands

*Genres:* All types of music

*Contact:* Tom O'Rourke

If submitting by email prefers links to your SoundCloud, YouTube or Facebook page. If you insist on sending MP3s, send no more than two. Include short bio, photo, social media links, and upcoming gig listings. CDs cannot be returned. Aims to listen to everything, but response not guaranteed if not interested.

## 141a Management

*Email:* admin@art19.co.uk
*Website:* https://www.141amanagement.co.uk
*Website:* https://www.facebook.com/141amanagementcompany/?fref=ts

*Represents:* Artists/Bands

*Genres:* All types of music

Music management company representing artists from all music genres.

## 140dB Management Limited

London
*Email:* info@140db.co.uk
*Email:* ros@140db.co.uk
*Website:* http://www.140db.co.uk
*Website:* https://www.facebook.com/140dBManagement/

*Represents:* Artists/Bands; Producers

*Genres:* All types of music

*Contact:* Ros Earls

Management company based in London. Represents artists and producers. Send query by email with links to music online.

## Ornadel Management

*Email:* info@ornadel.com
*Email:* guy@ornadel.com
*Website:* http://www.ornadel.com
*Website:* https://www.facebook.com/ OrnadelMGM/

*Represents:* Artists/Bands; DJs

*Genres:* Dance

*Contact:* Guy Ornadel

Mainly works with DJs.

## Paper House Music

89 Borough High Street
London
SE1 1NL
*Fax:* +44 (0) 20 7357 9750
*Email:* doug@paperhousemusic.co.uk
*Email:* matt@paperhousemusic.co.uk
*Website:* http://www.ma2music.com

*Represents:* Artists/Bands

*Genres:* All types of music

Management and promotion company based in London.

## Park Records

PO Box 651
Oxford
OX2 9RB
*Fax:* +44 (0) 1865 204556
*Email:* parkoffice@parkrecords.com
*Website:* http://www.parkrecords.com
*Website:* https://www.facebook.com/Park-Records-154023671336938/

*Represents:* Artists/Bands

*Genres:* Folk; Singer-Songwriter; Roots; Acoustic; Folk Rock

Music company based in Oxford, including record label and management and PR services. Send demo with photo by email. Particularly interested in hearing from female singer-songwriters.

## Perfect Havoc Ltd

Flat 7
46 De Beauvoir Crescent
London
N1 5RY
*Email:* info@perfecthavoc.com
*Website:* https://perfecthavoc.com
*Website:* https://soundcloud.com/ perfecthavocmusic

*Represents:* Artists/Bands

*Genres:* Dance; Disco; House

London-based music entertainment management, record label, club night and blog. Send query by email with soundcloud links.

## Perry Road Records

75 Perry Road
Buckden
Cambridgeshire
PE19 5XG
*Email:* enquiries@perryroadrecords.co.uk
*Website:* https://www. perryroadrecords.co.uk
*Website:* https://www.facebook.com/pages/ Perry-Road-Records/140101102757735

*Represents:* Artists/Bands

*Genres:* Country; Blues; Indie; Rock

*Contact:* Gilly Lee

Independent record label and artist management based in Buckden, Cambridge. Send demo by post or send links to music online by email.

## Petty Music Management

*Email:* hello@pettymanagement.com
*Website:* https://pettymanagement.com
*Website:* https://www.facebook.com/ pettymanagement

*Represents:* Artists/Bands

*Genres:* All types of music

UK management company.

## Pieces of 8 Music

London
*Email:* info@piecesof8music.com

*Website:* http://piecesof8music.com
*Website:* https://www.facebook.com/
Piecesof8Music

*Represents:* Artists/Bands; Producers;
Songwriters; Sound Engineers

*Genres:* All types of music

*Contact:* James Morgan; Thea Lillepalu

Boutique management company set up to
representing artists, producers, engineers,
mixers and songwriters on a professional
level. Send query by email with links to
music online. No attachments.

## Pierce Entertainment
Pierce House
London Apollo Complex
Queen Caroline Street
London W6 9QH
*Email:* info@pierce-entertainment.com
*Website:* http://www.pierce-
entertainment.com
*Website:* https://www.facebook.com/
PierceEnt/

*Represents:* Artists/Bands

*Genres:* Pop; R&B

Call in first instance. Send demo on
invitation only.

## Pillar Artists
Newcastle upon Tyne
*Email:* pillar.artists@gmail.com
*Website:* https://www.musicglue.com/pillar-
artists
*Website:* https://facebook.com/PillarArtists

*Represents:* Artists/Bands

*Genres:* Acoustic; Alternative; Guitar based;
Indie

Management agency based in Newcastle
Upon Tyne. Also involved with independent
gig promotion, PR, and booking. Send query
by email with bio and links to music online.

## Plus Music
Hoxton
London

*Email:* info@plusmusic.co.uk
*Website:* http://www.plusmusic.co.uk

*Represents:* Artists/Bands

*Genres:* Funk; Pop; R&B; Soul

*Contact:* Desmond Chisholm

Looking for male or female singers aged 16-
23. Send MP3 with recent photo(s) and
social media links by email. See website for
full details.

## PMS Music Management
122 London Road
Rayleigh
Essex
SS6 9BN
*Fax:* +44 (0) 1268 784807
*Email:* pmsmusicmgt@yahoo.co.uk
*Website:* http://pmsmusicmanagement.
weebly.com

*Represents:* Artists/Bands; Tribute Acts

*Genres:* All types of music

*Contact:* Peter Scott

Send demo by post or email. MP3 preferred
but not essential. Currently managing
Indie/pop/rock but open to all genres. 'If I
like it, I can represent it!' Welcomes all
submissions in the form of CD, MP3 or
video on DVD together with a biography and
links to your Website, Myspace and any
other relevant links. Particularly keen to
work with unsigned bands.

## Pond Life Songs
London
*Email:* info@pondlifesongs.com
*Website:* http://www.pondlifesongs.com
*Website:* https://soundcloud.com/
pondlifesongs

*Represents:* Artists/Bands

*Genres:* All types of music

*Contact:* Keith Aspden

Record label based in London, specialising
in artist development and management. Send
demos by email. Responds to all
submissions.

## Possessive Management
*Email:* contact@possessivemanagement.com
*Website:* https://www.facebook.com/
PossessiveManagement
*Website:* https://twitter.com/PossessiveMgmt

*Represents:* Artists/Bands

*Genres:* Metal; Punk; Rock; Progressive;
Thrash; Hardcore; Alternative

Management company specialising in rock,
metal and hardcore bands. Send query by
email with links to music online.

## Prolifica Management
London
*Email:* info@prolifica.co.uk
*Website:* http://www.
prolificamanagement.co.uk
*Website:* https://www.instagram.com/
prolificamanagement/

*Represents:* Artists/Bands

*Genres:* All types of music

London-based Music Management and
Production Company. Send demo by email.

## Psycho Management Company
*Email:* patrick@psycho.co.uk
*Website:* https://www.psycho.co.uk/
*Website:* https://twitter.com/psychomanco

*Represents:* Artists/Bands; Comedians; DJs;
Other Entertainers; Tribute Acts

*Genres:* All types of music

Management company representing circus
acts, entertainment acts, lookalikes, music
acts, name acts, and tribute acts.

## Push Music Management
London
*Email:* info@pushmusicmanagement.com
*Website:* http://www.
pushmusicmanagement.com
*Website:* https://twitter.com/pushmusicmgmt
*Website:* http://www.myspace.com/
pushmusicmanagement

*Represents:* Artists/Bands

*Genres:* All types of music

Management company based in London.
Send email with links to your music online.

## PVA Management Ltd
County House
St Mary Street
Worcester WR1 1HB

*Email:* md@pvmedia.co.uk
*Website:* http://pvmedia.co.uk/

*Represents:* Artists/Bands

*Genres:* Classical

Broadcasting and Media Consultants, PVA
Payroll Services, PVA Training and PVA
Music.

## Quest Management
*Email:* quest@maverick.com
*Website:* http://www.quest-management.com
*Website:* https://www.instagram.com/
questartistmgmt/

*Represents:* Artists/Bands

*Genres:* All types of music

A collective of experienced management
executives, renowned for innovations in
creating lasting revenue strategies for artists.

## Qveen Management
Way Out Studios
London
E14 7DE
*Email:* qv@qveenmanagement.com
*Website:* https://www.
qveenmanagement.com

*Represents:* Artists/Bands

*Genres:* Commercial; Electronic; Urban

Female-led management company based in
London. Send query by email with bio and
links to music online.

## Raven Black Music
*Email:* info@ravenblackmusic.com
*Website:* https://www.facebook.com/
ravenblackmusic

*Represents:* Artists/Bands

*Genres:* Rock

*Contact:* Dean G. Hill

UK-based record label. Contact by email. No physical submissions.

## Raw Power Management
London
*Fax:* +44 (0) 845 331 3500
*Email:* info@rawpowermanagement.com
*Website:* http://www.
rawpowermanagement.com
*Website:* http://www.facebook.com/
rawpowermanagement
*Website:* http://www.myspace.com/
rawpowermanagement

*Represents:* Artists/Bands

*Genres:* Punk Rock; Alternative; Metal; Rock

Punk rock management company based in London. Send demos as MP3s or links to music online by email.

## Real Media Music
*Email:* info@realmediamusic.co.uk
*Website:* http://www.realmediamusic.co.uk
*Website:* https://www.facebook.com/
RealMediaMusic

*Represents:* Artists/Bands

*Genres:* All types of music

International artist booking and management. Send query by email with links to music online. No submissions by post. Response only if interested.

## Reckless Yes
*Email:* pete@recklessyes.com
*Email:* sarah@recklessyes.com
*Website:* http://recklessyes.com
*Website:* https://www.facebook.com/
RecklessYes/

*Represents:* Artists/Bands

*Genres:* Acoustic; Alternative; Guitar based; Indie

*Contact:* Pete; Sarah

Independent record label, management and live music agency. Closed to submissions as at October 2019. Check website for current status.

## Red Afternoon Management
*Email:* submissions@
redafternoonmanagement.co.uk
*Email:* info@redafternoonmanagement.co.uk
*Website:* https://www.
redafternoonmanagement.co.uk
*Website:* https://www.facebook.com/Red-
Afternoon-Management

*Represents:* Artists/Bands

*Genres:* All types of music

*Contact:* Lewis Forrest

Management company founded in 2016, set up to champion up and coming bands and artists. Services include: Artist Management, Booking, Promotion, and Consulting. Willing to consider all music types, but background is in rock, indie, and punk. Send submissions by email or through online form on website.

## Red Grape Music
82 Chestnut Grove
New Malden
Surrey
KT3 3JS
*Email:* info@redgrapemusic.com
*Website:* https://www.redgrapemusic.com

*Represents:* Artists/Bands

*Genres:* Acoustic; Folk; Pop; Singer-Songwriter

Management company and record label based in New Malden, Surrey. Not accepting submissions as at January 2019. Check website for current status.

## RGM Production
*Email:* info@ryangloveronline.com
*Website:* http://ryangloveronline.com
*Website:* https://www.facebook.com/
RGMproductionLtd/

*Represents:* Artists/Bands

*Genres:* Pop; R&B; Soul

A Dorset and Hampshire based music production, management and artist development company. Send query by email with Soundcloud or Youtube links.

## Rhythmic Records Management and Production

*Email:* info@rhythmic-records.co.uk
*Website:* https://www.rhythmic-records.co.uk
*Website:* https://www.facebook.com/RhythmicRecordsUK/?ref=bookmarks

*Represents:* Artists/Bands

*Genres:* Dance; Hip-Hop; House; Pop

Independent record label and management company based in London. Submit query with links to music online through form on website or by email.

## Richard Lipman

*Email:* richardlipmanfilms@gmail.com
*Website:* https://www.richardlipman.co
*Website:* https://www.facebook.com/richardlipman.co

*Represents:* Artists/Bands

*Genres:* Classical; Pop; Rock; World

Freelance filmmaker, photographer, and music manager.

## Rock Hippie Management & Music

*Email:* info@rockhippiemanagement.com
*Email:* rebecca@rockhippiemanagement.com
*Website:* https://www.facebook.com/rockhippiem/
*Website:* https://twitter.com/RockHippieM

*Represents:* Artists/Bands; Comedians; DJs; Songwriters; Tribute Acts

*Genres:* All types of music

*Contact:* Rebecca

Management company based in London. For management enquiries send email with subject "[management] + your name or the name of your band" with link to your music

and short bio. Include details of what you expect from a manager, in more detail than simply "I/We want a record deal". No MP3 attachments.

## Rock People Management (RPM)

*Email:* terri@rockpeoplemanagement.com
*Email:* heidi@rockpeoplemanagement.com
*Website:* https://www.rockpeoplemanagement.com
*Website:* https://www.facebook.com/rockpeoplemanagement/

*Represents:* Artists/Bands

*Genres:* Blues; Rock

*Contact:* Terri Chapman; Heidi Kerr

Send query by email with links to music, videos, and social media, plus EPK.

## Rollover

29 Beethoven Street
London
W10 4LG
*Fax:* +44 (0) 20 8968 1047
*Website:* http://www.rollover.co.uk

*Represents:* Artists/Bands

*Genres:* All types of music

Management company based in London. Contact by phone in first instance, then submit demo by post upon request.

## Rosier Artist Management (RAM)

*Website:* https://twitter.com/steverosier

*Represents:* Artists/Bands

*Genres:* Americana; Rock

*Contact:* Steve Rosier

UK manager focusing on Rock and Americana.

## Rough Diamond

London
*Website:* https://www.roughdiamondmusic.org

*Website:* https://twitter.com/
roughdiamondldn

*Represents:* Artists/Bands

*Genres:* All types of music

Artist development and production company
based in London.

## Roundface Music Management
Dunfermline
Scotland
*Email:* george@roundfacemusic.com
*Website:* http://www.roundfacemusic.com
*Website:* https://www.facebook.com/
RFmusicmanagement/

*Represents:* Artists/Bands

*Genres:* All types of music

*Contact:* George Murray

Offers Music Management and Consultancy
to Artists based in Dunfermline, Scotland.
Send query by email with MP3 attachments
or links to music online.

## S&B Creative
*Email:* info@snbcreative.com
*Website:* http://www.snbcreative.com

*Represents:* Artists/Bands; Film / TV
Composers; Producers; Songwriters

*Genres:* All types of music

Talent management, record label, brand
consultancy, and scors for film and TV. Send
query by email with links to music online.

## Salvation Records
*Email:* info@salvationrecords.co.uk
*Website:* https://www.facebook.com/
thesoundofsalvationrecords
*Website:* https://soundcloud.com/
salvationrecords

*Represents:* Artists/Bands

*Genres:* Electronic; Garage; Psychedelic
Rock; Punk

*Contact:* Anthony Nyland

Record label and artist management.

## Saviour Management
London
*Email:* james@svrmgmt.com
*Email:* angelo@svrmgmt.com
*Website:* http://saviourmgmt.tumblr.com
*Website:* https://www.facebook.com/
saviourmanagement

*Represents:* Artists/Bands

*Genres:* Alternative; Metal; Pop Punk

*Contact:* James Illsley; Angelo Pandolfi

Management company based in London.
Send query by email with bio and links to
social media and music online.

## SB Management
Greenhouse Studios
8 Mackintosh Lane
London
E9 6AB
*Email:* info@sb-management.com
*Website:* https://www.sb-management.com/
*Website:* https://twitter.com/sbmanagement

*Represents:* Artists/Bands; Producers;
Songwriters

*Genres:* All types of music

Management company based in London and
Los Angeles.

## September Management (UK)
London
*Email:* info@septembermanagement.com
*Website:* https://septembermanagement.com

*Represents:* Artists/Bands; Producers; Sound
Engineers

*Genres:* All types of music

Represents a roster of internationally
renowned recording artists, producers and
mix engineers who have collectively
amassed 44 Grammys, 12 Brit Awards, 2
Oscars, 2 Golden Globes and sold over 100
million albums worldwide. The company has
offices in London, New York and Los
Angeles.

## Serious

51 Kingsway Place
Sans Walk
Clerkenwell
London
EC1R 0LU
*Website:* https://serious.org.uk
*Website:* http://www.facebook.com/
seriouslivemusic

*Represents:* Artists/Bands

*Genres:* Jazz; World; Contemporary

Management company based in London
producing jazz, international, and
contemporary music, and offering
management, music publishing and the
production of concerts, tours and special
events. Send query via form on website,
including links to music online.

## 74 Promotions

94 Centurion Road
Brighton
BN1 3LN
*Email:* andy@74promotions.com
*Website:* http://www.74promotions.com
*Website:* https://www.facebook.com/74-
Promotions-181204548583646/

*Represents:* Artists/Bands

*Genres:* All types of music

*Contact:* Andy Hollis

Management company based in Brighton.
Send demo by email or by post.

## SGM Music Group Ltd

Base Studios
Unit 14
Rufford Road Trading Estate
Stourbridge
West Midlands
DY9 7ND
*Email:* info@sgmmusicgroup.com
*Website:* https://www.sgmmusicgroup.com
*Website:* https://www.facebook.com/
sgmmusicgroup/

*Represents:* Artists/Bands

*Genres:* Pop; Rock

*Contact:* Scott Garrett

Management company based in Stourbridge,
West Midlands. Send demos by post or send
query by email with links to music online.

## SGO Ltd

PO Box 2015
Salisbury
SP2 7WU
*Fax:* +44 (0) 1747 870678
*Email:* sgomusic@sgomusic.com
*Website:* http://www.sgomusic.com
*Website:* http://www.facebook.com/
SGOMusic

*Represents:* Artists/Bands

*Genres:* All types of music

*Contact:* Stuart Ongley

Management company based in Salisbury.
Send query in first instance. No unsolicited
demos.

## Shaw Thing Management

20 Coverdale Road
London
N11 3FG
*Email:* info@shawthingmanagement.com
*Website:* https://www.
shawthingmanagement.com
*Website:* https://www.facebook.com/Shaw-
Thing-Management-2205412639509595/?
modal=admin_todo_tour

*Represents:* Artists/Bands

*Genres:* Pop

Send demo as MP3 file by email, including
any additional information, such as photos
etc.

## Sidewinder Management Ltd

*Email:* sdw@sidewindermgmt.com
*Website:* http://www.sidewindermgmt.com

*Represents:* Artists/Bands

*Genres:* All types of music

*Contact:* Simon Watson

Management company based in Brighton and Hove. Send query by email with links to music online. No MP3 attachments.

## Silverword Music Group
*Website:* https://www.silverword.co.uk

*Represents:* Artists/Bands

*Genres:* Urban; Dance; Pop; Rock; Jazz; Soul; Classical; Country; Gospel; R&B

Part of music group incorporating record label, promotion, publishing, distribution, etc.

## Solar Management
Unit 10 Union Wharf
23 Wenlock Road
London
N1 7SB
*Email:* info@solarmanagement.co.uk
*Website:* http://www.solarmanagement.co.uk
*Website:* http://soundcloud.com/solarmanagement
*Website:* http://www.myspace.com/solarmanagement

*Represents:* Artists/Bands; Producers

*Genres:* All types of music

*Contact:* Carol Crabtree

Eexperience in producer and artist development, recording, touring, budgeting and all producer and artist contracts. Send email with links to music online. No MP3 attachments.

## Sound Consultancy
Resound Media
Kingsley House
Church Lane
Shurdington
Cheltenham
GL51 4TQ
*Email:* hey@soundconsultancy.co.uk
*Website:* http://www.soundconsultancy.co.uk
*Website:* https://www.facebook.com/soundconsultancy

*Represents:* Artists/Bands

*Genres:* All types of music

Cheltenham music company offering artist development, mentoring, and promotion packages. Considers all genres, but mainly acoustic, rock, and folk. Send MP3s by email.

## The Soundcheck Group
29 Wardour Street
London
W1D 6PS
*Email:* daniel@thesoundcheckgroup.com
*Website:* http://www.thesoundcheckgroup.com
*Website:* https://www.facebook.com/thesoundcheckgroup1

*Represents:* Artists/Bands

*Genres:* All types of music

*Contact:* Daniel Hinchliffe

Management company based in London. Send query by email with links to music online.

## South Star Music
PO BOX 1350
Southampton
SO15 5WX
*Email:* admin@southstarmusic.co.uk
*Website:* http://www.southstarmusic.co.uk

*Represents:* Artists/Bands

*Genres:* All types of music

Based in Southampton, offers artist management and promotion, songwriting services, and studio recording, mixing, and mastering facilities.

## Steve Allen Entertainments
The Coach House
163 Broadway
Peterborough
PE1 4DH
*Fax:* +44 (0) 1733 561854
*Email:* sales@sallenent.co.uk
*Website:* https://steveallenentertainments.co.uk
*Website:* https://www.facebook.com/steveallenentertainments/

*Represents:* Artists/Bands; Comedians; Other Entertainers; Tribute Acts

*Genres:* All types of music

*Contact:* Steve Allen

Based in Peterborough, in Cambridgeshire. Supplies entertainers and entertainments for private events and corporate occasions. Client base includes many National companies as well as most of the major Hotel Chains.

## Storm5 Management
Resound Media
Brincliffe House
59 Wostenholm Road
Sheffield
S7 1LE
*Email:* info@storm5management.com
*Website:* http://www.storm5management.com
*Website:* https://www.facebook.com/storm5management/

*Represents:* Artists/Bands

*Genres:* All types of music

Management company based in Sheffield. Send query by email with links to music online.

## Stormcraft Music
*Email:* info@stormcraftmusic.com
*Website:* https://www.stormcraftmusic.com
*Website:* https://www.facebook.com/stormcraftmusic

*Represents:* Artists/Bands

*Genres:* Alternative Pop; Singer-Songwriter; Guitar based

Specialises in the management and development of up and coming talented artists. Send query by email with links to music online, or use online form.

## Sugar House Music
*Email:* info@sugarhousemusic.co.uk
*Website:* http://www.sugarhousemusic.co.uk
*Website:* http://www.soundcloud.com/sugarhousemusic

*Website:* http://www.myspace.com/sugarhousemusicuk

*Represents:* Artists/Bands

*Genres:* Indie; New Wave; Pop; Rock

*Contact:* Lee McCarthy; Ady Hall

Send email with links to music online (soundcloud / myspace etc. only – no MP3 attachments).

## SugarNova
St John St
London
*Email:* info@SugarNova.com
*Website:* http://sugarnova.com
*Website:* https://www.facebook.com/SugarNovaGroup

*Represents:* Artists/Bands

*Genres:* Hip-Hop; Indie; Jazz; Pop; R&B; Urban

Management company dealing mainly with musicians, but also actors, models, fashion designers and athletes. Send demo by email, including three tracks, photo, and links to social networking sites.

## Tap Music
*Email:* info@tapmgmt.com
*Website:* https://tap-music.com
*Website:* https://www.facebook.com/tapmusicofficial/

*Represents:* Artists/Bands

*Genres:* All types of music

Music management company with offices in London, Berlin and LA. Make initial contact by email.

## Tape
London
*Email:* info@taperec.com
*Website:* http://www.taperec.com
*Website:* https://www.facebook.com/TAPEWORLD

*Represents:* Artists/Bands

*Genres:* All types of music, except: Metal; Techno

Management company with offices in London and Barcelona. Send demos by email as MP3 attachments.

## Third Bar Artist Development
C/O Oh yeah Music Centre
15-21 Gordon Street
Belfast
BT1 2GH
*Email:* candice@thirdbar.co.uk
*Email:* thirdbarsubmissions@gmail.com
*Website:* http://thirdbar.co.uk
*Website:* https://www.facebook.com/thirdbar

*Represents:* Artists/Bands

*Genres:* All types of music

*Contact:* Davy Matchett

Artist development business based in Belfast. Send music via online file transfer system (see website).

## Third Rock Music
*Email:* info@thirdrockmusic.co.uk
*Website:* http://www.thirdrockmusic.co.uk
*Website:* https://soundcloud.com/third-rock-recordings

*Represents:* Artists/Bands

*Genres:* All types of music

Management and publishing company. Send query with MP3s by email.

## This Is Music Ltd
Studio 2
Excel Building
6-16 Arbutus Street
Haggerston
London
E8 4DT
*Email:* simon@thisismusicltd.com
*Website:* http://thisismusicltd.com
*Website:* https://www.soundcloud.com/this-is-music

*Represents:* Artists/Bands; Producers

*Genres:* Electronic; Underground; Indie; Pop

*Contact:* Simon Gold

Music company based in London and Los Angeles. Provides management and label services for artists and producers.

## Tileyard Music
15 Tileyard Studios
Tileyard Road
Kings Cross
London
N7 9AH
*Email:* Jason@tileyardmusic.co.uk
*Email:* info@tileyardmusic.co.uk
*Website:* http://www.tileyard.co.uk/music

*Represents:* Artists/Bands

*Genres:* Dance; Hip-Hop; Folk; Pop; Rock; Urban

Boutique management and publishing company, formed in October 2012. Send query by email with soundcloud links.

## Tone Management
22 The Close
Saxton
Leeds
West Yorkshire
LS9 8HW
*Email:* hello@tonemgmt.com
*Website:* http://tonemgmt.com
*Website:* https://www.facebook.com/ToneMGMT

*Represents:* Artists/Bands

*Genres:* Metal; Rock; Pop; Post Rock; Hardcore; Punk

*Contact:* Tom Bellhouse; Tom Ghannad; Tony Boden; Kim Kelly; Sofi Nowell

Management company with offices in Leeds, London, Bristol, and New York. Send query by email with links to streaming music online. No attachments.

## Toonteen Industries: Management & Promotions
*Email:* demos@toonteen.co.uk
*Email:* joe@toonteen.co.uk
*Website:* https://www.toonteen.co.uk
*Website:* https://www.myspace.com/toonteenindustries

*Represents:* Artists/Bands

*Genres:* Acoustic Alternative Heavy
Progressive Ambient Emo Hardcore Indie
Metal Pop Punk Rock

*Contact:* Joe Weaver

Management company based in Bury St
Edmunds. Promotes shows with various
bands in venues all over East Anglia, but
mainly focued within Bury St Edmunds.
Also manages bands and solo artists. Send
query by email with links to music online.
No attachments.

## Travelled Music
*Email:* alan@travelledmusic.co.uk
*Email:* ian@travelledmusic.co.uk
*Website:* https://www.travelledmusic.co.uk
*Website:* https://soundcloud.com/
travelledmusic
*Website:* https://myspace.com/travelledmusic

*Represents:* Artists/Bands

*Genres:* Alternative; Rock; Electronic; Indie

*Contact:* Alan Thompson; Ian Thompson

Music company based in Berwick upon
Tweed offering artist and tour management,
websites and social media, direct-to-fan
marketing, bookings and promotions, event
management.

## Trinifold Management
12 Oval Road
London
NW1 7DH
*Fax:* +44 (0) 20 7419 4325
*Website:* https://www.trinifold.co.uk
*Website:* https://www.instagram.com/
trinifold

*Represents:* Artists/Bands

*Genres:* All types of music

Submit demo via form on website.

## TRYB Management
*Email:* alex@trybmanagement.com
*Website:* https://www.trybmanagement.com
*Website:* https://twitter.com/trybmanagement

*Represents:* Artists/Bands

*Genres:* Pop

Music management company, based in
Bristol. Currently managing new pop artist
LENN.

Feel free to get in touch!

## Tsunami Music
20–22 Wenlock Road
London
N1 7GU
*Email:* demos@tsunamimusic.com
*Email:* hello@tsunamimusic.com
*Website:* http://www.tsunamimusic.com

*Represents:* Film / TV Composers;
Supervisors

*Genres:* All types of music

Provides composed music for film, TV,
video games, etc.

## UAC Management
*Email:* hristo@uacmanagement.co.uk
*Email:* thrasher@uacmanagement.co.uk
*Website:* http://www.uacmanagement.co.uk
*Website:* https://www.facebook.com/
uacmanagement/?fref=nf

*Represents:* Artists/Bands

*Genres:* All types of music

*Contact:* Hristo Penchev; Kevin Thrasher

Full service management company based in
the UK. Make initial contact by email.

## Underplay
*Email:* chrisbellam@underplay.co.uk
*Website:* https://www.underplay.co.uk

*Represents:* Artists/Bands

*Genres:* All types of music

*Contact:* Chris Bellam

Artist management and promotion.

## United Stage International Ltd

Apartment 1
160 New Kings Road
London
SW6 4LZ
*Email:* valerie@unitedstage.co.uk
*Email:* info@unitedstage.co.uk
*Website:* https://www.unitedstage.co.uk
*Website:* https://www.facebook.com/
UnitedStageInternational

*Represents:* Artists/Bands

*Genres:* Electronic; Indie; Rock

International office of Scandinavia's largest
booking agency. Send query by email with
bio and links to music online.

## Universal Talent Group

71-75 Shelton Street
Covent Garden
London
WC2H 9JQ
*Email:* info@universaltalentgroup.co.uk
*Website:* http://www.
universaltalentgroup.co.uk

*Represents:* Artists/Bands

*Genres:* Pop

Management company based in London.
Send submissions through online form on
website.

## Uplifted Music Management

Manchester
M41
*Website:* https://www.
upliftedmusicmanagement.co.uk

*Represents:* Artists/Bands; DJs

*Genres:* Dance; Electronic

Electronic / Dance artist management, based
in Manchester.

## Various Artists Management

37 Lonsdale Road
London
NW6 6RA
*Email:* info@variousartistsmanagement.com
*Website:* http://

variousartistsmanagement.com
*Website:* https://www.facebook.com/
variousartistsmanagement

*Represents:* Artists/Bands; Producers

*Genres:* All types of music

Management company with offices in
London and Los Angeles.

## The Velvet Drum

*Email:* felix@thevelvetdrum.com
*Website:* http://www.thevelvetdrum.com

*Represents:* Artists/Bands

*Genres:* All types of music

Send submissions by email.

## Verdigris Management

London
*Email:* info@verdigrismanagement.com
*Website:* http://www.
verdigrismanagement.com

*Represents:* Artists/Bands

*Genres:* All types of music

*Contact:* Sam

Management company based in London.
Send demos by email.

## Viral Music

Brunswick Mill
Manchester
M40 7EZ
*Email:* info@viralmusicuk.com
*Website:* https://www.viralmusicuk.com
*Website:* https://www.facebook.com/
ViralMusicUK/

*Represents:* Artists/Bands; DJs

*Genres:* Dance; House; Commercial

Management company providing
conservatoire-trained, professionally-
accomplished musicians to the nightlife
entertainment industry, as well as for a wide
range of other events, including weddings
and private/corporate functions. Send query
by email or through contact form on website,
with links to music online.

## We Like Oliver

London
*Email:* olly@welikeoliver.com
*Website:* https://welikeoliver.com
*Website:* https://www.facebook.com/
welikeoliver

*Represents:* Artists/Bands

*Genres:* All types of music

*Contact:* Olly Andrews

Describes itself as an "all things digital
company for musicians, artists, visual artists
and creative types".

## The Weird and the Wonderful

London
*Email:* info@theweirdandthewonderful.com
*Website:* https://
theweirdandthewonderfulofficial.
tumblr.com/
*Website:* https://www.facebook.com/
theweirdandthewonderfulofficial

*Represents:* Artists/Bands

*Genres:* Electronic; Folk; House; Techno;
Urban

An international multi-discipline music and
arts talent consultancy and management
company.

## Wildlife Entertainment Ltd

*Email:* info@wildlife-entertainment.com
*Website:* https://www.wildlife-
entertainment.com

*Represents:* Artists/Bands

*Genres:* Indie; Rock; R&B

Management company based in South West
London. Send query by email and follow up
with demo upon request.

## XIX Entertainment Ltd

UNIT 5B
The Albion Riverside
London
SW11 4AX
*Email:* info@xixentertainment.com
*Website:* http://www.xixentertainment.com

*Represents:* Artists/Bands

*Genres:* All types of music

Management company responsible for such
shows as American Idol and Little Britain
USA. Has offices in London, Los Angeles,
New York, Paris, and Nashville. Send demos
by post or email.

## XVII Music Group

Brighton
*Email:* info@xviimusic.com
*Website:* https://xviimusic.com
*Website:* https://soundcloud.com/
xviimusicgroup

*Represents:* Artists/Bands

*Genres:* All types of music

Artists development and record label based
in Brighton. Send demos by email.

## Yearone Management

*Email:* pharris@yearonesm.com
*Website:* https://www.yearonesm.com
*Website:* https://www.facebook.com/
yearonesm/

*Represents:* Artists/Bands

*Genres:* All types of music

Looking for any sort of artist either up and
coming or established for us to take to the
next level. Contact via contact form on
website.

## Yellowbrick Music

5-7 Vernon Yard
London
W11 2DX
*Email:* info@yellowbrickmusic.com
*Email:* meredith@yellowbrickmusic.com
*Website:* https://yellowbrickmusic.com
*Website:* https://twitter.com/YellBrickMusic

*Represents:* Artists/Bands

*Genres:* All types of music

Label service company based in London,
offering artists a creative range of support
and tools. Send query by email with links to

streaming music online, or send submissions by post. No download links.

## YMU Group

Clifton Works
23 Grove Park Terrace
Chiswick
London
W4 3QE

180 Great Portland Street
London
W1W 5QZ

3rd Floor Colwyn Chambers
19 York Street
Manchester
M2 3BA
*Email:* enquiries@ymugroup.com
*Website:* https://www.ymugroup.com

*Represents:* Artists/Bands; DJs; Producers; Songwriters

*Genres:* Alternative Rock; Dance; Electronic; Pop

Management company with offices in London, Manchester, Washington DC, California, and New York.

## Young Guns

2 Princes Street
Mayfair
London
W1B 2LB
*Email:* hello@younggunsgroup.com
*Website:* https://www.younggunsgroup.com
*Website:* https://www.facebook.com/YoungGunsLtd

*Represents:* Artists/Bands; Producers; Studio Musicians

*Genres:* Classical; Jazz; Pop; Fusion

Management company based in London. Send two contrasting tracks as MP3s by email.

# Canadian Managers

*For the most up-to-date listings of these and hundreds of other managers, visit https://www.musicsocket.com/managers*

*To claim your **free** access to the site, please see the back of this book.*

## Bedlam Music Management

290 Gerrard St East
Toronto, ON M5A 2G4

LOS ANGELES
4525 Russell Ave #1
Los Angeles CA 90027

NASHVILLE
1300 Clinton St, Suite 205
Nashville, TN 37203
*Email:* info@bedlammusicmgt.com
*Website:* http://www.bedlammusicmgt.com

*Represents:* Artists/Bands

*Genres:* All types of music

A full service artist management company based in Toronto, Canada, with offices in Los Angeles and Nashville.

## Panacea Entertainment

2nd Floor, 9868a 33 Avenue
Edmonton, AB T6N 1C6

US OFFICE:
13587 Andalusia Drive East
Santa Rosa Valley, CA 93012
*Fax:* +1 (780) 490-5255
*Email:* info@panacea-ent.com
*Website:* http://panaceaentertainment.com

*Represents:* Artists/Bands; Film / TV Composers; Producers; Songwriters

*Genres:* All types of music

*Contact:* Eric Gardner

Management company based in Edmonton, Alberta. Not accepting submissions as at November 2019.

# Australian Managers

*For the most up-to-date listings of these and hundreds of other managers, visit https://www.musicsocket.com/managers*

*To claim your **free** access to the site, please see the back of this book.*

## Open Door Management
*Email:* info@opendoormgmt.com.au
*Website:* https://opendoormgmt.com.au/
*Website:* https://www.facebook.com/
OpenDoorMgt/

*Represents:* Artists/Bands

*Genres:* All types of music

Open door policy where artists will feel free to be a part of the process and be not left in the dark with anything happening in their careers.

## Wanted Management
*Email:* wantedgregg@gmail.com
*Website:* https://www.facebook.com/
WantedMgmt
*Website:* https://soundcloud.com/
wantedmgmt

*Represents:* Artists/Bands

*Genres:* Pop; Punk; Rock; Soul; Roots; Rock and Roll

*Contact:* Gregg Bell

Management company formed originally in the US in 2001, now based in Perth, Australia.

# Managers Index

*This section lists managers by their genres, with directions to the section of the book where the full listing can be found.*

*You can create your own customised lists of managers using different combinations of these subject areas, plus over a dozen other criteria, instantly online at https://www.musicsocket.com.*

*To claim your **free** access to the site, please see the back of this book.*

**All types of music**
!K7 (*UK*)
360 Artist Development (*UK*)
4 Tunes Ltd (*UK*)
A&R Factory (*UK*)
Abba-Tude Entertainment (*US*)
ACA Music & Entertainment (*US*)
AirMTM (*UK*)
Amber Artists (*UK*)
AMW Group Inc. (*US*)
Aneko Music (*UK*)
Anger Management (*UK*)
Anglo Management (*UK*)
The Animal Farm (*UK*)
APA (Agency for the Performing Arts) (*US*)
ASM Talent (*UK*)
ATC Management (*UK*)
Atomic (*UK*)
Atum Management Ltd (*UK*)
Autonomy Music Group (*UK*)
Avenoir (*UK*)
Azoff Music Management (*US*)
Backstage Entertainment (*US*)
Bandguru Management (*US*)
Bedlam Music Management (*Can*)
Big Hug Management (*UK*)
Big Life Management (*UK*)
Big Noise (*US*)
BiGiAM Promotions & Management (*UK*)

Bill Silva Management (*US*)
BK40 Productions (*UK*)
Black Fox Management (*UK*)
Blue Raincoat Music (*UK*)
BORDR (*UK*)
Brian Yeates Associates Ltd (*UK*)
Catalyst Management (*UK*)
Century Artists Management Agency, LLC (*US*)
Closer Artists Management & Publishing (*UK*)
CMP Entertainment (*UK*)
Conchord (*UK*)
Covert Talent Management (*UK*)
Creating Monsters (*UK*)
Creative Artists Agency (CAA) (*US*)
Creeme Entertainments (*UK*)
Crockford Management (*UK*)
Crush Music Media Management (*US*)
Culler Talent Management (*US*)
Culture City (*UK*)
Darren Adam (*UK*)
Deltasonic Records (*UK*)
Deluxxe Management (*UK*)
Denizen Artist Management (*UK*)
The Derek Power Company & Kahn Power Pictures (*US*)
Deuce Management & Promotion (*UK*)
Discovering Arts Music Group (DAMG) (*UK*)

DMF Music Ltd (*UK*)
Dog & Pony Industries (*US*)
East Coast Entertainment (ECE) (*US*)
Electric Pineapple Music (*UK*)
End of the Trail Creative (*UK*)
Fave Sounds (*UK*)
Ferocious Talent (*UK*)
Formidable Music Management (*UK*)
Friends Vs Music Ltd (*UK*)
Funzalo Records (*US*)
Gary Stamler Management (*US*)
Gayle Enterprises, Inc. (*US*)
The Gorfaine/Schwartz Agency, Inc. (*US*)
Grizzly Management (*UK*)
Guild Productions (*UK*)
Hannah Management (*UK*)
Happy House Management & Marketing
Services (*UK*)
Heard and Seen (*UK*)
Heart & Soul Artist Management (*US*)
Hot House Music Ltd (*UK*)
Hot Vox (*UK*)
Howard Rosen Promotion, Inc. (*US*)
ie:music (*UK*)
Impact Management (*UK*)
Indevine (*UK*)
Innate – Music Ltd (*UK*)
Interlude Artists (*UK*)
International Creative Management (ICM)
Partners (*US*)
Intune Addicts (*UK*)
Invasion Group, Ltd (*US*)
JA Artist Management (*UK*)
James Joseph Music Management (*UK*)
Jampol Artist Management (*US*)
JD & Co. (*UK*)
John Waller Management (*UK*)
Jost Music (*UK*)
Karma Artists Music LLP (*UK*)
KBH Entertainment (*US*)
KRMB Management & Consultancy (*UK*)
Laissez Faire Club (*UK*)
Liquid Management (*UK*)
MaDa Music Entertainment (*UK*)
Major Labl (*UK*)
Manners McDade Artist Management
(*UK*)
Manta Ray Music (*UK*)
MBM (Music Business Management Ltd)
(*UK*)
The MGMT Company (*US*)
Michael Kline Artists (*US*)
Million Dollar Artists (*US*)
MJM Agency (*UK*)
Monotone, Inc. (*US*)

Mother Artist Management (*UK*)
MPL Music Publishing, Inc. (*US*)
MSH Management (*US*)
Murphy to Manteo (MTM) Music
Management (*US*)
Music by Design (*UK*)
Music City Artists (*US*)
Nettwerk Management UK (*UK*)
New Heights Entertainment (*US*)
New Level Music Management (*UK*)
New Outlaw (*UK*)
Nightside Entertainment, Inc. (*US*)
No Half Measures Ltd (*UK*)
One Fifteen (*UK*)
141a Management (*UK*)
140dB Management Limited (*UK*)
Open Door Management (*Aus*)
Ozark Talent (*US*)
Pacific Talent (*US*)
Panacea Entertainment (*Can*)
Paper House Music (*UK*)
Paradigm Talent Agency (*US*)
Persistent Management (*US*)
Petty Music Management (*UK*)
Pieces of 8 Music (*UK*)
PMS Music Management (*UK*)
Pond Life Songs (*UK*)
Pretty Lights (*US*)
Prolifica Management (*UK*)
Psycho Management Company (*UK*)
Push Music Management (*UK*)
Quest Management (*UK*)
Real Media Music (*UK*)
Red Afternoon Management (*UK*)
Regime Seventy-Two (*US*)
Richard Varrasso Management (*US*)
Riot Squad (*US*)
Rock Hippie Management & Music (*UK*)
Rollover (*UK*)
Rosen Music Corp. (*US*)
Rough Diamond (*UK*)
Roundface Music Management (*UK*)
S&B Creative (*UK*)
SB Management (*UK*)
Selak Entertainment, Inc. (*US*)
September Management (UK) (*UK*)
September Management (US) (*US*)
74 Promotions (*UK*)
SGO Ltd (*UK*)
Sidewinder Management Ltd (*UK*)
SKH Music (*US*)
SMC Artists (*US*)
Solar Management (*UK*)
Solid Music Company (*US*)
Sound Consultancy (*UK*)

The Soundcheck Group (*UK*)
South Star Music (*UK*)
Sparks Entertainment Management Co. (*US*)
Steve Allen Entertainments (*UK*)
Storm5 Management (*UK*)
Take Out Management (*US*)
Talent Source (*US*)
Tap Music (*UK*)
Tape (*UK*)
Tenth Street Entertainment (*US*)
That's Entertainment International Inc. (TEI Entertainment) (*US*)
Third Bar Artist Development (*UK*)
Third Rock Music (*UK*)
Threee (*US*)
Tom Callahan & Associates (TCA) (*US*)
Trinifold Management (*UK*)
True Talent Management (*US*)
Tsunami Entertainment (*US*)
Tsunami Music (*UK*)
UAC Management (*UK*)
Uncle Booking (*US*)
Underplay (*UK*)
United Talent Agency (*US*)
Universal Attractions Agency (*US*)
Various Artists Management (*UK*)
The Velvet Drum (*UK*)
Velvet Hammer Music & Management Group (*US*)
Verdigris Management (*UK*)
Walker Entertainment Group (*US*)
We Like Oliver (*UK*)
Wolfson Entertainment, Inc. (*US*)
Worlds End Management (*US*)
XIX Entertainment Ltd (*UK*)
XVII Music Group (*UK*)
Yearone Management (*UK*)
Yellowbrick Music (*UK*)

**Acoustic**
A2E – Artists 2 Events (*UK*)
ADSRecords (*UK*)
Aspire Music Management (*UK*)
Audio Bay Management (*UK*)
Bandzmedia (*UK*)
Dawson Breed Music (*UK*)
Fat City Artists (*US*)
Fat Penguin Management (*UK*)
Heist or Hit (*UK*)
Hello! Booking, Inc. (*US*)
Kari Estrin Management & Consulting (*US*)
Moneypenny (*UK*)
musicmedia (*UK*)
Offbeat Management (*UK*)

Park Records (*UK*)
Pillar Artists (*UK*)
Purple Rhino Music (*US*)
Reckless Yes (*UK*)
Red Grape Music (*UK*)
TAC Music Management (*US*)
Toonteen Industries: Management & Promotions (*UK*)

**Alternative**
0114 Records (*UK*)
ADSRecords (*UK*)
Advanced Alternative Media (AAM) (*US*)
Apex Talent Group (*US*)
Arlon Music (*UK*)
Artist in Mind (*US*)
Associated London Management (*UK*)
Big Hassle Management (*US*)
Bitchin' Entertainment (*US*)
Black Bleach Records (*UK*)
Burgess World Co. (*US*)
BUT! Management (*UK*)
Claudia eRecords (*UK*)
Craft Management (*UK*)
DDB Productions (*US*)
Deep South Artist Management (*US*)
Dissention Records + Artist Management (*UK*)
Don't Try (*UK*)
Dreamboat Management (*UK*)
East City (*UK*)
Elephant Management (*UK*)
F&G Management (*UK*)
Fat Penguin Management (*UK*)
Feed Your Head (*UK*)
5B Artist Management (*US*)
Flow State Music (*UK*)
Freaks R Us (*UK*)
Ganbei Records (*UK*)
Golden Arm (*UK*)
Goo Music Management Ltd (*UK*)
Hardin Entertainment (*US*)
Heist or Hit (*UK*)
Holier than Thou (HTT) Music (*UK*)
Hornblow Group USA, Inc. (*US*)
Ignition Management (*UK*)
Impact Artist Management (*US*)
JBLS Management (*UK*)
Jude Street Management (*UK*)
Key Music Management (*UK*)
Kuper Personal Management (*US*)
Landstar Management (*UK*)
Listen to This Management (*UK*)
Loggins Promotion (*US*)
M. Hitchcock Management (*US*)
Metal Music Bookings (*UK*)

MOB Agency (*US*)
Moksha Management (*UK*)
Monqui Presents (*US*)
Musicarchy Media (*UK*)
musicmedia (*UK*)
Mustang Agency (*US*)
North Central Music (NCM) (*UK*)
Offbeat Management (*UK*)
Pillar Artists (*UK*)
Position Music (*US*)
Possessive Management (*UK*)
Prodigal Son Entertainment (*US*)
Purple Rhino Music (*US*)
Q Prime Management, Inc. (*US*)
Raw Power Management (*UK*)
Reckless Yes (*UK*)
Russell Carter Artist Management (*US*)
Saviour Management (*UK*)
Sharpe Entertainment Services, Inc. (*US*)
Siren Music Company (*US*)
Steve Stewart Entertainment (*US*)
Steven Scharf Entertainment (SSE) (*US*)
Stormcraft Music (*UK*)
Strike up the Brand (*US*)
TAC Music Management (*US*)
Toonteen Industries: Management &
Promotions (*UK*)
Travelled Music (*UK*)
Union Entertainment Group (*US*)
Vector Management (*US*)
YMU Group (*UK*)
**Ambient**
Angelica Arts & Entertainment (*US*)
Bitchin' Entertainment (*US*)
Hot Gem (*UK*)
Landstar Management (*UK*)
Offbeat Management (*UK*)
Toonteen Industries: Management &
Promotions (*UK*)
Tuscan Sun Music (*US*)
**Americana**
Artist in Mind (*US*)
Bitchin' Entertainment (*US*)
Brighthelmstone Promotions (*UK*)
Brilliant Productions (*US*)
Dawson Breed Music (*UK*)
Deep South Artist Management (*US*)
Fat Penguin Management (*UK*)
Hardin Entertainment (*US*)
Kari Estrin Management & Consulting
(*US*)
KCA Artists (*US*)
Kuper Personal Management (*US*)
Loggins Promotion (*US*)
Mike's Artist Management (*US*)

Moneypenny (*UK*)
Myriad Artists (*US*)
Nancy Fly Agency (*US*)
Purple Rhino Music (*US*)
Rosier Artist Management (RAM) (*UK*)
Russell Carter Artist Management (*US*)
Siren Music Company (*US*)
Steven Scharf Entertainment (SSE) (*US*)
TAC Music Management (*US*)
Vector Management (*US*)
**Atmospheric**
Landstar Management (*UK*)
**Black Metal**
Offbeat Management (*UK*)
Purple Rhino Music (*US*)
**Black Origin**
Purple Rhino Music (*US*)
**Blue Beat**
Purple Rhino Music (*US*)
**Blues**
A2E – Artists 2 Events (*UK*)
Act 1 Entertainment (*US*)
Artist Representation and Management
(ARM) Entertainment (*US*)
Big Bear Music (*UK*)
Bitchin' Entertainment (*US*)
Brilliant Productions (*US*)
Burgess World Co. (*US*)
Cantaloupe Music Productions, Inc. (*US*)
Collin Artists (*US*)
Columbia Artists Management Inc.
(CAMI) (*US*)
Concerted Efforts (*US*)
Emcee Artist Management (*US*)
Fat City Artists (*US*)
Fleming Artists (*US*)
Hardin Entertainment (*US*)
Harmony Artists (*US*)
Impact Artist Management (*US*)
KCA Artists (*US*)
The Kurland Agency (*US*)
Len Weisman, Personal Manager (*US*)
Max Bernard Management (*US*)
Myriad Artists (*US*)
Nancy Fly Agency (*US*)
Offbeat Management (*UK*)
Perry Road Records (*UK*)
Piedmont Talent (*US*)
Q Prime Management, Inc. (*US*)
Red Light Management (RLM) (*US*)
Rock People Management (RPM) (*UK*)
Ron Rainey Management Inc. (*US*)
Russell Carter Artist Management (*US*)
Siren Music Company (*US*)
Sterling Artist Management (*US*)

Steven Scharf Entertainment (SSE) (*US*)
TAC Music Management (*US*)
Tower Management Group (*US*)
Union Entertainment Group (*US*)
Universal Tone Management (*US*)
Val's Artist Management (VAM) (*US*)
**Break Beat**
Finger Lickin' Management (*UK*)
**Celtic**
A2E – Artists 2 Events (*UK*)
Columbia Artists Management Inc.
(CAMI) (*US*)
Fat City Artists (*US*)
Landstar Management (*UK*)
Purple Rhino Music (*US*)
Worldsound, LLC (*US*)
**Chill**
Involved Management (*UK*)
Offbeat Management (*UK*)
Purple Rhino Music (*US*)
**Christian**
25 Artist Agency (*US*)
The Brokaw Company (*US*)
Deep South Artist Management (*US*)
Hardin Entertainment (*US*)
Jeff Roberts & Associates (*US*)
Nettwerk Management (*US*)
Prodigal Son Entertainment (*US*)
Red Light Management (RLM) (*US*)
**Classic**
Act 1 Entertainment (*US*)
American Artists Corporation (*US*)
Arslanian & Associates, Inc. (*US*)
Artist Representation and Management
(ARM) Entertainment (*US*)
Big Beat Productions, Inc. (*US*)
Bill Hollingshead Productions, Inc. Talent
Agency (*US*)
Entertainment Services International (*US*)
IMG Artists (*US*)
Michael Anthony's Electric Events (*US*)
Moneypenny (*UK*)
Mustang Agency (*US*)
Suncoast Music Management (*US*)
TAC Music Management (*US*)
**Classical**
Askonas Holt Ltd (*UK*)
Audio Bay Management (*UK*)
BBA Management & Booking (*US*)
Bitchin' Entertainment (*US*)
Columbia Artists Management Inc.
(CAMI) (*US*)
Dawn Elder Management (*US*)
Domo Music Group Management (*US*)
Intertalent Rights Group (*UK*)

Jude Street Management (*UK*)
Opus 3 Artists (*US*)
Purple Rhino Music (*US*)
PVA Management Ltd (*UK*)
Richard Lipman (*UK*)
Silverword Music Group (*UK*)
Val's Artist Management (VAM) (*US*)
Young Guns (*UK*)
**Club**
Empire Artist Management (*US*)
Purple Rhino Music (*US*)
**Commercial**
B&H Management (*UK*)
Create Management (*UK*)
Freedom Management (*UK*)
GR Management (*UK*)
Handshake Ltd. (*UK*)
Insomnia Music UK (*UK*)
Island Music Management (*UK*)
Purple Rhino Music (*US*)
Qveen Management (*UK*)
TAC Music Management (*US*)
Viral Music (*UK*)
**Contemporary**
Amour:Music (*UK*)
Artist in Mind (*US*)
Big Beat Productions, Inc. (*US*)
Black Dot Management (*US*)
Booking Entertainment (*US*)
Chapman & Co. Management (*US*)
Collin Artists (*US*)
Columbia Artists Management Inc.
(CAMI) (*US*)
David Belenzon Management, Inc. (*US*)
Domo Music Group Management (*US*)
Fleming Artists (*US*)
Hardin Entertainment (*US*)
Impact Artist Management (*US*)
Kragen & Company (*US*)
M. Hitchcock Management (*US*)
Michael Hausman Artist Management Inc.
(*US*)
MM Music Agency (*US*)
Moksha Management (*UK*)
Nettwerk Management (*US*)
Purple Rhino Music (*US*)
Riot Artists (*US*)
Ron Rainey Management Inc. (*US*)
Russell Carter Artist Management (*US*)
Serious (*UK*)
Sharpe Entertainment Services, Inc. (*US*)
Spot Light Entertainment, Inc. (*US*)
Stiefel Entertainment (*US*)
Val's Artist Management (VAM) (*US*)
Vector Management (*US*)

Freaks R Us (*UK*)
Hardin Entertainment (*US*)
Holier than Thou (HTT) Music (*UK*)
Holy-Toto (*UK*)
Hot Gem (*UK*)
HQ Familia (*UK*)
Humans & Other Animals (*UK*)
Involved Management (*UK*)
JBLS Management (*UK*)
Landstar Management (*UK*)
Lucky Number Music Limited (*UK*)
Moksha Management (*UK*)
Music + Art Management (*US*)
Nettwerk Management (*US*)
OnDaBeat Talent Management (*UK*)
Position Music (*US*)
Purple Rhino Music (*US*)
Qveen Management (*UK*)
Red Light Management (RLM) (*US*)
Salvation Records (*UK*)
This Is Music Ltd (*UK*)
Travelled Music (*UK*)
United Stage International Ltd (*UK*)
Uplifted Music Management (*UK*)
Waxploitation (*US*)
The Weird and the Wonderful (*UK*)
YMU Group (*UK*)

**Emo**
Purple Rhino Music (*US*)
Toonteen Industries: Management & Promotions (*UK*)

**Ethnic**
Domo Music Group Management (*US*)
Purple Rhino Music (*US*)

**Experimental**
Bitchin' Entertainment (*US*)
F&G Management (*UK*)
Freaks R Us (*UK*)
Hot Gem (*UK*)
Landstar Management (*UK*)
Music + Art Management (*US*)
Purple Rhino Music (*US*)

**Extreme**
Purple Rhino Music (*US*)

**Folk**
0114 Records (*UK*)
21st Century Artists, Inc. (*US*)
AEC Music Management (*UK*)
Artist in Mind (*US*)
Audio Bay Management (*UK*)
Bernie Nelson Artist Management (*UK*)
Bitchin' Entertainment (*US*)
Brighthelmstone Promotions (*UK*)
Bulletproof Artist Management (*US*)
Case Entertainment Group Inc. (*US*)

Columbia Artists Management Inc. (CAMI) (*US*)
Concerted Efforts (*US*)
Dawson Breed Music (*UK*)
DCA Productions (*US*)
Domo Music Group Management (*US*)
Fat City Artists (*US*)
Fat Penguin Management (*UK*)
Fleming Artists (*US*)
Front Room Songs (*UK*)
Ganbei Records (*UK*)
Hardin Entertainment (*US*)
Hello! Booking, Inc. (*US*)
Humans & Other Animals (*UK*)
IMG Artists (*US*)
Impact Artist Management (*US*)
Kari Estrin Management & Consulting (*US*)
KCA Artists (*US*)
Kuper Personal Management (*US*)
M. Hitchcock Management (*US*)
Maine Road Management (*US*)
Mike's Artist Management (*US*)
musicmedia (*UK*)
Myriad Artists (*US*)
Nettwerk Management (*US*)
NSI Management (*US*)
Off the Chart Promotions (*UK*)
Park Records (*UK*)
Q Prime Management, Inc. (*US*)
Red Grape Music (*UK*)
Russell Carter Artist Management (*US*)
Siren Music Company (*US*)
Steven Scharf Entertainment (SSE) (*US*)
TAC Music Management (*US*)
Tileyard Music (*UK*)
Tractor Beam Managing & Consulting (*US*)
Two Chord Touring (*US*)
Val's Artist Management (VAM) (*US*)
Variety Artists International (*US*)
Vector Management (*US*)
The Weird and the Wonderful (*UK*)
Worldsound, LLC (*US*)

**Funk**
Bitchin' Entertainment (*US*)
Fat City Artists (*US*)
Plus Music (*UK*)
Purple Rhino Music (*US*)
Pyramid Entertainment Group (*US*)
Red Entertainment Agency (*US*)
TAC Music Management (*US*)

**Funky**
Purple Rhino Music (*US*)
TAC Music Management (*US*)

**Fusion**
Moksha Management (*UK*)
Purple Rhino Music (*US*)
TAC Music Management (*US*)
Young Guns (*UK*)
**Garage**
0114 Records (*UK*)
Black Bleach Records (*UK*)
Landstar Management (*UK*)
Offbeat Management (*UK*)
Purple Rhino Music (*US*)
Salvation Records (*UK*)
**Glam**
Purple Rhino Music (*US*)
**Gospel**
Celebrity Talent Agency Inc. (*US*)
Circle City Records USA (*US*)
Concerted Efforts (*US*)
Fat City Artists (*US*)
Fresh Flava Entertainment (*US*)
IMG Artists (*US*)
KCA Artists (*US*)
Len Weisman, Personal Manager (*US*)
Music World Entertainment (*US*)
Pyramid Entertainment Group (*US*)
Red Entertainment Agency (*US*)
Silverword Music Group (*UK*)
Spot Light Entertainment, Inc. (*US*)
Vector Management (*US*)
**Gothic**
Bitchin' Entertainment (*US*)
Holier than Thou (HTT) Music (*UK*)
Landstar Management (*UK*)
Musicarchy Media (*UK*)
Purple Rhino Music (*US*)
**Grime**
Purple Rhino Music (*US*)
**Grind**
Purple Rhino Music (*US*)
**Guitar based**
Crosstalk Management (*UK*)
Landstar Management (*UK*)
Offbeat Management (*UK*)
Pillar Artists (*UK*)
Purple Rhino Music (*US*)
Reckless Yes (*UK*)
Stormcraft Music (*UK*)
TAC Music Management (*US*)
**Hard**
0114 Records (*UK*)
Landstar Management (*UK*)
Musicarchy Media (*UK*)
Offbeat Management (*UK*)
Prodigal Son Entertainment (*US*)
Purple Rhino Music (*US*)

TAC Music Management (*US*)
**Hardcore**
Hardin Entertainment (*US*)
Position Music (*US*)
Possessive Management (*UK*)
Purple Rhino Music (*US*)
Red Light Management (RLM) (*US*)
Steve Stewart Entertainment (*US*)
Tone Management (*UK*)
Toonteen Industries: Management &
Promotions (*UK*)
**Heavy**
Landstar Management (*UK*)
Lokation (*UK*)
Musicarchy Media (*UK*)
Offbeat Management (*UK*)
Purple Rhino Music (*US*)
TAC Music Management (*US*)
Toonteen Industries: Management &
Promotions (*UK*)
**Hip-Hop**
Bitchin' Entertainment (*US*)
The Brokaw Company (*US*)
Celebrity Talent Agency Inc. (*US*)
Chicken Grease Presents (*UK*)
Claudia eRecords (*UK*)
DAS Communications Ltd (*US*)
Finger Lickin' Management (*UK*)
First Access Entertainment (*US*)
Fresh Flava Entertainment (*US*)
Hello! Booking, Inc. (*US*)
Holy-Toto (*UK*)
Len Weisman, Personal Manager (*US*)
Lippman Entertainment (*US*)
Loggins Promotion (*US*)
The Lost Atlantis Records (*UK*)
Lupo Entertainment (*US*)
Mauldin Brand Agency (*US*)
Nettwerk Management (*US*)
NSB Artist Management (*UK*)
OnDaBeat Talent Management (*UK*)
Position Music (*US*)
Purple Rhino Music (*US*)
Pyramid Entertainment Group (*US*)
Red Entertainment Agency (*US*)
Red Light Management (RLM) (*US*)
Rhythmic Records Management and
Production (*UK*)
Spectrum Talent Agency (*US*)
Spot Light Entertainment, Inc. (*US*)
Steven Scharf Entertainment (SSE) (*US*)
SugarNova (*UK*)
Tileyard Music (*UK*)
Union Entertainment Group (*US*)
Val's Artist Management (VAM) (*US*)

Waxploitation (*US*)
**Horror**
Purple Rhino Music (*US*)
**House**
Bitchin' Entertainment (*US*)
F&G Management (*UK*)
House of Us (*UK*)
Involved Management (*UK*)
The Lost Atlantis Records (*UK*)
M24 Management (*UK*)
OnDaBeat Talent Management (*UK*)
Perfect Havoc Ltd (*UK*)
Rhythmic Records Management and
Production (*UK*)
Spectrum Talent Agency (*US*)
Viral Music (*UK*)
The Weird and the Wonderful (*UK*)
**House**
Bitchin' Entertainment (*US*)
F&G Management (*UK*)
House of Us (*UK*)
Involved Management (*UK*)
The Lost Atlantis Records (*UK*)
M24 Management (*UK*)
OnDaBeat Talent Management (*UK*)
Perfect Havoc Ltd (*UK*)
Rhythmic Records Management and
Production (*UK*)
Spectrum Talent Agency (*US*)
Viral Music (*UK*)
The Weird and the Wonderful (*UK*)
**Indie**
0114 Records (*UK*)
ADSRecords (*UK*)
Advanced Alternative Media (AAM) (*US*)
Apex Talent Group (*US*)
Artist in Mind (*US*)
Audio Bay Management (*UK*)
Bear Music Management (*UK*)
Bernie Nelson Artist Management (*UK*)
Big Dipper Productions Ltd (*UK*)
Big Hassle Management (*US*)
Black Bleach Records (*UK*)
Bold Management (*UK*)
Brighthelmstone Promotions (*UK*)
Claudia eRecords (*UK*)
Columbia Artists Management Inc.
(CAMI) (*US*)
Dawson Breed Music (*UK*)
Disaster Artist Management (*UK*)
Domo Music Group Management (*US*)
Don't Try (*UK*)
Dreamboat Management (*UK*)
Dusty Studio Productions (*UK*)
East City (*UK*)

Equator Music (*UK*)
Fat Penguin Management (*UK*)
Feed Your Head (*UK*)
Freedom Management (*UK*)
Fruition Music (*UK*)
Golden Arm (*UK*)
Goo Music Management Ltd (*UK*)
Hand in Hive Independent Records &
Management (*UK*)
Hardin Entertainment (*US*)
Heist or Hit (*UK*)
Hello! Booking, Inc. (*US*)
Hornblow Group USA, Inc. (*US*)
House of Us (*UK*)
Humans & Other Animals (*UK*)
Ignition Management (*UK*)
Impact Artist Management (*US*)
In De Goot Entertainment (*US*)
Island Music Management (*UK*)
Jude Street Management (*UK*)
Landstar Management (*UK*)
Listen to This Management (*UK*)
Lucky Number Music Limited (*UK*)
Lyricom (*UK*)
Madrigal Music artist management (*UK*)
Maine Road Management (*US*)
Max Bernard Management (*US*)
Memphia Music Management (*UK*)
Mike's Artist Management (*US*)
Miller Music Management (*UK*)
Monqui Presents (*US*)
Musicarchy Media (*UK*)
Nettwerk Management (*US*)
NSI Management (*US*)
Off the Chart Promotions (*UK*)
Perry Road Records (*UK*)
Pillar Artists (*UK*)
Purple Rhino Music (*US*)
Reckless Yes (*UK*)
Red Light Management (RLM) (*US*)
Russell Carter Artist Management (*US*)
Sharpe Entertainment Services, Inc. (*US*)
Steven Scharf Entertainment (SSE) (*US*)
Stiefel Entertainment (*US*)
Street Smart Management (*US*)
Sugar House Music (*UK*)
SugarNova (*UK*)
TAC Music Management (*US*)
This Is Music Ltd (*UK*)
Toonteen Industries: Management &
Promotions (*UK*)
Tractor Beam Managing & Consulting
(*US*)
Travelled Music (*UK*)
United Stage International Ltd (*UK*)

Val's Artist Management (VAM) (*US*)
Waxploitation (*US*)
Wildlife Entertainment Ltd (*UK*)
**Industrial**
Landstar Management (*UK*)
Purple Rhino Music (*US*)
**Instrumental**
Bitchin' Entertainment (*US*)
Collin Artists (*US*)
Columbia Artists Management Inc.
(CAMI) (*US*)
Offbeat Management (*UK*)
Prodigal Son Entertainment (*US*)
Purple Rhino Music (*US*)
**Jazz**
Act 1 Entertainment (*US*)
B.H. Hopper Management Ltd. (*UK*)
BBA Management & Booking (*US*)
Big Bear Music (*UK*)
Big Beat Productions, Inc. (*US*)
Bitchin' Entertainment (*US*)
Black Dot Management (*US*)
Booking Entertainment (*US*)
Burgess World Co. (*US*)
Cantaloupe Music Productions, Inc. (*US*)
Celebrity Talent Agency Inc. (*US*)
Chapman & Co. Management (*US*)
Chicken Grease Presents (*UK*)
Collin Artists (*US*)
Columbia Artists Management Inc.
(CAMI) (*US*)
Concerted Efforts (*US*)
Dawn Elder Management (*US*)
DDB Productions (*US*)
DFJ Artists (*UK*)
Emcee Artist Management (*US*)
Entourage Talent Associates, Ltd (*US*)
Fat City Artists (*US*)
Fresh Flava Entertainment (*US*)
Harmony Artists (*US*)
Hello! Booking, Inc. (*US*)
IMG Artists (*US*)
Impact Artist Management (*US*)
Ina Dittke & Associates (*US*)
The Kurland Agency (*US*)
Loggins Promotion (*US*)
Maine Road Management (*US*)
The Management Ark, Inc. (*US*)
Mars Jazz (*US*)
Mascioli Entertainment (*US*)
Max Bernard Management (*US*)
MM Music Agency (*US*)
Music + Art Management (*US*)
Myriad Artists (*US*)
Opus 3 Artists (*US*)

PRA [Patrick Rains & Associates] (*US*)
Purple Rhino Music (*US*)
Pyramid Entertainment Group (*US*)
Red Entertainment Agency (*US*)
RPM Music Productions (*US*)
Russell Carter Artist Management (*US*)
Serious (*UK*)
Silverword Music Group (*UK*)
Sterling Artist Management (*US*)
Steven Scharf Entertainment (SSE) (*US*)
SugarNova (*UK*)
TAC Music Management (*US*)
Tony Margherita Management (*US*)
Tractor Beam Managing & Consulting
(*US*)
Val's Artist Management (VAM) (*US*)
Variety Artists International (*US*)
Young Guns (*UK*)
**Latin**
BBA Management & Booking (*US*)
Cantaloupe Music Productions, Inc. (*US*)
Celebrity Talent Agency Inc. (*US*)
Collin Artists (*US*)
Columbia Artists Management Inc.
(CAMI) (*US*)
Hardin Entertainment (*US*)
Harmony Artists (*US*)
IMG Artists (*US*)
Impact Artist Management (*US*)
Ina Dittke & Associates (*US*)
Nettwerk Management (*US*)
Red Entertainment Agency (*US*)
Red Light Management (RLM) (*US*)
Universal Tone Management (*US*)
Val's Artist Management (VAM) (*US*)
**Lounge**
Angelica Arts & Entertainment (*US*)
**Mainstream**
GR Management (*UK*)
Max Bernard Management (*US*)
Purple Rhino Music (*US*)
**Melodic**
Aspire Music Management (*UK*)
Holier than Thou (HTT) Music (*UK*)
Purple Rhino Music (*US*)
**Melodicore**
Purple Rhino Music (*US*)
**Metal**
Artist Representation and Management
(ARM) Entertainment (*US*)
Bitchin' Entertainment (*US*)
Creative International Artist Management
(*UK*)
Enso Music Management (*UK*)
5B Artist Management (*US*)

Holier than Thou (HTT) Music (*UK*)
In De Goot Entertainment (*US*)
Incendia Music (*UK*)
Landstar Management (*UK*)
Lokation (*UK*)
McGhee Entertainment (*US*)
Metal Music Bookings (*UK*)
Musicarchy Media (*UK*)
Mustang Agency (*US*)
Northern Music Co. Ltd (*UK*)
Offbeat Management (*UK*)
Position Music (*US*)
Possessive Management (*UK*)
Purple Rhino Music (*US*)
Q Prime Management, Inc. (*US*)
Raw Power Management (*UK*)
Red Light Management (RLM) (*US*)
Saviour Management (*UK*)
Steven Scharf Entertainment (SSE) (*US*)
Street Smart Management (*US*)
TAC Music Management (*US*)
Tone Management (*UK*)
Toonteen Industries: Management &
Promotions (*UK*)
Vector Management (*US*)
**Modern**
Artist in Mind (*US*)
Purple Rhino Music (*US*)
**Mystical**
Landstar Management (*UK*)
**New Age**
Angelica Arts & Entertainment (*US*)
Domo Music Group Management (*US*)
Landstar Management (*UK*)
Tuscan Sun Music (*US*)
**New Wave**
Purple Rhino Music (*US*)
Sugar House Music (*UK*)
**Noise Core**
Purple Rhino Music (*US*)
**Nostalgia**
Purple Rhino Music (*US*)
**Pop**
ADSRecords (*UK*)
Advanced Alternative Media (AAM) (*US*)
AEC Music Management (*UK*)
AJM (*UK*)
American Artists Entertainment Group (*US*)
Angelica Arts & Entertainment (*US*)
Apex Talent Group (*US*)
Arlon Music (*UK*)
Artist in Mind (*US*)
Aspire Music Management (*UK*)
Audio Bay Management (*UK*)

B&H Management (*UK*)
Bandzmedia (*UK*)
Bear Music Management (*UK*)
Big Dipper Productions Ltd (*UK*)
Big Hassle Management (*US*)
Bitchin' Entertainment (*US*)
Black Bleach Records (*UK*)
Blue Shell Music (*UK*)
Bold Management (*UK*)
Booking Entertainment (*US*)
Brick Wall Management (*US*)
The Brokaw Company (*US*)
Bulletproof Artist Management (*US*)
BUT! Management (*UK*)
Career Artist Management (CAM) (*US*)
Case Entertainment Group Inc. (*US*)
Circle City Records USA (*US*)
Claudia eRecords (*UK*)
Columbia Artists Management Inc. (CAMI) (*US*)
Consolidated Artists (*UK*)
Create Management (*UK*)
Creative International Artist Management (*UK*)
D. Bailey Management, Inc. (*US*)
DAS Communications Ltd (*US*)
David Belenzon Management, Inc. (*US*)
Dawn Elder Management (*US*)
Dawson Breed Music (*UK*)
DCA Productions (*US*)
Deep South Artist Management (*US*)
Direct Management Group (DMG) (*US*)
Disaster Artist Management (*UK*)
Domo Music Group Management (*US*)
Dusty Studio Productions (*UK*)
East End Management (*US*)
Entourage Talent Associates, Ltd (*US*)
Equator Music (*UK*)
Fat City Artists (*US*)
First Access Entertainment (*US*)
Flat50 (*UK*)
Fleming Artists (*US*)
Freedom Management (*UK*)
Front Room Songs (*UK*)
Future Songs (*UK*)
Golden Arm (*UK*)
Guvnor Management (*UK*)
Hand in Hive Independent Records & Management (*UK*)
Handshake Ltd. (*UK*)
Hardin Entertainment (*US*)
Hello! Booking, Inc. (*US*)
Holy-Toto (*UK*)
Hornblow Group USA, Inc. (*US*)
Hot Gem (*UK*)

Offbeat Management (*UK*)
Salvation Records (*UK*)
**Punk**
0114 Records (*UK*)
Bitchin' Entertainment (*US*)
Black Bleach Records (*UK*)
Blackheart Records Group (*US*)
Dissention Records + Artist Management (*UK*)
Freaks R Us (*UK*)
Ganbei Records (*UK*)
Landstar Management (*UK*)
Nettwerk Management (*US*)
Possessive Management (*UK*)
Purple Rhino Music (*US*)
Raw Power Management (*UK*)
Salvation Records (*UK*)
Saviour Management (*UK*)
Tone Management (*UK*)
Toonteen Industries: Management & Promotions (*UK*)
Tractor Beam Managing & Consulting (*US*)
Val's Artist Management (VAM) (*US*)
Wanted Management (*Aus*)
**Ragga**
Purple Rhino Music (*US*)
**R&B**
Act 1 Entertainment (*US*)
American Artists Corporation (*US*)
American Artists Entertainment Group (*US*)
Bandzmedia (*UK*)
Big Beat Productions, Inc. (*US*)
Bitchin' Entertainment (*US*)
Black Dot Management (*US*)
Booking Entertainment (*US*)
Case Entertainment Group Inc. (*US*)
Celebrity Talent Agency Inc. (*US*)
Collin Artists (*US*)
Columbia Artists Management Inc. (CAMI) (*US*)
D. Bailey Management, Inc. (*US*)
David Belenzon Management, Inc. (*US*)
Defenders Ent (*UK*)
Fat City Artists (*US*)
First Access Entertainment (*US*)
Fresh Flava Entertainment (*US*)
Future Songs (*UK*)
Holy-Toto (*UK*)
IMC Entertainment Group (*US*)
Impact Artist Management (*US*)
Len Weisman, Personal Manager (*US*)
Lippman Entertainment (*US*)
Little White Bear Music (*UK*)

Loggins Promotion (*US*)
Lokation (*UK*)
Lupo Entertainment (*US*)
Major Bob Music, Inc. (*US*)
Mascioli Entertainment (*US*)
Mauldin Brand Agency (*US*)
Max Bernard Management (*US*)
Music World Entertainment (*US*)
Offbeat Management (*UK*)
Pierce Entertainment (*UK*)
Plus Music (*UK*)
Position Music (*US*)
Purple Rhino Music (*US*)
Pyramid Entertainment Group (*US*)
Red Entertainment Agency (*US*)
RGM Production (*UK*)
Silverword Music Group (*UK*)
Spectrum Talent Agency (*US*)
Spot Light Entertainment, Inc. (*US*)
Starkravin' Management (*US*)
SugarNova (*UK*)
TAC Music Management (*US*)
True Talent Entertainment (*US*)
Val's Artist Management (VAM) (*US*)
Wildlife Entertainment Ltd (*UK*)
**Rap**
Bitchin' Entertainment (*US*)
Case Entertainment Group Inc. (*US*)
Claudia eRecords (*UK*)
Defenders Ent (*UK*)
First Access Entertainment (*US*)
Flat50 (*UK*)
Len Weisman, Personal Manager (*US*)
Lippman Entertainment (*US*)
Loggins Promotion (*US*)
The Lost Atlantis Records (*UK*)
Mauldin Brand Agency (*US*)
Nettwerk Management (*US*)
OnDaBeat Talent Management (*UK*)
Position Music (*US*)
Purple Rhino Music (*US*)
Red Light Management (RLM) (*US*)
Spot Light Entertainment, Inc. (*US*)
Steven Scharf Entertainment (SSE) (*US*)
Union Entertainment Group (*US*)
Val's Artist Management (VAM) (*US*)
Variety Artists International (*US*)
Waxploitation (*US*)
**Reggae**
0114 Records (*UK*)
Act 1 Entertainment (*US*)
Celebrity Talent Agency Inc. (*US*)
Defenders Ent (*UK*)
Fat City Artists (*US*)
Purple Rhino Music (*US*)

Waxploitation (*US*)
**Reggaeton**
Purple Rhino Music (*US*)
**Regional**
Big Beat Productions, Inc. (*US*)
Brilliant Productions (*US*)
Cantaloupe Music Productions, Inc. (*US*)
MM Music Agency (*US*)
Siren Music Company (*US*)
TAC Music Management (*US*)
**Rhythm and Blues**
Offbeat Management (*UK*)
Purple Rhino Music (*US*)
TAC Music Management (*US*)
**Rock and Roll**
Fat City Artists (*US*)
Handshake Ltd. (*UK*)
Paradise Artists (*US*)
Purple Rhino Music (*US*)
TAC Music Management (*US*)
Wanted Management (*Aus*)
Worldsound, LLC (*US*)
**Rock**
0114 Records (*UK*)
21st Century Artists, Inc. (*US*)
Act 1 Entertainment (*US*)
Advanced Alternative Media (AAM) (*US*)
AEC Music Management (*UK*)
American Artists Corporation (*US*)
American Artists Entertainment Group (*US*)
Apex Talent Group (*US*)
Arslanian & Associates, Inc. (*US*)
Artist in Mind (*US*)
Artist Representation and Management (ARM) Entertainment (*US*)
Aspire Music Management (*UK*)
Bandzmedia (*UK*)
BBA Management & Booking (*US*)
Bear Music Management (*UK*)
Big Beat Productions, Inc. (*US*)
Big Dipper Productions Ltd (*UK*)
Big Hassle Management (*US*)
Bill Hollingshead Productions, Inc. Talent Agency (*US*)
Bitchin' Entertainment (*US*)
Black Bleach Records (*UK*)
Blackheart Records Group (*US*)
Bold Management (*UK*)
Booking Entertainment (*US*)
Brick Wall Management (*US*)
The Brokaw Company (*US*)
Bulletproof Artist Management (*US*)
Burgess World Co. (*US*)
BUT! Management (*UK*)

Career Artist Management (CAM) (*US*)
Case Entertainment Group Inc. (*US*)
Claudia eRecords (*UK*)
Concerted Efforts (*US*)
Consolidated Artists (*UK*)
Creative International Artist Management (*UK*)
D. Bailey Management, Inc. (*US*)
DAS Communications Ltd (*US*)
Dave Kaplan Management (*US*)
David Belenzon Management, Inc. (*US*)
Dawn Elder Management (*US*)
DCA Productions (*US*)
Deep South Artist Management (*US*)
Disaster Artist Management (*UK*)
Domo Music Group Management (*US*)
Don't Try (*UK*)
East End Management (*US*)
Elephant Management (*UK*)
Emcee Artist Management (*US*)
Entertainment Services International (*US*)
Entourage Talent Associates, Ltd (*US*)
Epic Venom (*UK*)
Equator Music (*UK*)
Fat Penguin Management (*UK*)
5B Artist Management (*US*)
Flat50 (*UK*)
Fleming Artists (*US*)
Fresh Flava Entertainment (*US*)
Ganbei Records (*UK*)
Golden Arm (*UK*)
Goo Music Management Ltd (*UK*)
Guvnor Management (*UK*)
Hand in Hive Independent Records & Management (*UK*)
Hardin Entertainment (*US*)
Hello! Booking, Inc. (*US*)
Holier than Thou (HTT) Music (*UK*)
Hornblow Group USA, Inc. (*US*)
Humans & Other Animals (*UK*)
Ignition Management (*UK*)
Impact Artist Management (*US*)
In De Goot Entertainment (*US*)
Incendia Music (*UK*)
Intrigue Music (*US*)
Kuper Personal Management (*US*)
Landstar Management (*UK*)
Lippman Entertainment (*US*)
Listen to This Management (*UK*)
Little White Bear Music (*UK*)
Loggins Promotion (*US*)
Lupo Entertainment (*US*)
M. Hitchcock Management (*US*)
Madrigal Music artist management (*UK*)
Maine Road Management (*US*)

Mascioli Entertainment (*US*)
McDonough Management LLC (*US*)
McGhee Entertainment (*US*)
Memphia Music Management (*UK*)
Metal Music Bookings (*UK*)
Michael Anthony's Electric Events (*US*)
Michael Hausman Artist Management Inc. (*US*)
Mike's Artist Management (*US*)
Miller Music Management (*UK*)
MOB Agency (*US*)
Moneypenny (*UK*)
Monqui Presents (*US*)
Music + Art Management (*US*)
Musicarchy Media (*UK*)
Mustang Agency (*US*)
N.O.W. Music Management (*UK*)
Nancy Fly Agency (*US*)
Nettwerk Management (*US*)
Northern Music Co. Ltd (*UK*)
NSI Management (*US*)
Off the Chart Promotions (*UK*)
Offbeat Management (*UK*)
Paradise Artists (*US*)
Park Records (*UK*)
Perry Road Records (*UK*)
Position Music (*US*)
Possessive Management (*UK*)
PRA [Patrick Rains & Associates] (*US*)
Prodigal Son Entertainment (*US*)
Progressive Global Agency (PGA) (*US*)
Purple Rhino Music (*US*)
Q Prime Management, Inc. (*US*)
Rainmaker Artists (*US*)
Raven Black Music (*UK*)
Raw Power Management (*UK*)
Red Entertainment Agency (*US*)
Red Light Management (RLM) (*US*)
Richard Lipman (*UK*)
Rock People Management (RPM) (*UK*)
Ron Rainey Management Inc. (*US*)
Rosier Artist Management (RAM) (*UK*)
Russell Carter Artist Management (*US*)
Salvation Records (*UK*)
SGM Music Group Ltd (*UK*)
Sharpe Entertainment Services, Inc. (*US*)
Silverword Music Group (*UK*)
So What Media & Management (*US*)
Starkravin' Management (*US*)
Steve Stewart Entertainment (*US*)
Steven Scharf Entertainment (SSE) (*US*)
Stiefel Entertainment (*US*)
Street Smart Management (*US*)
Sugar House Music (*UK*)
Suncoast Music Management (*US*)

TAC Music Management (*US*)
Tileyard Music (*UK*)
Tone Management (*UK*)
Tony Margherita Management (*US*)
Toonteen Industries: Management & Promotions (*UK*)
Tower Management Group (*US*)
Tractor Beam Managing & Consulting (*US*)
Travelled Music (*UK*)
Union Entertainment Group (*US*)
United Stage International Ltd (*UK*)
Universal Tone Management (*US*)
Val's Artist Management (VAM) (*US*)
Variety Artists International (*US*)
Vector Management (*US*)
Wanted Management (*Aus*)
Waxploitation (*US*)
Wildlife Entertainment Ltd (*UK*)
Worldsound, LLC (*US*)
YMU Group (*UK*)

**Rockabilly**
Act 1 Entertainment (*US*)
Fat City Artists (*US*)
Hello! Booking, Inc. (*US*)
Purple Rhino Music (*US*)
TAC Music Management (*US*)
Two Chord Touring (*US*)

**Roots**
21st Century Artists, Inc. (*US*)
Act 1 Entertainment (*US*)
Brilliant Productions (*US*)
Dawn Elder Management (*US*)
Fleming Artists (*US*)
Front Room Songs (*UK*)
Hardin Entertainment (*US*)
Impact Artist Management (*US*)
Kari Estrin Management & Consulting (*US*)
KCA Artists (*US*)
Kuper Personal Management (*US*)
Nancy Fly Agency (*US*)
Park Records (*UK*)
Piedmont Talent (*US*)
Purple Rhino Music (*US*)
Siren Music Company (*US*)
Steven Scharf Entertainment (SSE) (*US*)
TAC Music Management (*US*)
Tractor Beam Managing & Consulting (*US*)
Val's Artist Management (VAM) (*US*)
Wanted Management (*Aus*)

**Shoegaze**
Black Bleach Records (*UK*)
Elephant Management (*UK*)

**Singer-Songwriter**
0114 Records (*UK*)
ADSRecords (*UK*)
AEC Music Management (*UK*)
Amour:Music (*UK*)
Apex Talent Group (*US*)
Arlon Music (*UK*)
Artist in Mind (*US*)
Bernie Nelson Artist Management (*UK*)
Bitchin' Entertainment (*US*)
Brick Wall Management (*US*)
Burgess World Co. (*US*)
BUT! Management (*UK*)
Concerted Efforts (*US*)
Create Management (*UK*)
Domo Music Group Management (*US*)
Entourage Talent Associates, Ltd (*US*)
Fat Penguin Management (*UK*)
Future Songs (*UK*)
Hardin Entertainment (*US*)
Hornblow Group USA, Inc. (*US*)
IMG Artists (*US*)
Impact Artist Management (*US*)
JBLS Management (*UK*)
KCA Artists (*US*)
Kragen & Company (*US*)
Lippman Entertainment (*US*)
Little White Bear Music (*UK*)
Lyricom (*UK*)
Madrigal Music artist management (*UK*)
Max Bernard Management (*US*)
McGhee Entertainment (*US*)
Michael Hausman Artist Management Inc. (*US*)
Miller Music Management (*UK*)
Nettwerk Management (*US*)
NSI Management (*US*)
Off the Chart Promotions (*UK*)
Offbeat Management (*UK*)
Park Records (*UK*)
Position Music (*US*)
Purple Rhino Music (*US*)
Q Prime Management, Inc. (*US*)
Red Grape Music (*UK*)
Red Light Management (RLM) (*US*)
Russell Carter Artist Management (*US*)
Sharpe Entertainment Services, Inc. (*US*)
Siren Music Company (*US*)
Sterling Artist Management (*US*)
Steven Scharf Entertainment (SSE) (*US*)
Stiefel Entertainment (*US*)
Stormcraft Music (*UK*)
TAC Music Management (*US*)
Vector Management (*US*)

**Ska**
0114 Records (*UK*)
Fat City Artists (*US*)
Purple Rhino Music (*US*)
**Soul**
Act 1 Entertainment (*US*)
Bandzmedia (*UK*)
Chicken Grease Presents (*UK*)
Claudia eRecords (*UK*)
Concerted Efforts (*US*)
Len Weisman, Personal Manager (*US*)
Little White Bear Music (*UK*)
The Lost Atlantis Records (*UK*)
Major Bob Music, Inc. (*US*)
Max Bernard Management (*US*)
NSB Artist Management (*UK*)
Piedmont Talent (*US*)
Plus Music (*UK*)
RGM Production (*UK*)
Silverword Music Group (*UK*)
Wanted Management (*Aus*)
**Soulful**
Max Bernard Management (*US*)
Purple Rhino Music (*US*)
TAC Music Management (*US*)
**Soundtracks**
Kraft-Engel Management (*US*)
Max Bernard Management (*US*)
Purple Rhino Music (*US*)
Soundtrack Music Associates (SMA) (*US*)
Steven Scharf Entertainment (SSE) (*US*)
**Spoken Word**
Bitchin' Entertainment (*US*)
Purple Rhino Music (*US*)
**Surf**
Bill Hollingshead Productions, Inc. Talent Agency (*US*)
Purple Rhino Music (*US*)
**Swing**
Act 1 Entertainment (*US*)
American Artists Corporation (*US*)
Big Bear Music (*UK*)
Cantaloupe Music Productions, Inc. (*US*)
Collin Artists (*US*)
Fat City Artists (*US*)
Harmony Artists (*US*)
Mascioli Entertainment (*US*)
Purple Rhino Music (*US*)
**Synthpop**
Purple Rhino Music (*US*)
**Techno**
Bitchin' Entertainment (*US*)
Empire Artist Management (*US*)
F&G Management (*UK*)
The Lost Atlantis Records (*UK*)

OnDaBeat Talent Management (*UK*)
Purple Rhino Music (*US*)
The Weird and the Wonderful (*UK*)
**Thrash**
Holier than Thou (HTT) Music (*UK*)
Landstar Management (*UK*)
Offbeat Management (*UK*)
Possessive Management (*UK*)
Purple Rhino Music (*US*)
**Traditional**
Dawn Elder Management (*US*)
Nancy Fly Agency (*US*)
Riot Artists (*US*)
TAC Music Management (*US*)
**Trance**
Bitchin' Entertainment (*US*)
Involved Management (*UK*)
**Tribal**
Purple Rhino Music (*US*)
**Trip Hop**
Purple Rhino Music (*US*)
**Twisted**
Purple Rhino Music (*US*)
**Underground**
In De Goot Entertainment (*US*)
North Central Music (NCM) (*UK*)
Purple Rhino Music (*US*)
This Is Music Ltd (*UK*)
**Urban**
B&H Management (*UK*)
Bitchin' Entertainment (*US*)
Black Dot Management (*US*)
HQ Familia (*UK*)
Lippman Entertainment (*US*)
Loggins Promotion (*US*)
Lokation (*UK*)
The Lost Atlantis Records (*UK*)
Lyricom (*UK*)
Max Bernard Management (*US*)
Music World Entertainment (*US*)
NSB Artist Management (*UK*)
Position Music (*US*)

Purple Rhino Music (*US*)
Pyramid Entertainment Group (*US*)
Qveen Management (*UK*)
Red Entertainment Agency (*US*)
Silverword Music Group (*UK*)
SugarNova (*UK*)
Tileyard Music (*UK*)
Val's Artist Management (VAM) (*US*)
The Weird and the Wonderful (*UK*)
**World**
Angelica Arts & Entertainment (*US*)
Bitchin' Entertainment (*US*)
Cantaloupe Music Productions, Inc. (*US*)
Collin Artists (*US*)
Columbia Artists Management Inc.
(CAMI) (*US*)
Concerted Efforts (*US*)
Dawn Elder Management (*US*)
DDB Productions (*US*)
Domo Music Group Management (*US*)
Fat City Artists (*US*)
Front Room Songs (*UK*)
Hardin Entertainment (*US*)
IMG Artists (*US*)
Impact Artist Management (*US*)
Ina Dittke & Associates (*US*)
Landstar Management (*UK*)
Line-Up pmc (*UK*)
McGhee Entertainment (*US*)
Music + Art Management (*US*)
Nancy Fly Agency (*US*)
Nettwerk Management (*US*)
Position Music (*US*)
Progressive Global Agency (PGA) (*US*)
Purple Rhino Music (*US*)
Red Light Management (RLM) (*US*)
Richard Lipman (*UK*)
Riot Artists (*US*)
Serious (*UK*)
Steven Scharf Entertainment (SSE) (*US*)
Val's Artist Management (VAM) (*US*)
Worldsound, LLC (*US*)

# Get Free Access to the MusicSocket Website

To claim your free access to the **MusicSocket** website simply go to https://www.musicsocket.com/subscribe and begin the subscription process as normal. When you are given the opportunity to enter a voucher / coupon enter the following code:

- MSC-TXL-878

You should then be able to take out a subscription for free, or a longer term subscription at a reduced price.

Please note that this code will only remain valid until the release of the next edition, and is only permitted for use in the creation of one account for the owner of this book.

If you need any assistance please email support@musicsocket.com.

**If you have found this book useful, please consider leaving a review on the website where you bought it!**

## What you get

Once you have set up access to ths site you will be able to benefit from all the following features:

### Databases

All our databases are updated almost every day, and include powerful search facilities to help you find exactly what you need. Searches that used to take you hours or even days in print books or on search engines can now be done in seconds, and produce more accurate and up-to-date information. You can try out any of our databases before you subscribe:

- Search **over 1,800 record labels**
- Search **over 700 managers**

PLUS advanced features to help you with your search:

- Save searches and save time – set up to 15 search parameters specific to your work, save them, and then access the search results with a single click whenever you log in. You can even save multiple different searches if you have different types of work you are looking to place.
- Add personal notes to listings, visible only to you and fully searchable – helping you to organise your actions.

- Set reminders on listings to notify you when to submit your work, when to follow up, when to expect a reply, or any other custom action.
- Track which listings you've viewed and when, to help you organise your search – any listings which have changed since you last viewed them will be highlighted for your attention!

### Daily email updates

As a subscriber you will be able to take advantage of our email alert service, meaning you can specify your particular interests and we'll send you automatic email updates when we change or add a listing that matches them. So if you're interested in labels dealing in hard rock in the United States you can have us send you emails with the latest updates about them – keeping you up to date without even having to log in.

### User feedback

Our databases all include a user feedback feature that allows our subscribers to leave feedback on each listing – giving you not only the chance to have your say about the markets you contact, but giving a unique artist's perspective on the listings.

### Save on copyright protection fees

If you're sending your work away to record labels or managers, you should consider first protecting your copyright. As a subscriber to **MusicSocket** you can do this through our site and save 10% on the copyright registration fees normally payable for protecting your work internationally through the Intellectual Property Rights Office.

---

## Terms and conditions

*The promotional code contained in this publication may be used by the owner of the book only to create one subscription to MusicSocket at a reduced cost, or for free. It may not be used by or disseminated to third parties. Should the code be misused then the owner of the book will be liable for any costs incurred, including but not limited to payment in full at the standard rate for the subscription in question. The code may be used at any time until the end of the calendar year named in the title of the publication, after which time it will become invalid. The code may be redeemed against the creation of a new account only – it cannot be redeemed against the ongoing costs of keeping a subscription open. In order to create a subscription a method of payment must be provided, but there is no obligation to make any payment. Subscriptions may be cancelled at any time, and if an account is cancelled before any payment becomes due then no payment will be made. Once a subscription has been created, the normal schedule of payments will begin on a monthly, quarterly, or annual basis, unless a life Subscription is selected, or the subscription is cancelled prior to the first payment becoming due. Subscriptions may be cancelled at any time, but if they are left open beyond the date at which the first payment becomes due and is processed then payments will not be refundable.*